MENG JIANGNÜ

BRINGS DOWN THE GREAT WALL

MENG JIANGNÜ

BRINGS DOWN THE GREAT WALL

Ten Versions of a Chinese Legend

TRANSLATION AND INTRODUCTION BY
WILT L. IDEMA

WITH AN ESSAY BY
HAIYAN LEE

A China Program Book

UNIVERSITY OF WASHINGTON PRESS   SEATTLE & LONDON

This book was supported in part by the China Studies Program, a division of the Henry M. Jackson School of International Studies at the University of Washington, and by the Donald R. Ellegood International Publications Endowment.

UNIVERSITY OF WASHINGTON PRESS

PO Box 50096, Seattle, WA 98145   www.washington.edu/uwpress

LIBRARY OF CONGRESS CATALOGING-IN-PUBLICATION DATA

Meng Jiangnü brings down the Great Wall : ten versions of a Chinese legend /
translation and introduction by Wilt L. Idema ; with an essay by Haiyan Lee.

p.   cm. — (A China program book)

Includes bibliographical references and index.

ISBN 978-0-295-98783-5 (alk. paper) — ISBN 978-0-295-98784-2 (pbk. : alk. paper)

1. Mengjiangnü (Legendary character)   2. Legends—China.   I. Idema, Wilt L.

GR335.4.M45M45 2008   398.20951—dc22

2007035751

The paper used in this publication is acid-free and 90 percent recycled
from at least 50 percent post-consumer waste. It meets the minimum
requirements of American National Standard for Information Sciences—
Permanence of Paper for Printed Library Materials, ANSI z39.48–1984.

FRONTISPIECE: Meng Jiangnü (right) and Wan Xiliang (left), from
Meng Jiang xiannü baojuan, undated lithographic edition, early 20th century.
Courtesy of the Harvard-Yenching Library, Harvard College Library

CONTENTS

❧ PART II ❧
Ballads Collected in the Countryside

ACKNOWLEDGMENTS

T HE MAJORITY OF THE TRANSLATIONS IN THIS VOLUME
were finalized during the academic year of 2005–6, when I had the
luxury of a full year's sabbatical. I would like to express my gratitude
to the Dean of the Faculty of Arts and Sciences at Harvard for granting me this
rare opportunity to indulge myself for such a long and uninterrupted period
in the fascinating world of traditional Chinese popular lore and literature.

This project, however, could not have been brought to fruition without
the full support of the staff at the Harvard-Yenching Library, who went out
of their way to answer all my inquiries and went well beyond the call of duty
in order to make sure I would be provided with hard-to-get materials from
China. In this respect, I would especially like to thank Mrs. Ellen McGill,
Mrs. Sharon Yang, and Mr. Ma Xiao-he. At the Fung Library, Mrs. Nancy
Hearst provided me with rare materials. I also would like to thank all those
colleagues and friends around the globe who answered my queries about the
lithographic editions of *The Revised Version of the Complete Story of the Steadfast Chastity of the Maiden Meng Jiang, Who, Searching for her Husband,
Brought Down the Long Wall by Her Weeping.*

I am very grateful to the two anonymous readers at the University of

Washington Press. Their detailed comments were very helpful in my rethinking and revising of the manuscript. I would also like to express my gratitude to Professor Haiyan Lee, who not only allowed us to reprint her essay about the May Fourth Folklore Movement's views on the legend of Meng Jiangnü but also graciously agreed to revise it for this volume—and did so on short notice.

I also would like to express my thanks to the University of Washington Press for publishing this volume. It has been a pleasure to work with the highly efficient staff of the Press, especially Lorri Hagman and Mary Ribesky. I count myself very lucky in having had Laura Iwasaki as my copy editor, as she has saved me from many infelicities of style and inconsistencies of fact. All remaining infelicities and mistakes are of course purely my own.

TRANSLATOR'S NOTE

ALL TRANSLATIONS IN THIS COLLECTION ARE MY OWN, AND I have scrupulously distinguished between prose and verse. I have attempted to give lines of verse of the same length in Chinese roughly the same length in English but have made no attempt to impose any metrical schema on the verse sections or to rhyme them. In the original, the same rhyme may on occasion be maintained throughout the whole text. Longer verse passages tend to be constructed out of four-line building blocks. In order to help the reader, the beginning of such a four-line group is marked by a half-inch indentation.

The most common line of verse in the translated texts is the seven-syllable line. Texts that are based on recordings of oral performances show that one or two syllables quite often were added to this basic pattern. Some genres allow for the occasional insertion of a three-character phrase in front of a seven-syllable line for emphasis or variation. In printed versions, such three-character phrases are in a smaller size, a convention I have followed in this collection. On occasion, a seven-syllable line has been replaced by a six-syllable line made up of two half-lines of three syllables each. In my translation, these two half-lines are separated by a slash (/). The closer we come to modern times, the more frequent becomes the use of ten-syllable lines. A ten-syllable line consists of two groups of three syllables followed by a four-syllable phrase or of a four-syllable phrase preceded and followed by a three-character phrase. In my translations, I have tried to bring out the tripartite construction of these ten-syllable lines by typographical means.

The common way to refer to our heroine nowadays is Meng Jiangnü. The standard American library transcription of this name is Mengjiangnü, which is questionable, as Meng is usually understood as a surname. However, strictly speaking, *nü* is not part of her name and is rarely treated as such in the texts translated in this collection. While *nü* has the more general meaning of "woman," its primary meaning is "daughter" or "maiden," a young woman who has not yet married and is living with her parents. Some of the texts in this volume prefer the form Meng Jiang. In such cases, Meng is taken to be her family name, while Jiang is her personal name. One of our texts, however, states that her surname is Jiang, and that *meng* in ancient times had the meaning of "the eldest of siblings." Other texts call our heroine simply Jiangnü (the maiden Jiang). And in yet other versions of the text, our heroine has acquired the name Xu Mengjiang. My translations reflect the interpretation of the name in each of the translated texts. In the same way, the name of her husband is different in almost every text.

Married women, such as Meng Jiangnü's mother, are usually designated by their natal surname. I refer to such married women as "lady." Some married women are designated by the title *furen*, which I translate as "Lady."

I have preferred to be somewhat more literal than is common by translating "Changcheng" as "Long Wall" and not as "Great Wall." The length of the wall is usually hyperbolically said to be "a myriad of miles." In this and comparable expressions, "miles" is the translation for the Chinese *li*, which is roughly equivalent to one-third of an English mile.

All translation involves a certain degree of guesswork, but for those cases in which my translation is nothing but guesswork, I have placed a (?) at the end of the line.

MENG JIANGNÜ

BRINGS DOWN THE GREAT WALL

MENG JIANGNÜ

The Development of a Legend

WILT L. IDEMA

THE TALE OF THE MAIDEN MENG JIANG, OR MENG JIANGNÜ, was one of the most popular and widespread legends of traditional China during the Ming (1368–1644) and Qing (1644–1911) dynasties. It features a teenage widow who, out of loyalty to a husband she has barely lived with, brings down the Great Wall with her weeping, and some versions of the legend pit her against the greatest tyrant of Chinese history, the First Emperor of the Qin (Qin Shi huangdi). In the twentieth century, the legend was extensively studied by Gu Jiegang (1893–1980) and other members of the Folklore Movement of the 1920s and 1930s. To this very day, most Chinese are well acquainted with the tale, usually on the basis of one of the modern retellings they have encountered in their schoolbooks. Many Western visitors hear the story on the occasion of a visit to the Great Wall, especially if they visit Shanhaiguan (Mountain-Sea Pass), where the Wall meets the Bohai Sea. It is here, according to one widespread version of the legend, that Meng Jiangnü committed suicide by jumping into the ocean after she had seduced the lust-besotted First Emperor into conducting state funeral rites for her husband, a conscript laborer who had died and been buried in the body of the Wall.

It is not difficult to imagine why this story enjoyed such a long and continued popularity. Like *Romeo and Juliet*, it focuses on the tragic love of a young couple: once Meng Jiangnü has found her husband, she is fully committed to her partner and shirks no ordeal to be reunited with him. The young lovers in this case are separated not by the inveterate feuding of their respective families but by the cruel despotism of the state. The state here is the tyrannical regime of the First Emperor of the Qin dynasty (221–208 B.C.E.). The First Emperor had succeeded in uniting the whole known Chinese world under his dominion, but the massive construction projects for the building of his palaces, his grave, and the Great Wall soon exhausted the population, and immediately after his death, rebellions erupted across the empire. Meng Jiangnü's husband was conscripted to work on the Wall, where he soon died. Traditionally the construction of the Great Wall was widely considered to have been a meaningless folly: according to one legend, the First Emperor had embarked on the project following a prediction that his dynasty would be brought down by *hu*, which he took to refer to the *hu* (barbarians), nomadic inhabitants of the steppes to the north of China, but which actually referred to his son, Huhai. Little remains of the wall of Qin-dynasty times or of the walls that were built in later ages. The walls that may be visited nowadays to the north of Beijing, and which are touted as the Great Wall, were constructed only in the sixteenth and seventeenth centuries during the Ming dynasty, which carefully avoided the use of the term "Long Wall" (Changcheng) for these extensive border fortifications because of the negative implications kept alive by the popular legend of Meng Jiangnü. Seventeenth-century Jesuit missionaries from Europe actually were the first to identify the wall of Qin times with the Ming fortifications, to feature it prominently on their maps, and to claim an unbroken history of almost two thousand years for the Great Wall. Not until the twentieth century, and especially the period of the Anti-Japanese War of 1937–45, did the Great Wall become the proud symbol of the Chinese nation in China itself.[1]

Thematizing both absolute devotion and the relation between an all-powerful state and a single individual, against the backdrop of a formative moment in Chinese history and one of China's most fabled monuments, the legend of Meng Jiangnü was bound to exert an abiding attraction and to generate multiple retellings and widely divergent interpretations. In the last century, Meng Jiangnü has inspired modern and contemporary writers as diverse as Zhang Henshui and Su Tong, and the story has repeatedly been adapted for the screen. During the Cultural Revolution (1966–78), the legend's negative characterization of the First Emperor (beloved by Mao Zedong) resulted in a strident ideological condemnation of the tale as "a poisonous weed," but this judgment was reversed in the 1980s. Yet, while almost every Chinese knows about the legend nowadays, few except specialists are aware of the immense richness and variety of its many versions in late-imperial times and in the popular traditions of the twentieth century.

During the Qing dynasty and throughout the last century, the legend of Meng Jiangnü circulated in numerous popular genres all over China. These versions show many differences, depending on region, genre, and function, but despite this considerable variation, all would appear to derive from a tale that originated, at the latest, in the Tang dynasty (618–906). This tale, in its turn, is at least partly derived from much earlier legends, which can be traced back to *The Zuo Tradition* (Zuo zhuan), of the fourth or third century B.C.E., and Liu Xiang's *Biographies of Exemplary Women* (Lienü zhuan), of the final years of the first century B.C.E. In these earliest versions, the Great Wall and the First Emperor are still absent—they enter our legend only in Tang-dynasty times.

EARLIEST BEGINNINGS

The legend of Meng Jiangnü can be traced back over 2,500 years. When, in 549 B.C.E., Duke Zhuang of Qi tried to take the city of Ju by surprise, his troops were rebuffed, and one of the fighters of Qi who died in the engagement was Qi Liang (also known as Qi Zhi), who earlier had refused to take a bribe from the lord of Ju. As recounted in *The Zuo Tradition*, Qi Liang's widow distinguished herself by her strong sense of propriety, as she refused to accept the duke's condolences when they were offered to her on the road, an inappropriate location. Other sources from the Warring States period (fifth–third centuries B.C.E.) mention that Qi Liang's widow was "good at weeping." "Weeping" (*ku*, perhaps better translated as "wailing") here refers not to a spontaneous emotion but to the deliberate, loud, and public expression of grief or other forms of deep distress that, as a performance of sadness, often is very close to song (*ge*).[2]

When Liu Xiang (79–6 B.C.E.) compiled his *Biographies of Exemplary Women* and included her story, he added the detail that Qi Liang's widow by her weeping had brought down the wall (of Ju?). He also extended the story further by having her commit suicide once she had provided her husband with a proper funeral:

The Wife of Qi Liang of Qi

She was the wife of Qi Liang (Zhi) of Qi. Zhi died in battle during the raid of Duke Zhuang on Ju. On his way back, Duke Zhuang encountered Qi's wife and had a servant offer his condolences to her there on the road. Qi Liang's wife riposted, "Why would our lord take this trouble if Zhi had committed some crime? But if Zhi committed no crime, the humble abode of his father is still standing. It is unacceptable to offer me condolences out in the fields." Thereupon Duke Zhuang had his carriage return and visited her at home, and he departed only after all the rites had been completed.

The wife of Qi Liang was without a son, and she also had no relatives in any of the five grades of mourning. Resting her head on the corpse of her husband at the foot of the wall [of Ju?], she wept,[3] and her inner sincerity moved the passers-by to such a degree that none of them did not shed tears. After ten days, the wall collapsed on her account.

After she had completed the burial, she said, "Where can I take refuge? A woman needs a person on whom she can rely. As long as her father is alive, she relies on her father. As long as her husband is alive, she relies on her husband. As long as her son is alive, she relies on her son. Now I have no father, no husband, and no son. Inside the home I have no one to rely on to display my sincerity, and outside the home I have no one to rely on in order to display my chastity. And how could I ever marry a second husband? All I can do is to die!" She then died after jumping into the Zi River.

A gentleman will call the wife of Qi Liang "chaste and conversant with the rites." The following lines of the Book of Odes are apposite: "My heart is wounded by grief, / With you I will seek refuge together."

The hymn reads:

When Qi Liang had died in battle,
His wife collected his corpse for burial.
When Zhuang of Qi offered his condolences on the road,
She refused to accept them there.
She wept for her husband by the wall,
And the wall tumbled down on her account.
And because she was bereft of relatives,
She committed suicide by jumping into the Zi.[4]

Early authors disagree as to which wall came tumbling down because of the weeping of Qi Liang's widow. The account as quoted in the *Imperial Reader of the Taiping Reign* (Taiping yulan), a huge encyclopedia compiled in 977, which is based largely on the *Biographies of Exemplary Women* as we know it, adds the detail that "the people of Ju had built a wall of corpses as a victory monument (*jingcheng*). When his wife went there to bring him back home for burial, she wept before this wall until the earth collapsed on her behalf and she could bury him."[5]

In these stories, Qi Liang is a warrior, not a conscript. For a story of a man who is forced to work on the construction of walls as a conscript laborer, we must turn to the tale of Han Ping and his wife, which may be found, for instance, in Gan Bao's *In Search of the Supernatural* (Soushenji), of the fourth century C.E. When the last ruler of the state of Song, King Kang (r. 328–286 B.C.E.) took a fancy to the wife of Han Ping and she remained steadfast in her loyalty to her husband, the king had the husband condemned to forced labor on the construction of walls and terraces. Following Han Ping's death, his wife committed suicide by jumping from a high terrace.[6] This story continued to be quite popular in later ages. An adaptation from the ninth or tenth century in the form of a "narrative rhapsody" (*sufu*), titled "Rhapsody on Han Peng" (Han Peng fu), is among the Dunhuang manuscripts.[7] In this version, Han Ping's wife suggests to the king that she will follow his wishes once he has properly buried her deceased husband, but when she is allowed to inspect the grave, she joins her husband in death by jumping into the grave pit.[8] Boris Riftin, the Russian scholar of Chinese folklore and popular literature, has argued that this story of Han Ping and his faithful wife should be seen as the true origin of the later Meng Jiangnü legend, but up to the tenth century, the two tales appear to have circulated side by side.[9]

EARLIEST VERSIONS OF THE MENG JIANGNÜ LEGEND

When we reencounter the story of the wife of Qi Liang in Tang-dynasty sources, the setting has been moved from the sixth century B.C.E. to the Qin dynasty (221–208 B.C.E.), and the wall that crumbles because of her weeping is now the Great Wall. Scholars see in the emergence of this new form of the tale a reflection of the frantic wall-building activities of the fifth and sixth centuries in northern China, when that area was divided into contesting kingdoms.

During the Han dynasty (206 B.C.E.–220 C.E.), authors in general had very little to say on the First Emperor's Great Wall. The famous historian Sima Qian (145–87 B.C.E.) provided the following account of its construction in chapter 88 of his *Records of the Historian* (Shi ji):

After Qin had unified the world [in 221 B.C.E., the great general] Meng Tian was sent to command a host of three hundred thousand to drive out the Rong and the Di along the north. He took from them the territory to the south of the [Yellow] River and built the Great Wall, constructing its defiles and passes in accordance with the configuration of the terrain. It started in Lintao [in the west] and extended to Liaodong [in the east], reaching a distance of more than ten thousand *li*.[10]

Other Han-period references to the Great Wall add little of substance. It is only from the late second century onward, when China once again is wracked by civil war, that the Wall becomes a quite common topic in lyrical poetry as a site of desolation and misery, of battlefields strewn with white bones. In the lyrical poetry of the Tang, the making of winter clothes for soldiers serving on the northern borders, and the sending or taking of these to them, also becomes a popular theme.

A relatively complete version of the new legend is provided in the preserved fragments of a Japanese manuscript of 747, the anonymous *Carved Jade* (Diaoyuji); the specific section is *juan* 12, "Divine Responses" (Ganying pian). Little is known about the provenance and date of composition of this encyclopedic compendium of excerpts, and even less about its reputed source for the legend, *Being with the Wise* (Tongxian ji). The version in *Carved Jade* may be rendered as follows:

Qi Liang was a man from Qi in the times of the Zhou dynasty. When Duke Zhuang attacked Ju by surprise, Qi Liang died in battle. When his wife retrieved his corpse and was on her way home, Duke Zhuang offered her his condolences on the road. Liang's wife replied: "If Liang died of some crime, his wife and children also should be cast off. But if he did not commit any crime, he has his house, so how could I dare accept your condolences here, out on the road?" Duke Zhuang then retreated, deeply ashamed. From *Annals of Spring and Autumn*.[11]

Another version goes: Qi Liang was a man who in the time of the First Emperor [had been conscripted to work] in the north on the building of the Long Wall.[12] Fleeing the hardship, he escaped [from the construction site] and ran away. Because of this, he entered the garden behind [the house of] Meng Qi [and hid himself] in a tree. Qi's daughter Zhongzi took a bath in the [garden] pond. When she looked up, she noticed Qi Liang and called him down. She asked him, "Where are you from? And why are you here?"

He answered her, "My name is Qi Liang and I hail from Yan. Because I was conscripted and worked on building the Long Wall, I could not stand the bitter hardship, and subsequently I fled to this place." Zhongzi said, "I want to be your wife!" Liang replied, "Young lady, you are the daughter of a rich man, and you grew up in the inner apartments. Your beauty is dazzling—how can you be the spouse of a conscript?" Zhongzi said, "A woman's body cannot be seen by a second man, so please don't refuse!" Subsequently she informed her father of the circumstances, and her father assented.

After husband and wife had consummated their marriage, Liang went back to the construction site. His supervisor, who was furious that Liang had escaped, had him beaten to death and buried in the section of the wall that was being built. [Meng] Qi, who did not know Liang had died, sent a servant, whom he wanted to be Liang's *remplaçant*, and so learned that Liang had died and been buried in the wall. When Zhongzi heard this, she was choked by grief, and went [to the Long Wall]. She wailed and wept before the Long Wall. The wall in front of her suddenly collapsed. The white bones of the deceased were all mixed up, so she did not know which ones were the right ones. Zhongzi then pricked her finger in order to drip drops of blood on the white bones. Saying, "If these are the bones of Qi Liang, may the blood penetrate them," she sprinkled the bones with her blood. When she indeed came to Liang's bones, the blood promptly penetrated the bones. She then brought the bones back home with her and buried them. From *Being with the Wise.*

These two accounts are not the same, and I do not know which one is correct.[13]

A chapter from an undated, annotated version of the sixth-century anthology *Selections of Refined Literature* (Wenxuan)[14] provides a somewhat different account of this new tale:

Li Shan says: The *Biographies of Exemplary Women* states: The [loyal widow from] Qi was the wife of Qi Liang (Zhi). When Duke Zhuang of Qi [attacked Ju], Liang died in battle. Qi Liang's wife had no relatives to rely on. As she had no place to return to, she went to her husband's corpse at the foot of the wall and wept over him. Her inner sincerity moved people to such an extent that of those who passed by on the road none did not wipe away his tears. After ten days, the wall collapsed on her account. . . . The *Biographies of Exemplary Women* states: [Meng Zi] was not yet married, and she lived close

9

to the Long Wall. Qi [Liang could not stand the hardship of building the Wall] and fled from his corvée to the flower garden of this Meng Zi, where he hid among the trees by the pond. When Zi was taking a bath under him, she saw the reflection of a man in the water. When she got out of the water, she addressed him and said, "Let's become man and wife!" But Liang replied, "At this moment I have been conscripted for a killing corvée, and I am here fleeing that corvée. I would not dare hope to be considered by such a noble person as you!" Zi said, "A woman is not seen twice. [As you have seen me in the nude, I cannot] marry someone else." She thereupon had intercourse with him. [After he had returned to the construction site, she prepared to bring him] food. But when she later learned he had died, she went [to the Wall] with food and wine in order to reclaim his bones. When she arrived at the foot of the Wall and asked about his corpse, she saw that the laborers had been buried inside the Wall. She then wept at the Wall that had been built, and the Wall subsequently collapsed on her behalf. The bones in the Wall were all mixed up, so she could not recognize [those of her husband]. She sprinkled them with her tears, which turned into blood.[15]

This new legend is reflected in a poem written by the late-Tang-dynasty monk Guanxiu (832–912):

When Qin was without the Way, the four seas dried up:
They built a Long Wall to keep out the northern barbarians.
For a myriad of miles they built it of men and of mud,
So Qi Liang's chaste wife fell to weeping and wailing.
    "Above I have no father, at my side I have no husband,
Below me I have no son, I am all alone and lonely."
At her first cry the wall collapsed under a bitterly cold sky;
At her second cry the bones of Qi Liang appeared from the mud.
    As her wearied soul and his starving spirit return home together,
You young men on the road should speak no words of abuse![16]

But it is only in one of the anonymous songs recovered from Dunhuang, which most likely dates from the ninth or the tenth century, that we first encounter the name Meng Jiang ("the maiden Meng Jiang," Meng Jiangnü). The song also contains the detail of her delivering winter clothes to her conscript husband, which would become such a major element in later versions of the legend:

MENG JIANGNÜ

The maiden Meng Jiang, / the wife of Qi Liang—
Once he had left for the northern mountains, he never returned.
When she had made winter clothes, she had no one to deliver them,
So she had no alternative but to go and deliver those clothes herself.[17]

The name Meng Jiang itself has a long pedigree, as it already occurs in the *Book of Odes*, one of the Five Classics, as the name of beautiful women. In the *Book of Odes*, however, the word *meng* is not used as a surname, and *meng Jiang* has the meaning "the eldest [daughter of the] Jiang family." In the Tang legend, *meng* is understood as the common surname Meng. As in some later versions of the legend Jiang is still recognized as a family name, added details explain how our heroine ended up with a name consisting of two surnames. Some later versions of the legend change the heroine's name to Xu Mengjiang and then must explain a name made up of three surnames!

One of the manuscripts recovered from Dunhuang contains a prosimetric version of the legend, telling the story through alternating prose and verse. This is a quite popular format among the longer narrative texts intended for performance recovered from Dunhuang. Together with the long verse narrative, the prosimetric format would remain popular with professional storytellers through later centuries and engender many genres of popular literature. Unfortunately, the manuscript containing this prosimetric retelling of the legend of Meng Jiang is heavily damaged, and both the beginning and ending are missing. The text is probably best dated to the ninth or tenth century. The preserved fragment of the text begins when Meng Jiang has arrived at the Great Wall, and the ghost of Qi Liang appears to her in a dream:

"Young lady, you have been so kind as to bring me winter gear.
I do not know how I would ever be able to repay your kindness.

When we said good-bye, we believed it wouldn't have to be long,
As I intended to come back home again in a day or so at most.
Who could know I would be buried in the body of the Wall,
That my soul would dissolve, my life end here at the border!

After I had departed from you and arrived at the Long Wall,
The official in charge of my work subjected me to hardship.

When my life was finished, I was buried in the body of the Wall,
And my roving soul dispersed on the trail of brambles and thorns.

You have been so kind as to come and find me despite the long journey;
Traveling through wind and frost, you have exhausted your energy.
By all means, take good care of yourself, and quickly go home.
You'll always be remembered by this poor conscript below the earth."

When his wife heard these words, she wept loudly and said,
"I did not know you had met a violent end at the Long Wall!
As you say that your bones have been buried inside the Wall,
I do not know what more I can say."

Meng Jiang threw herself to the ground and wept to High Heaven,
Lamenting at length that her husband had died much too early.
A woman's determination till death can move rivers and mountains:
Because of her piteous weeping, the Long Wall collapsed!

An ancient poem reads:

Somber clouds rose over the mountains of Long,[18]
As the sound of her weeping saddened the wasteland.
If you say that man is bereft of the power to move,
Then why did the Long Wall come tumbling down?
    Over a thousand fathoms the stone wall was torn;
The wide world of rivers and mountains turned over.
Of course the Wall should never have collapsed;
It all occurred because of this single woman!

Beyond the border—too bad for words:
A shuddering heart does not dare listen.

After she had finished weeping, her heart was overcome by grief. She was saddened by the thought that her husband had suddenly passed away as a conscript. Alas, because of her chastity, her depression was only deepened. The skeletons were without number, not from a single deceased. The bones were heaped in a pile, so how could she choose the right ones? She bit her finger till she drew blood and sprinkled it on the Long Wall to display her determination. So she chose her husband's bones.

Meng Jiang wept as she said, "How do I choose them?
Your jade-like face is now mixed with the yellow earth.
I would have thought that your grave would have a marker,
But which ones are the right ones in this pile of bones?"
　　Alas, it was really impossible to make a rational choice;
The very sight filled one with sad and sorrowful thoughts.
One by one she picked up the bones to inspect them, and
Bit her finger till she drew blood, and then tested them all.
　　"If you are my husband, may the blood penetrate the bone;
If you are not Qi Liang, may it stay away from the bone.
If you allow me to recognize you, I will take you back home;
It is my dearest hope I will not have to leave you behind."
　　Loudly she wept till her voice was hoarse and choked up;
From her eyes flowed tears—a stream that couldn't be stopped.
"If High Heaven does not go against people's wishes,
May I too be allowed to die here before the Long Wall!"

Three times she stepped forward, three times she stepped back; now she was overcome by sadness, then she expressed her grief. Birds and beasts all cried and shrieked, mountains and forests all were shaking. . . . As the drop of blood dissolved, it immediately penetrated [the bone] completely. Of all the more than three hundred bones and joints, not a single piece was missing. . . . There were several other skeletons who had no one to take them home. The beauty, crying sadly, approached them and asked, "All you skeletons, where do you hail from? Because I am taking my husband back, I can convey a message on your behalf. And if you have a spirit, I can guide it home."

When the skeletons were asked about their situation,
They were able to communicate their hometowns in words.
Their souls replied to the wife of Qi Liang,
"We were all the sons of renowned families.
　　We were conscripted by the Qin to build the Long Wall;
Because we couldn't stand the hardship, we died on the job.
Our corpses lie in the fields, unknown to our relatives;

From spring till winter we rest in the sand of the desert.
    Please tell her who is grieving for us in the inner apartment
To make every effort to summon our souls and offer sacrifices.
And please remember these words very well in your heart,
And only disclose them to our parents when you see them."

The next six lines of verse are too damaged to allow for a translation. The text continues as follows:

Meng Jiang wrapped up her husband's bones in order to carry them back home with her. Aggrieved by the fact that her husband had passed away as a conscript, she composed a sacrificial text:

On day X of the X Month of the X year,[19] [I prepared] a sacrificial offering of all kind of victuals, which I respectfully offer in sacrifice to [you, my dear husband]. You were perfect in the hundred deportments and fully conversant with the seven texts. In the days you were among the living, your name reverberated through village and country. Toward superiors and inferiors you were without malice, finding the mean between harshness and pliability. But how could you serve as a conscripted laborer, building the Long Wall in faraway regions? You could not stand the hardship, and your soul found refuge in the realm of the dead. You may be compared to a red petal that falls to the ground, so we will forever lack the splendor of watching the blossom, or to the white snowflake that drifts down from heaven and never will be able to return to the clouds. Alas, your wife in her diligence provides you with this single cup: I display this orchid beaker on this jade mat, so you may enjoy the offerings from this golden goblet. If your soul has intelligence, may it take and accept these offerings!

When she had presented the offerings, she wrapped up her husband's bones and carried them with her on her back. . . . [20]

Here the text fragment ends, so the conclusion is unclear, but this version most likely ended with her return home.[21] In some later versions, Meng Jiangnü returns home and provides her husband with a proper funeral, while in the legend that was later current in Tongguan county, she dies of exhaustion in Tongguan on her way home.[22] But in many later versions, Meng Jiangnü's beauty attracts the attention of the First Emperor of the Qin, who wants to marry her. She agrees to do so if the emperor meets her conditions, but once he does, she commits suicide by drowning herself.

MENG JIANGNÜ

Once Meng Jiangnü had acquired her own name, she also acquired a cult. We find mention of temples dedicated to Meng Jiangnü (and her husband) from the eleventh century onward. Among the earliest places where such temples were erected are Ansu (Xushui) and Tongguan. In Yongqiu in 1176, the temple was devoted to Qi Liang, who was accompanied by his wife, and General Meng Tian. Here Qi Liang was given the surname Fan, which may derive either from a misrecognition of the character used to write his surname or from a mishearing of the phrase "the criminal Qi Liang" (*fan Qi Liang*). In the later tradition, Qi Liang thereupon became Fan Qilang. The number of temples to Meng Jiangnü increased greatly under the Ming dynasty, when constant conflicts with the Mongols along the northern border eventually resulted in the resumption of large-scale wall-building projects. Apart from the places already mentioned, temples to Meng Jiangnü were also found at Qixian (the birthplace of Qi Liang) and at Shanhaiguan, often presented as the site of the final confrontation between Meng Jiangnü and the First Emperor. Most of the temples dedicated to Meng Jiangnü were found in northern China; however, there were also temples in southern China, such as in Lizhou, in northwestern Hunan, which claimed to be her birthplace. Our information about the establishment or restoration of such temples usually is based on relevant documents found in local gazetteers. Often these documents also contain a potted version of the legend.

However, no complete account of the legend as novel, play, or ballad has been preserved from the period spanning the eleventh to the sixteenth century, despite the lament of the learned scholar Zheng Qiao (1104–1162) that the story of characters who had earned only a few words in the Classics, such as the wife of Qi Liang, might be developed into tales "of millions of words" by fiction writers, who relied only on their fertile tongues.[23] We know that the tale was adapted for the stage from early on, but of these plays only fragments have been preserved. The *Brocade Bag of Breeze and Moonlight* (Fengyue jin-nang), an anthology of song and drama printed in 1553, contains the arias of a number of scenes from an adaptation as "southern play" (*nanxi*) titled *Jiangnü's Winter Clothes* (Jiangnü hanyi ji), which may well date back to the fifteenth century. It comes with the following summary:

The style name of Meng Guang from Zhuguang county in Guazhou prefecture was Ziming. His daughter Jiangnü had studied the *Documents* and

Odes from an early age, and she was deeply conversant with the rites and righteousness. She swore an oath before Heaven that she would marry the man who had seen her undressed naked body, whether he was rich or poor. Later it happened that the talented student Fan Qiliang hid himself in the shade of the willows, below the flowers, because he was fleeing his corvée. When Jiangnü was taking a pleasure stroll and was about to take a bath, a wasp hid inside her gown, and she mistakenly opened her clothes. When she looked up, she saw Fan Qiliang, whom she took home with her; there she informed her parents and immediately married him. But they were husband and wife for only two days. Because Fan Qiliang suffered his corvée, she made the long trip to deliver him his winter clothes, and by her weeping brought down the Long Wall. When she saw her husband's corpse, the broken mirror was at his side. But by the grace of Heaven, he was raised to become a human being again, and husband and wife were once more reunited. When the king of Qin noticed her pure chastity, he appointed all members of her family to noble rank.[24]

Southern plays by convention end with a grand reunion scene, so playwrights were strongly tempted to provide even tragic stories with a happy ending of sorts, either by resurrecting dead lovers or by envisioning a reunion in heaven. The conventions of typecasting also turned Fan Qiliang from an undistinguished conscript into a student, and many later versions added plot details to explain why he was conscripted for corvée labor when students, as a status group, usually were exempted from such duties. Jiangnü's vow is here encountered for the first time. The playwright has also been quite inventive in dealing with episodes that must have been hard to stage, such as our heroine taking a bath and identifying her husband's remains by dropping blood on the jumbled bones.[25] The legend of Meng Jiangnü continued to be a favorite of the popular stage, and many versions are known from the regional forms of traditional Chinese opera of the late nineteenth and early twentieth centuries.[26]

The earliest full-length narrative account of the legend of Meng Jiangnü that has been preserved in its entirety is the *Precious Scroll as Spoken by the Buddha of the Chaste and Virtuous, Wise and Filial Meng Jiangnü at the Long Wall* (Foshuo zhenlie xianxiao Meng Jiangnü Changcheng baojuan). This work, printed around 1680, most likely dates from the final decades of the Ming dynasty.[27] The work belongs to the genre of "precious scrolls" (*baojuan*), also known as "precious volumes," which originated (perhaps as early as the twelfth century) as pious tales on Buddhist themes, written in a mixture of prose and verse. During the Ming and Qing dynasties, teachers of many new religions and sects also used this prosimetric format. These sectarian precious scrolls often consist of a considerable number of small chapters, each made up of song, prose, and verse. The *Precious Scroll as Spoken by the Buddha of the Chaste and Virtuous, Wise and Filial Meng Jiangnü at the Long Wall* clearly adheres to this format and also makes extensive use of the religious terminology of these new sectarian religions. At the very end, when all characters have returned to heaven, the Jade Emperor discloses that the First Emperor had been an incarnation of the "old Buddha," and that Fan Qiliang and Meng Jiangnü are the bodhisattvas of summer heat and winter cold, respectively, who created the four seasons by their intervention. The *Precious Scroll as Spoken by the Buddha of the Chaste and Virtuous, Wise and Filial Meng Jiangnü at the Long Wall* may well have been connected with a cult of Meng Jiangnü in the milieu of these sectarian religions; it also may have been more widely connected with the custom, once common in northern China, of burning winter clothes made of paper as a sacrifice to the deceased on the first day of the Tenth Month, the first day of winter.

In this precious scroll, Fan Qiliang is introduced as a student who, as a filial son, is the *remplaçant* for his elderly father when the latter is conscripted to work on the Wall. Once he arrives at the work site, he visits his uncle Meng Tian, who introduces him to the First Emperor. But when the First Emperor places Fan Qiliang in charge of the construction, a jealous Meng Tian plots Fan Qiliang's downfall. He tells Fan Qiliang that he should visit his parents, but as soon as he leaves, Meng Tian reports him for desertion. Fan Qiliang at first escapes, as a supernatural wind deposits him in Meng Jiangnü's flower garden, but soon after the wedding, he is arrested and taken back to the Wall, where Meng Tian engineers his death. Meng Jiangnü will take revenge on Meng Tian: she has not only made winter clothes for her husband but also woven a beautiful dragon-robe for the emperor; however, when Meng Tian offers the emperor what he believes to be this dragon-robe, he finds that she has substituted a set of winter clothes, and the greatly offended First Emperor has Meng Tian put to death. In the *Precious Scroll as Spoken by the Buddha of the Chaste and Virtuous, Wise and Filial Meng Jiangnü at the Long Wall*, the First Emperor is immediately impressed by Meng Jiangnü's virtue and happily accedes to her request to have her husband's bones buried in the eastern ocean. There she joins Fan Qiliang in death by jumping in after him.

In his 1958 collection of songs and prosimetric ballads on Meng Jiangnü, the editor Lu Gong preceded an excerpted edition of this very long text with the following disparaging remarks:

> On the basis of its contents, this text differs greatly from the Meng Jiangnü stories that are found among the people; moreover, the standpoint and viewpoint of the author are different. From the standpoint of the landowning class, the author proclaims the "virtuous administration by the imperial court." The whole work is permeated with feudal ideals, and it expounds a fatalistic viewpoint. Its artistic quality also is not very high, and it lacks emotive power.[28]

Lu Gong's ire may have been roused by one aspect of the text, which is that this version plays down the confrontation between the chaste maiden and the lustful tyrant, an episode that provides the high point of many other versions. But such a conclusion is far from universal, and the plot elements of the filial son, the jealous general, and the switched dragon-robe are reencountered in other adaptations of the legend as a precious scroll, including the one translated in this volume, which circulated till the 1980s in western Gansu (see chapter 6).

VERSIONS FROM THE EIGHTEENTH TO TWENTIETH CENTURIES

Of the many adaptations of the Meng Jiangnü legend from the last few centuries, the one in the "women's script" (*nü shu*) of Jiangyong still adheres closely to the outline of events as presented in the Tang-dynasty tales (for a brief explanation of women's script, see chapter 9). This version focuses consistently on the inner feelings of Meng Jiangnü, from her earliest yearnings for love to her grief at retrieving the bones of her husband, which she takes back to her home, where from that time on, "Each night she slept alongside her husband's bones, / And never in her life did she marry another man" (translated in chapter 9). Many versions, however, conclude the tale with a confrontation between the young widow and the ruler who acts inappropriately. Only this time, the muddle-headed ruler is not the duke of Qi, who offended against the rules of the mourning ritual, but the First Emperor of the Qin, the most redoubtable tyrant in Chinese history, who wants to have sex with her. Usually, the lascivious emperor is smitten by her beauty at first sight and is willing to do anything in order to make her his own. Many versions compete in developing the confrontation between Meng Jiangnü and the First Emperor. She demands more and more of him before she will consent to a marriage and then betrays the emperor's fevered hopes by committing suicide as soon as he has fulfilled all her requirements. In some, but certainly not all, versions of the tale, this confrontation between the First Emperor and Meng Jiangnü takes place at Shanhaiguan, to the northeast of Beijing, where the sixteenth-century Ming-dynasty wall reached the Bohai. Over the years, more and more local features would be associated with the characters and incidents in the story. It should be pointed out, however, that in some versions of the legend, the First Emperor is so impressed by Meng Jiangnü's virtue that he immediately grants her high honors.

Broadly speaking, the many versions of the legend can be divided into a northern and a southern group. The versions in the northern group tend to dispense with the bathing scene (see chapters 1, 5, and 7 for representative texts), perhaps because bathing customs changed over time or because it seemed reasonable to conclude that such a loyal wife must have been a perfect daughter-in-law too. Some retellings of the story give considerable space to Meng Jiangnü's care for her mother-in-law after her husband departs to work on the Wall and specify that she sets out to deliver the winter clothes only after her mother-in-law has died and properly been buried. As a rule, however, the stories stress Meng Jiangnü's single-minded devotion to her husband, alive or dead, to the detriment of her filial duties.

The southern versions retain the bathing scene. One group of texts maintains the vow described in the play *Jiangnü's Winter Clothes* and has her then take a bath on a stiflingly hot summer day. But other versions, originating from the Jiangnan area (Hangzhou, Suzhou, Shanghai), often seem to reflect the need to come up with some kind of explanation as to why a properly educated upper-class girl such as Meng Jiangnü would go skinny-dipping in the garden pond (see, for instance, the ballad translated in chapter 3). In these southern versions from the Jiangnan area, the name of Fan Qiliang has been changed to Wan Xiliang, a pampered young student from Suzhou who is on the run because the First Emperor wants to bury him in the Wall in order to ensure the stability of the project. As *wan* also has the meaning "ten thousand," the name change in these versions plays off the emperor's belief that the sacrificial victim Wan can replace ten thousand ordinary men (for more on this theme, see chapter 4). As soon as the wedding has taken place, Wan Xiliang is arrested and taken to the north, in some cases even before the wedding has been consummated. In texts from the Jiangnan area, descriptions of Meng Jiangnü's trek to the Long Wall develop the section of her journey from her hometown Huating, in Songjiang prefecture, to Zhenjiang by way of Suzhou, Wuxi, and Danyang.[29] Crossing Hushu Pass (between Suzhou and Wuxi) becomes a crucial episode, and she is allowed to continue her journey only after singing "the names of the flowers," that is, singing about her feelings of loneliness in each month of the year. This song also circulated independently. The southern versions from the Jiangnan region also maintain the servant who travels to the Wall and learns of Wan Xiliang's death, but the servant becomes more and more evil in each subsequent adaptation.

In a relatively late adaptation of the legend as precious scroll, which clearly shows the influence of the southern versions, Wan Xiliang and Meng Jiangnü are introduced as minor denizens of heaven. The future Wan Xiliang, filled with compassion for the people, who are suffering under the cruel regime of the First Emperor, decides on his own authority to descend to earth and serve as substitute for the ten thousand victims of the Long Wall. The future Meng Jiangnü decides to follow him, but as she is unwilling to be born "on a river of blood," she chooses vegetable birth instead and is born from a gourd. Once the emperor has given Wan Xiliang a great state funeral, she jumps into the burning pile of sacrificial offerings and returns to heaven as a whiff of smoke.

STUDIES AND TRANSLATIONS

The many versions of the legend were eagerly studied by the members of the Folklore Movement of the 1920s and 1930s, with Gu Jiegang in a leading role. His studies, based on an exhaustive collection of materials from classical stories and folkloric fieldwork, set a model in tracing both the development of the story over time and its variation regionally.[30] The members of the Folklore Movement very much wanted to read Meng Jiangnü as a direct expression of the emotions and feelings of "the people" in traditional society: as an expression of the yearning of women for freedom in love (being able to choose one's husband) and as an expression of the common people's hatred of political abuse and their daring to confront those in power. In order to do so, they had to ignore the wide differences between versions as well as the obvious intent of many of these versions. Summarizing this approach, Lu Gong in 1958 hailed the legend of Meng Jiangnü, in the Marxist jargon of the day, as "reflecting in a concentrated manner the resentment and resistance of the laboring people in feudal society against their cruel servitude under the ruling classes and exposing the crimes of the exploitative government of the feudal ruling classes."[31] This reading of course ran into trouble after 1949, and especially after 1966, because of Mao Zedong's admiration for the First Emperor of the Qin. During the Cultural Revolution, Meng Jiangnü did not escape classification as a "poisonous weed." In the words of a tract published in 1975, "This story viciously maligns the First Emperor and attacks the Great Wall, one of the greatest historical achievements of the Chinese people; it propagates reactionary Confucian ritualism with its loyalty and chastity, the Three Obediences, and the Five Norms; and it also propagates religious superstition, a fatalist viewpoint, and low taste."[32] Since then, however, Meng Jiangnü's status as an embodiment of all the suffering of the people in the old society has been reaffirmed, and the many versions of the tale have been the subject of a constant stream of articles since the early 1980s.[33] Recent decades have also seen the publication of a series of English-language articles on the historical development of the story by Ch'iu-kuei Wang (based on his Oxford dissertation, supervised by H. C. Chang and Piet van der Loon) and exhaustive monographs on the development and variety of the legend, also in oral literature, by Yang Zhenliang (1985), Wu Ruishu (2001), and Huang Ruiqi (2003).

The earliest English-language version of the legend of Meng Jiangnü most likely is the rhymed retelling offered by George Carter Stent as "Mêng Chêng's Journey to the Great Wall," in his *Entombed Alive, and other songs, ballads, etc. (from the Chinese)*, of 1878. This rendition would appear to be based on the "southern ballad" (*nanci*) version "Retrieving the Fan" (see chapter 3), or a closely related text. Not quite fifty years later, in 1934, Genevieve Wimsatt and Geoffrey Chen (Chen Sun-han) published *The Lady of the Long Wall, a Ku Shih or Drum Song, translated from the Chinese*. This translation, in rhymed verse, is based on a repeatedly reprinted text of an anonymous "youth book" (*zidishu*), also referred to as "bannerman's tales," in five chapters, *Weeping at the Wall* (Kucheng). Youth books were not performed in the early part of the twentieth century, but the texts were used by performers of "big-drum ballads" (*dagushu*), a very popular entertainment in northern China in late-Qing and Republican China. The earliest rendition of a prosimetric version is the translation by Joseph Needham and Liao Hongying, "The Ballad of Meng Jiang nu Weeping at the Great Wall (A Broadsheet from the City God's Temple at Lanchow, Kansu)," of 1948. This short text may well derive from Sichuan, as Meng Jiangnü and her husband are said to hail from that province. The translators do not specify the genre of their version, but its introduction has a strong Buddhist coloring. The main body of the text is written in seven-syllable verse interspersed with a few passages in ten-syllable lines. The passages in seven-syllable verse have been rendered using "William Langland's metre."

THE DUAL AIM OF THIS COLLECTION

First of all, this collection will serve to introduce a contemporary readership to the great variety in the retellings of the Meng Jiangnü legend. There is no single essential tale of Meng Jiangnü; there are only many versions, each with its own idiosyncrasies. While some versions focus very much on the difficulties of Meng Jiangnü's journey to the Great Wall, others pass over that episode in a few lines, and still others mention the weeping at the Wall only in passing. In addition to the variations discussed in this introduction, the reader should expect many more points of divergence, depending on period, region, and function of the text, and should realize that this collection contains but a small sampling of the myriad versions.

A second aim of this collection is to present to the Western reader a small selection of popular genres of verse narrative and prosimetric ballads. While earlier works of prosimetric narrative from the Tang and Song dynasties have been translated into English, translations of the voluminous and rich literature in the many genres of prosimetric literature of the Qing dynasty and Republican China are scarce. Many of these works are of considerable merit, and our ignorance impoverishes our appreciation of the variety of Chinese literature. The formal characteristics of the genres concerned are briefly discussed in the introductions to the translated texts.

In making this selection, I have been guided both by my own literary preference and pleasure in translating and by considerations of size. Many works of prosimetric literature are of great length and defy the endurance of all but the most committed translator. The works selected for this collection are all relatively short, if not very short, by the standards of traditional prosimetric narrative. Some of the most widespread versions of the legend in modern times are therefore not included. For example, the anonymous sixteen-chapter *Meng Jiangnü Travels a Myriad Miles to Search for Her Husband* (Meng Jiangnü wanli xunfu), of 1917, which tells its story through an alternation of prose and ten-syllable verse, and greatly expands the role of the evil servant Meng Xing, is not part of this collection.[34]

The translated texts fall naturally into two groups. The first comprises versions of the legend preserved in printed versions from the period of the Qing dynasty (and the early years of the Republic). The second is made up of texts collected in the final decades of the twentieth century. The texts belonging to the first group were printed (and probably written) in the biggest and most advanced cities of late-imperial China, such as Beijing, Suzhou, Shanghai, Xiamen, and Xi'an. While these texts definitely were intended for a large and popular urban and rural readership, their authors often display considerable literary skills: they may not have belonged to the bureaucratic and scholarly elite, but they also were far from illiterate peasants. Most likely they were members of the educated urban middle class of lower literati and literate professionals such as doctors, schoolteachers, priests, geomancers, and even professional entertainers. After modern printing technologies, such as lithography, were introduced into China by the last quarter of the nineteenth century, these texts, though now often quite rare, were printed in such quantities that they reached the remotest corners of the realm, often exerting considerable influence on local, oral traditions.

The texts belonging to the second group usually were collected in out-of-the-way and backward corners of the countryside.[35] A few are based on recordings of oral performances, and others are based on partially reconstructed texts. While many of these rural areas may have preserved traditions that were lost in other parts of China, it does not mean that these areas did not share in the vicissitudes of twentieth-century Chinese history and were immune to outside influences. The texts also have been edited more or less intrusively by modern scholars of folklore, who brought to their task not only their ardent love of folk literature but also their preconceptions about the nature of the materials they were collecting (so well described by Haiyan Lee in her contribution to this volume). In addition, after 1949, these scholars often had to meet very strict demands of correctness in order to see their editions published.

MENG JIANGNÜ AND THE
MAY FOURTH FOLKLORE MOVEMENT

HAIYAN LEE

N 1924, THE RENOWNED HISTORIAN GU JIEGANG PUBLISHED a pathbreaking essay on the origins and transformations of the Meng Jiangnü legend. In the following years, the effort Gu initiated grew into a collective one involving his Beijing-based colleagues as well as folklore enthusiasts from around the country. They gathered, collated, and analyzed a wide array of versions and genres from different parts of China and published their research findings in nine special issues of Beijing University's *Folksong Weekly* (Geyao zhoukan), which were reprinted in anthologies and formed the founding texts of modern Chinese folklore studies. Why did a folktale about a woman whose weeping for her dead husband is said to have brought down the Great Wall generate so much enthusiasm among the May Fourth folklorists? The answer must first be sought in the larger ideological context of modern folklore movements.

Modern folklore studies owes its origins to the Romantic movement in Europe, particularly Germany. Romanticism ushered in an expressive theory of language that privileged the spoken over the written and motivated the discovery of the timeless folk as a site of authenticity. It canonized the belief that poetry was the most natural expression of feeling and that the folk spoke

24

an eminently poetic language because they spoke directly from the heart. German Romanticism was also intimately bound up with German nationalism, and the localization of national essence in the poetic language of the folk became the guiding principle of modern folklore movements in Germany and among other latecomers to modernity such as Japan and China. The expressive theory of language, introduced to China as part of the conceptual baggage of Romanticism, enabled the leaders of the May Fourth movement to accelerate the language reform initiated in the late Qing.[1] Adoption of the vernacular was intended not only to facilitate the modernization projects of the nation-state but also to connect the May Fourth generation to the imaginary roots that had been rendered invisible by the encrusted overgrowth of Confucian culture. May Fourth folklorists set out to excavate an emotional fullness of being from beneath the written word and to establish folk culture as an alternative (albeit vanishing) tradition that preserved the authentic values and sentiments of the people. From its inception, folklore was wedded to May Fourth emancipatory agendas: the liberation of the individual, woman, and nation. This political orientation motivated two intersecting endeavors: the engendering of folklore as feminine and the translation of emotion across moral and epistemic divides.

May Fourth folklorists deployed the following typical narrative in order to account for the origin and nature of folklore. For the entire duration of history, the folk were oppressed by the ruling classes and their voices excised from the annals of official history. But the indomitable folk were able to articulate their feelings and protests in folksong—a medium that Confucian literati, with few exceptions, considered beneath their attention. Folksong and other folk genres, therefore, offer us a rare glimpse into the lives and sentiments of vast segments of the populace who are otherwise "without history." The folklore movement pursued a dual mission: on the one hand, the quest for the lost voice of the people "within the interior of the scriptural systems," or the archives, and, on the other, the quest for the songs and myths that the folklorists believed could still be heard "behind the doors of our cities, in the nearby distance of the countryside."[2] Yet the positing of an essential, timeless folk culture blended the two quests into a fundamental search for the "Voice" of the other, an operation of retrieval and rescue. The folklorists' task was to collect as many ballads and rhymes from as many places as possible, thereby rescuing the folk tradition from the ravages of historical prejudice and modern indifference.

25

Bearing in mind the larger context, we now return to our question about the Meng Jiangnü legend: What was it about the story that made it the founding legend of the May Fourth folklore movement? And how were its meanings and messages construed and constructed by the pioneering folklorists represented by Gu Jiegang? The earliest written record that can be linked to the legend is a meager episode about rites and proper womanhood. And yet the later versions invariably present a colorful legend replete with an accidental voyeur, a plucky and independent-spirited woman, a heartbreaking separation, a lonely and perilous journey, and a miracle at China's most famous landmark. This was precisely what puzzled Gu Jiegang. In his first essay on Meng Jiangnü, the one that astonished his colleagues and became their model, he recalled having first become aware of the linkage between the two stories, that is, the folk legend of Meng Jiangnü and the official record about the wife of Qi Liang, when he stumbled upon an intriguing reference in Zheng Qiao's (1104–1162) *Comprehensive Treatise on Institutions* (Tongzhi). It stated that although Qi Liang's wife was mentioned only in passing in the classics, storytellers had developed her life into tales of "tens of millions of words." Gu followed the lead and went back to *The Zuo Tradition*, China's oldest narrative history. There he found the terse episode about Qi Liang's wife encountering the duke of Qi outside the city wall.

Gu noted wryly that aside from commending Qi Liang's wife for knowing ritual propriety, *The Zuo Tradition* gives no explanation as to why she was outside the city wall, how she grieved for her husband, or whether she followed him in death in an act of self-immolation.[3] All these would become central ingredients in the Meng Jiangnü legend. A subsequent record, for example, makes the weeping of Qi Liang's wife a key feature of her story. She is said to be such an expert at ritual wailing that she single-handedly inspired a vocal fad in the state of Qi. To Gu the astute historian, this was patently a case of inverted cause and effect. He confidently argued that the emphasis on her ability to wail was in fact a reflection of the musical trends in the state of Qi.[4] But Gu's interest was most roused by the ideological implications of a woman's magical tears. Thus when he turned next to Liu Xiang's (77–6 B.C.E.) *Biographies of Exemplary Women*, he was delighted to find that a whole new plot sequence had been added to the original story of Qi Liang's wife observing ritual propriety. The new sequence tells how she grieved for her dead husband and how her tears caused the city wall to collapse. Gu became fascinated by her bold act of weeping over her husband's corpse beneath the city wall, that is, in full public view, an act so contrary to her conduct in the earliest record and so full of subversive implications. He asked triumphantly, "How could the city wall be the proper place for ritual observance?" Moreover, she is said to have wept for ten days, which eventually caused the wall to crumble— "is this something permitted by ritual laws (*lifa*)?"[5]

Lest his readers fail to grasp the thrust of his rhetorical questions, Gu Jiegang spelled out the subversive message that Liu Xiang's text betrays despite itself: *li* (ritual), is meant to regulate people's emotions so that there is neither excess nor inadequacy. Qi Liang's wife, however, fails to moderate her grief and acts like a barbarian, going so far as to bellow in the field and frighten people. Thus one can hardly consider her a proper woman as the ancient records would have one believe.[6] Furthermore, *li* has always stipulated strict gender segregation, a rule that applies even to husbands and wives. Widows, therefore, are not allowed to weep at night lest they be suspected of "harboring sexual yearnings" (*si qing xing*).[7] It follows that Qi Liang's wife's immoderate and demonstrative wailing not only is highly subversive in itself but also casts a shadow of suspicion on the husband, who may have been so "uxorious" (*hao nei*) as to be "negligent of rites" (*kuang li*). In other words, there seems to have been too much feeling or attachment between husband and wife, which is a horizontal, reciprocal emotional bond seldom encouraged in the hierarchical kinship order. Gu could not help asking rhetorically again, "How did such a woman get into the sacrosanct pages of *Biographies of Exemplary Women*?"[8] Amazed by his "discovery" of a bold, even insurrectional, subtext in the pages of Confucian hagiographies, Gu attributes it to the Confucian scribe's absentmindedness: the episodes of the "crumbling wall" (*bengcheng*) and "suicide by drowning" (*toushui*) were invented by uneducated villagers who projected their own feelings and sufferings onto Qi Liang's wife. Liu Xiang perchance heard these unadorned stories and accidentally included them in his book alongside the original story; "nonetheless, we have a lot to thank him for," Gu notes.[9]

Gu then went on, with his signature historian's flourish, to explicate the process by which Qi Liang's wife became Meng Jiangnü and how the story of the city wall became intertwined with the resentment of the populace (particularly the lonely wives of corvée laborers) over the unending building of the Great Wall.[10] What emerged from Gu's excavation of the archives is a heroic narrative of the triumph of *qing* (feeling) over *li*, or ritual. From the vantage point of the May Fourth valorization of freedom in love,[11] Gu reads the legend as first and foremost a tale of sorrow, the sorrow of separation between a husband and wife, and a tale of protest, the individual's protest against the state's arbitrary power. Once sorrow and protest are identified as the core of the legend, the moral message about ritual propriety appears extraneous and awkwardly tacked on by Confucian literati who were ignorant of the sentiments of the common people. This is borne out, it seemed to Gu, by the fact that as the story evolved, the episode of Qi Liang's wife's refusing to accept condolences from a lord for ritualistic reasons was gradually lost and, by contrast, Meng Jiangnü's expressions of grief became more and more flamboyant. The evolution of the legend thus proves that the people's living feelings ultimately prevailed over the dead doctrines of the literati.

In another essay, Gu Jiegang recapitulates his earlier findings and dwells extensively on the thematic and regional variations of the legend by taking stock of the growing trove of materials that he and his fellow folklorists had gathered across the country. In conclusion, he argues, the myriad stories of Meng Jiangnü were the product of protean folk sentiment and imagination, not the result of corruption of an official story by the folk. If anything, he considered it odiously intrusive that the literati should insist on foregrounding such plot elements as Meng Jiangnü submitting to an arranged marriage, cheerfully serving her in-laws in her husband's absence, and setting out to find her husband only after burying her mother-in-law—elements highlighted in several ballads in this volume. He notes flatly: "when the story returned to the hands of the literati, it changed beyond recognition."[12]

Oftentimes Gu could not help acknowledging the literati provenance of a particular song or story, but he was reluctant to question the plebeian authorship of folklore or the existence of a folk culture that was distinct from elite culture. He lamented the fact that he and his colleagues had to rely heavily on written materials and contend with the literati's distorting renditions while striving to capture the faint echoes of folk voices in the interior of the scriptural systems. He nonetheless averred that "the story of Meng Jiangnü was not a creation of the literati; rather, it was the cumulative creation of commoners that was then appropriated by the literati."[13] For him, the traffic between elite and common cultures did not run both ways. The May Fourth movement's search for an alternative tradition drove even a discerning historian such as Gu to discount orthodox elements (such as Meng Jiangnü's filiality) in folklore as either a negligible or an artificial imposition that the folk would just as soon do without.

Gu Jiegang was grateful to those who sent him their field findings and "enabled [him] to see the true face of the story from around the country."[14] That he should speak of "a true face" when confronted precisely with a heterogeneity of narratives is paradoxical. If the original Voice was hard to discern because of "textual corruptions and the avatars of history,"[15] a symphony of "voices" was nonetheless gathered to attest to the Voice's veracity, vitality, and unity. Few folklorists paused to ponder the disjunction between the singular Voice of the people posited by modern nationalism, on the one hand, and the heterogeneous voices "retrieved" from the scriptural economy of tradition and/or "transcribed" directly by the field researchers, on the other hand. Their preferred way of dealing with the inherent instability of the folkloric "text" was to submit it to the scientific methods of folklore studies. For them, the sheer diversity and variability of folk genres posed no obstacle to the scientific classificatory schemes that they believed would lend coherence to everything collected under the rubric of folklore. Gender was a common category of classification with which they approached folkloric materials. They firmly believed that folklore for the most part was created by women, about women's lives, and for women's own amusement and catharsis.

Gu Jiegang maintained that folklore authorship was largely female because women were at the bottom of the social hierarchy and had the most to grieve about. Commenting on a ballad titled "Meng Jiangnü's Names of the Flowers of the Twelve Months" (Meng Jiangnü shieryue huaming), popular in the Jiangnan region, Gu wrote:

> We know that "Meng Jiangnü's Names of the Flowers of the Twelve Months" articulated the shared sorrow of all lonely wives. They humanized the story of the collapse of the Great Wall with their own sad experiences. When they saw their neighbors live in harmony and enjoy life's simple pleasures, their hearts ached and tears flowed; they imagined that Meng Jiangnü must have also wept like themselves. Thus whatever sorrows they experienced they projected onto Meng Jiangnü. She became their patron saint in suffering and she changed correspondingly to the way their feelings changed. Because she embodied all the feelings of pain and misery, her character became extraordinarily great.[16]

Here, Gu maps the transformation of the legend directly onto the shifting contours of women's emotional landscapes, and Meng Jiangnü becomes a folkloric symbol that condenses the cumulative sufferings of women through-out the ages. Through her, the folklorists hope to gain access to the hearts and minds of those who, like themselves, have protested against a cruel and unjust social order and whose emotional fullness of being holds the hope of regeneration for the nation. In their eyes, the Meng Jiangnü legend evokes a powerful imagery of a frail, empty-handed, and grief-stricken woman bringing down the monstrous Great Wall with nothing but her tears.

The imagery is so powerful precisely because the Great Wall has become a potent symbol of the traditional social order in the twentieth century. True, the folklorists were, to a large extent, following the pervasive Confucian literati view of the Wall as the ruins of failed moral rulership. As Arthur Waldron's study of the Great Wall myth shows, the Wall has carried a predominantly negative valence for most of Chinese history on both the elite and popular levels. During the Ming dynasty (1368–1644), for instance, despite the court's conscientious efforts to distinguish the Ming fortifications from the Qin walls, critics deliberately lumped them together in order to associate contemporary political practice with "despotism, cruelty, and ultimately, political failure."[17] Only in the twentieth century and, crucially, via a "detour" of mythologization in the West, however, did the Wall take on national-historical significance and become part and parcel of the crisis of modern nationhood.[18] Thus, for the folklorists, the Great Wall ceased to stand merely for the wrong kind of politics (ruling by force instead of by virtue) but rather for the entire traditional political and moral edifice, the inhuman feudal China that they wished to make human as well as modern. The imagery of Meng Jiangnü wailing at the Wall allowed the folklorists to posit woman as a prepolitical being and the feelings she expresses as external to everything that the Wall symbolized in their eyes. Her agency is thus entirely defined by her utopian location vis-à-vis the political. The contrast between the power of emotion (the tears) and the fragility of power (the crumbling Wall) must have been very seductive to the iconoclastic and romanticist mind-set of May Fourth intellectuals. Liu Fu (aka Liu Bannong) (1891–1934), another pioneer of the folklore movement, expressed his sense of wonderment at the discrimination of folk memory in the following poem:

> To this day people are still talking of Meng Jiangnü,
> Yet no more is said of the First Emperor of the Qin or the Martial Emperor of the Han.

Throughout the ages nothing is sadder than an ordinary tragedy;
In her tears Meng Jiangnü lives through all eternities.[19]

We may gloss the poem this way: The rich and powerful might aspire to immortality by recourse to brute force (the Great Wall) or hegemonic culture (dynastic histories), but in the end it is the heartfelt voices of the people that truly endure. An emperor's death might be mourned in the most sumptuous ceremony, but it was "an ordinary tragedy" that moved generation after generation to tears because ordinary tragedies, such as the absence or death of a husband, continued to devastate ordinary people, particularly women. Through the poignant symbols of Meng Jiangnü and the Great Wall, people passed on their feelings from heart to heart without or despite the alienating mediation of the written word, or so the folklorists seemed to believe.

The vision of the individual as an apolitical being who is able to confront power from without has so long shaped humanist scholarship and appealed to the liberatory impulses of Marxism and feminism that few have sought to complicate the May Fourth reading of the Meng Jiangnü legend as an allegory of subaltern protest. The folklorists cut through a web of significations that situated the story meaningfully in its immediate historical, moral, and epistemic context. Their scholarship is thus a process of translation and negotiation with alterity, a process that entails epistemological violence but also leaves behind visible traces of that violence in the forms of unassimilated and unassimilable "remainders." These traces and remainders come to us in the immediate form of citations, as when the folklorist cites a textual fragment, an oral anecdote, or a particular folk belief without being able fully to render it in (usually) his own terms or induct it into a new system of meanings. Such citations, by retaining their stubborn unintelligibility, point to the possibility of an alternative epistemological framework from which they have been severed. It therefore behooves us to attend to moments when the folklorist seems puzzled by, or deliberately dismisses, a particular article of his materials as an oddity or a literati fabrication. My contention is that there is enough in the citational texts of the legend that permits a reading of Meng Jiangnü as representing the claims of kinship rather than of an individual woman and that these claims are implicated within rather than outside the structures of power.

In his miscellaneous research notes on the legend, Gu Jiegang cites from an episode in the dynastic history of the Liang in which blood is used to ascertain father-son descent relations. The story concerns a royal heir named Zong who was able to establish his legitimacy by disinterring the deceased king's remains and dripping his blood onto the bones, which miraculously absorbed the blood. He then counterproved this by having another (non-related) man butchered and testing his blood on the royal bones. As Ann Waltner shows in her work on adoption, while concepts of consanguinity in late-imperial China were overshadowed by much stronger notions of reincarnation and retribution in the conceptualization of heredity, both medical texts and popular legends expressed a belief in the efficacy of blood in establishing paternity ties. When this belief was extended to the spousal relation, as in the Meng Jiangnü legend, however, there was no lack of skepticism. One commentary to a nineteenth-century edition of the Song forensic medicine text *Washing Away of Wrongs* (Xi yuan lu), for example, regarded the Meng Jiangnü episode as "unfathomable."[20] Gu, bolstered by Enlightenment confidence in science, came to the conclusion that the folk authors had simply gotten it wrong when they supposed that Meng Jiangnü could tell her husband's bones apart from those of other men by using her own blood:

> Because Xiao Zong and Dong Hun were presumed to be father and son, one could arguably allow for the idea of identifying bones by blood. But the relationship between Meng Jiangnü and Qi Liang was that of love [*lian'ai guanxi*] rather than blood ties. How could the method of dripping blood have worked for them? . . . The commoners must have thought that if it worked for father and son, it could work for husband and wife too, little knowing that it is all nonsense according to modern forensic science.[21]

Gu resolved the puzzle by pointing to the fanciful or at least not entirely logical way in which the folk mind works. But the folk "misapplication" of a folk belief points to something beyond just erratic logic. Perhaps in the folk imagination, the conjugal relationship is conceptualized more as one of kinship than that of contract or what Gu called "love" (*lian'ai guanxi*). Nancy Jay writes of the various ways to which kinship resorts in order to counter the obstacle women's reproductive powers pose to the "ideal of perfect patrilineal continuity."[22] The trope of "consanguinity" between spouses may well be such a strategy for converting women from outsiders to insiders so that their childbearing capacity does not "pollute" the purity of the paternal line.[23] As a corollary, it also converts marriage into a kinship institution that operates fully within the ascriptive, corporate logic of patriliny as opposed to a contractual institution predicated on individual rights and obligations or even a dyadic union based on private affective bonds. In other words, the trope articulates the desire to assimilate the conjugal relationship within the kinship structure of hierarchy, filiality, and continuity. If a wife is to a husband as a son is to a father, then the ties of blood and their ethical expression, filial piety, should ideally underwrite both relationships.

Indeed, Meng Jiangnü's story turns on an archetypal plot chronicling the trials and tribulations of a filial son or daughter searching for a lost parent or going to the rescue of a parent in distress. In a note appended to Zhong Jingwen's (1903–2002) contribution to his research volume, Gu Jiegang revealed that he had found textual evidence (by way of a colleague) that renders Meng Jiangnü a "filial woman" (*xiaonü*): A ballad from Guangxi compares her act of bringing winter garments to her husband to the magical acts of filiality immortalized in the *Classic of Filial Piety* (Xiaojing). Another ballad similarly lauds her weeping at the Great Wall, searching for her husband's bones, and bringing them home as "filial" acts on a par with that of the Buddha's disciple Mulian (Maudgalyayana), who descended to hell to save his mother from eternal damnation. Gu remarked that the folk mind seemed to have made an analogy between the parent-son and husband-wife relation and that this analogy even engendered variations about "searching for a father" (*xunfu*).[24] But he did not seem to perceive the logical consistency between the trope of consanguinity and the image of the filial Meng Jiangnü. Yet one may reasonably argue from such untranslated remainders of folklore scholarship that the Meng Jiangnü story is essentially a story about kinship virtue that deploys the tried and true formula of supernatural response as cosmic validation of human ethical heroism.

This reading of the trope of blood and bone as affirming the primacy of kinship, however, by no means presupposes the simple opposition of kinship and politics. In a way, this goes without saying, given the traditional conceptualization of the family and the state as analogous and mutually dependent institutions. Moreover, as historians have shown in recent decades, the late-imperial state as well as local authorities played an increasingly active role in promoting and sponsoring female virtue—enacted by chaste widows, self-immolating wives, sacrificial mothers, and filial daughters.[25] The inclusion of biographies of exemplary women in local histories was a way of articulating community pride and identity; quest for state commendation and sponsorship of virtuous womanhood was a constituent element in the "cultural nexus of power" that enabled the state to communicate its authority to local leaders and allowed the latter to articulate their political aspiration and buttress their moral legitimacy.[26]

In certain versions of the legend, after her tears have caused the Great Wall to crumble, Meng Jiangnü is summoned before the First Emperor of the Qin, who desires her for her virtue and beauty. She is said to have duped him into honoring her husband with a ceremonial burial and then jumped into a river and drowned herself. That a woman's virtue should make her an object of desire for the sovereign ruler seems to affirm the fact that kinship is never truly outside the state but, rather, inhabits a common moral universe with the latter. What the emperor desires is not so much an individual woman, alluring as she may be, but the extraordinary bond of kinship of which her virtue is an index. The emperors of China are proverbially benighted owing to the fecklessness of their political cronies and sexual subjects. The First Emperor's wish to wed Meng Jiangnü only accentuates his inability to cultivate lasting bonds of loyalty and devotion among his court ministers, courtiers, and harem. His attempt to appropriate what the ordinary folk are able to enjoy in their apparently abject powerlessness is thwarted only because, in popular historical memory, he is the epitome of politics as brute force, something that is utterly incompatible with virtue and inherently disruptive of the folk way of life. But like that of Antigone, Meng Jiangnü's defiance of the emperor partakes of the same political structure that robs her of her husband, a structure that grants the sovereign absolute power of life and death over his subjects.[27] Thus a ceremonial burial authorized and officiated by the emperor is the highest honor she can bring upon her dead husband after his life has been summarily extinguished by that ruler.

The legend, at least in the versions that figure the emperor as a desiring sovereign, can therefore be read both as a celebration of kinship's resistance to the illegitimate exercise of political power *and* as a commentary on the cultural nexus of power in which kinship virtues compulsively seek the recognition and validation of the ultimate political authority. This is perhaps why not a few versions actually feature the First Emperor in a positive role magnanimously conferring the honorable title of chaste widow on Meng Jiangnü. This, to be sure, is a typical practice of the late-imperial state and a crucial component of the cultural nexus of power. And it is apposite that the First Emperor becomes a player in the story only after the Ming dynasty.[28]

However, when the legend is translated by May Fourth folklorists, kinship is entirely eclipsed, and the individual stands alone in a heroic confrontation with the state. The exclusive focus on the individual, framed by the expressive theory of language that informs folklore studies, also explains why the most compelling imagery for the folklorists is that of Meng Jiangnü weeping at the foot of the Great Wall until it collapses. For them, weeping is expression par excellence, for the heart, in its uncontrollable grief, has dispensed with the clumsy medium of language and has "spoken" directly, spontaneously. In the same way that kinship is eclipsed in favor of the free-standing individual, the glossing of weeping as a cri de coeur elides the question of ritual, a crucial dimension of public mourning in traditional China. Ritual becomes yet another remainder of folklore translation.

In some of the early records scrutinized by Gu Jiegang, the ritual quality of Qi Liang's wife's wailing is underscored by its public enactment as well as the presence of instrumental accompaniment. Her virtuosity as a vocal performer sets a musical trend for others to emulate. Gu, however, placed her wailing on a continuum with acts of weeping, howling, or sobbing documented in later records—all as signs referencing the same psychosomatic reality of crying. In doing so, he inscribed the modern notion of psychological interiority on a ritual practice not necessarily grounded in personal feelings. In an essay on emotion and praise in India, Arjun Appadurai invokes the Hindi dramaturgic theory of *rasa* in order to highlight a different regime of feeling and expression. He characterizes *rasa* as an impersonal feeling expressed in a set of codified gestures so as to create a chain of communication in feeling. Crucially, this chain is forged "not by unmediated empathy between the emotional 'interiors' of specific individuals but by recourse to a shared, and relatively fixed, set of public gestures."[29] The same delinking of shared feeling and the emotional authenticity of individual performers also informs relatively stylized and semiscripted performances of ritual wailing. Indeed, Gu made the connection himself when he used the example of a famous opera singer's ability to carry a "weeping tune" (*kutou*) for four or five minutes in one breath as a way of helping his readers imagine Qi Liang's wife's consummate art of wailing.[30]

Yet the theatrical aspects of wailing did not deter Gu Jiegang from insisting on its personal expressive quality. Steven Feld points out that the expressive or cathartic model is based on the modern, largely Western assumption that "when emotions 'build up' to a 'boiling point' they must be released."[31] In this model, expressive behavior is taken in a functionalist sense to represent "a bursting of the social seam, an overflow, a chaotic falling apart."[32] In his study of Kaluli ritual wailing, Feld insists that we put aside such assumptions. In his view, the key quality of Kaluli ritual wailing is a creative "pulling together" of affect rather than its "falling apart." This socially organized and positively evaluated form of emotional articulation expresses identities as "deeply felt." Thus, traditionally, no attempts were made to constrain ritual wailing. In the catharsis model, by contrast, mourners can arouse a sense of unease and ambivalence in those around them who may, on the one hand, see crying as a salutary discharge of emotion (lest it build up and do harm to the bereaved) and, on the other, also be apprehensive of "the chaotic indication of personal aggressive impulses."[33]

The crumbling of the Great Wall seems so pregnant with the chaos of personal aggressive impulses that the folklorists gladly bring the cathartic model to bear on the story of Qi Liang's wife or Meng Jiangnü. Her performance of ritual wailing is translated into a spontaneous, passionate, and uncontrollable outpouring of grief; her tears become a transparent corporeal sign pointing to an inner emotional reality. In mythological terms, her tears burst the social seam and precipitate "a chaotic falling apart" of the orthodox social order. However, the classical records that cast Qi Liang's wife as an exemplar of ritual propriety apparently proceed from a different understanding of emotion and social order, one that is more akin to the concept of *rasa* or Kaluli ritual. Her public performance of ritual wailing may well be a codified gesture initiating a chain of communication in feeling that involves not only human spectators but also cosmic forces, to the extent that Heaven reciprocates her feeling with a supernatural sign: the collapse of the city wall. For the classical historian, the human-cosmic communion could well take place without reference to the "emotional interiors" of specific individuals. Even Meng Jiangnü's suicide need not be an ultimate gesture of undying passion; instead, it may simply complete the set of codified behavior expected of a new widow, particularly one who is being coerced into remarriage and who is therefore unable to consecrate her life to kinship solidarity. Her wailing and suicide suggest not a falling apart of the social order but, rather, an expression of deeply felt identity through a series of socially organized and positively evaluated performances. Her entry in *Biographies of Exemplary Women* is perhaps not so accidental as Gu Jiegang believed, for Liu Xiang probably had no reason to perceive a glaring contradiction between her observance of ritual propriety and her magical acts of mourning.

If the expressive theory of language has enabled May Fourth folklorists to replace the claims of kinship with those of the individual and to dismiss ritual formality in favor of emotional authenticity, it has also inspired the anachronistic discovery of romantic love in folklore. Disappointed with the relative reticence on the subject in elite classical poetry, the folklorists were ecstatic over the open and bold manner in which folksongs and legends dealt with eros. Chang-tai Hung explains that "love songs" (*qingge*) "ranked high with Chinese intellectuals, both because love had acquired a new meaning in modern China, and because more than half the songs they collected concerned love."[34] Hung does not ask how the "new meaning" of love came to constitute the very category of "love songs" and how the primacy of the category might account for the preponderance of love songs collected. To May Fourth folklorists, of course, what they found in amorous folksongs was love *pure and simple*. Love was a fundamental idiom of self-fashioning for the May Fourth generation.[35] The discovery of "love" in folklore enabled intellectuals to revise the bleak picture, sketched by Lu Xun (1881–1936) and others, of rural society as a breeding ground for misery and injustice and of the peasantry as unfeeling, cowardly, and chauvinistic. For the folklorists, the creators of erotic songs seemed to possess the quintessence of modern subjectivity: emotive expressiveness driven by unfettered sexuality.

Gu Jiegang, without exception, found himself especially drawn to the erotic flights of fancy that the folk inventors of the Meng Jiangnü story were fond of taking. In some versions, for example, Meng Jiangnü is said to have decided then and there that the young man who chanced upon her bathing in the garden would have to marry her. She then forthrightly demands that they immediately consummate their future marriage under a willow tree before bringing him to meet her parents. Here, the folk imagination seems to have been cross-fertilized by a popular narrative genre that features a sexually aggressive woman, or the femme fatale; for Gu, it is simply an expression of the free-spiritedness of the folk. He wrote:

As the folk legend became more and more elaborate, the meaning of the story was increasingly concentrated in the unrestrained expression of feeling. Before Meng Jiangnü was married, she had already harbored amorous thoughts. When she caught a man [peeping at her], she immediately demanded to mate with him under a willow tree. She embarked on a ten-thousand-*li* journey to search for her husband despite the strenuous objec-

37

tions of her parents and relatives. When the First Emperor wanted to marry her, she extracted three promises from him through subterfuge and then killed herself once her wishes were granted.... [In the folk imagination], the prim and proper wife of Qi Liang turned into an advocate of free love who dared to sacrifice her life for love.[36]

Indeed, romantic love is about the only subject on which folklore anthologists offer songs with an upbeat, even playful, spirit. Liu Jing'an, who compiled *Folksongs and Women* (Geyao yu funü), in 1927, explained that most of the songs he collected were sad because Chinese women lived in privation both materially and spiritually. They had little comfort in life, and their husbands treated them as playthings, or they were downright neglected and forced to live like widows. Nevertheless, even if a woman's person could be imprisoned, her love could not. Passion did not recognize "chastity" or the "memorial archway."[37] The happiest moment in a woman's life was her secret tryst with her lover, without which her life would be a living hell. Love songs came into being spontaneously at the zenith of romantic passion; either joyful or melancholy, they were always genuine, frank, and artless.[38]

May Fourth folklorists saw romantic love as something timeless and universal as they set out to document its historical lineage and regional variations. Philosophers and cultural historians, however, have long demonstrated the relative novelty, in the scale of human history, of the idea of romantic love. As a distinctly modern (eighteenth-century) concept, romantic love presupposes specific ideas about the individual, gender, marriage, family, and the meaning of life.[39] In particular, it involves a psychological model of the self, a new valuation of sentiment, as well as women's growing independence. Although women's liberation and gender equality did not become goals of social movements in China until the turn of the twentieth century, the folklorists did not hesitate to claim an uninterrupted history for love stretching back to antiquity. Under the rubric of love, they consolidated a range of expressions concerning the male-female relationship, even though most of them had little to do with the concepts of interiority, individual liberty, or gender equality.

Gu Jiegang's rendering of Meng Jiangnü as "an advocate of free love" is thus a classic instance of ideologically motivated epistemological anachronism. As an essentialized sexual being, Meng Jiangnü's actions can be nothing other than manifestations of her inner sexual truth. Her startling lack of inhibition in the matter of sex is read as nature's triumph over ritual; her courage to defy both her family and the emperor bespeaks nature's heroic self-assertion and contempt for repressive authorities. As a folklore character, Meng Jiangnü belongs to the tradition of folk protest, a tradition that was accommodated within the ideological framework of the Confucian social order. Rulers, in fact, are enjoined to pay heed to the voices of folk discontent because they have an ethical obligation to their subjects' well-being and their legitimacy rests partly on fulfilling that obligation. Those rulers whose political fortunes take a bad turn have, in historical reckoning, necessarily turned a deaf ear to folk anger and therefore hastened their own downfall. But as a fighter for free love, Meng Jiangnü is no longer merely a figure of protest against unjust rule and a medium of communicating folk anguish to the sovereign and appealing to his benevolence. Instead, she is endowed with a politicized agency and becomes a player in the mighty struggle between the dominant and the subaltern, between cultural artifice and natural emotion. The postulation of a reified subaltern subjectivity is precisely what allowed Gu to move freely between history and folklore and construct woman, eros, and defiance as signifiers of a fundamental human truth.

Through folklore studies, May Fourth intellectuals fashioned their self-identity vis-à-vis a reified notion of the Voice of the Chinese "people." But "people," particularly the peasantry, was a profoundly ambiguous entity, both seductive and dangerous, the object of nostalgic longing and of observation and regulation.[40] One of the questions that deeply troubled the intellectuals was whether or not the average peasant was capable of love or sympathy. The folklorists offered the most affirmative answer, mitigating Lu Xun's famously grim view and reinventing rural society as a site of emotional authenticity and pastoral nostalgia. Drawing inspiration from European and Japanese folklore studies, the folklorists projected folk culture as a vital alternative tradition suppressed by Confucian orthodoxy and threatened by modernity. They embarked on a rescue operation, aiming to save the endangered folk culture from its enemies old and new and to appropriate it for modern emancipatory goals.

Gu Jiegang's study of the Meng Jiangnü legend was exemplary of such efforts. By juxtaposing later versions of the story that celebrated passion and free will with the earlier story that emphasized ritual propriety, Gu drove home the point that folklore was an expression of women's sentiments and grievances, which Confucian scholars neither understood nor valued. The legend, which comes to us through the powerful mediation of the folklorists, seems to furnish just the right material for a radical agenda: the self-chosen spouse, the solitary traveler, and the weeping that brought down the Great Wall. But this is only so thanks to the scriptural labor of the folklorists qua translators, who took it upon themselves to transform the heteroglossic "noises" of the people into cogent "messages."[41] These messages are invariably linked to the May Fourth imperative of rebelling against a stultifying tradition in the name of sentimental emancipation. The folklorists thus translated folklore by mapping the problematic dichotomy of ritual/emotion onto the equally problematic oppositions of state/individual, aristocracy/folk, and patriarchy/women, depicting women in particular as prepolitical, subaltern subjects who spoke poetic truth from their bleeding hearts.

The archaeology of the Meng Jiangnü legend signaled the crucial shift, aided by the expressive theory of language, to the modern episteme wherein weeping was no longer a ritualized instrument of social-cosmic integration, but a protestation of subaltern subjectivity. With the epistemological complacency of Enlightenment humanism, the folklorists approached the folkloric materials "as though they were individual expressions rather than social institutions."[42] They read folksongs and legends as "expressions" indexed to individual interiorities rather than as collectively produced myths that made little reference to "inner nature." They mobilized the repressive hypothesis to establish love as the irrepressible essence of humanity, to invent "woman" as a universal category and as the progenitor of folk culture, and to construct the folk as the subject of the modern nation. The movement supplied a crucial idiom for negotiating the aporia in the nationalist project of remaking the "people" on whom the nation staked its legitimacy. Its celebration of distinct regional cultures also inspired a new way of writing about the "native soil" (*xiangtu*), one that drew on older native-place loyalties but represented local cultural idiosyncrasies and everyday sentiments as profoundly human and thereby universal.

Today, we may no longer identify strongly with the emancipatory goals of the May Fourth movement, but we still operate largely within the moral and epistemological framework of Enlightenment humanism that informed May Fourth folklore scholarship. It is therefore crucial that we reckon with the May Fourth legacy as we reengage the folkloric materials on Meng Jiangnü. The volume at hand is very much a collection of "remainders" that demand historically situated and analytically reflexive readings. The ten ballads were chosen to represent not only distinctive genres and sources but also divergent narrative and moral preoccupations. Ostensibly, they all tell the story of Meng Jiangnü journeying to the Great Wall and retrieving her dead husband's bones through a magical act of weeping, but what each text chooses to dramatize (and omit) and the manners of dramatization invite us to explore larger questions about kinship, gender, emotion, morality, and the political order. We must come to them with a sense of wonder and empathy as well as vigilance against our preference for affective and erotic expressiveness over moral or religious pietism. We must be ready and willing to ask questions that the May Fourth folklorists did not ask. For example, why does the youth-book ballad offer us an elaborate account of Meng Jiangnü's excruciating trek to the Great Wall, whereas the Buddhist precious scrolls dwell on the couple's heavenly identity as immortals who descend to the world of red dust to save the multitudes? Again, why does the "exposition" make Meng Jiangnü out to be a filial daughter-in-law who sets out for the Great Wall only after her mother-in-law has died and been properly buried and mourned, whereas the women's-script song depicts her as an impassioned bride who sends her spouse off with many words of tender affection?

The selection here, which does not come close to representing the sheer vastness of the Meng Jiangnü repertoire, impresses upon us that there is no true or original Meng Jiangnü story and that each version should be taken on its own terms even as we explore questions of intertextuality and interpretive community. Together these tales should dispel any illusion we might harbor about the singularity or authenticity of the folk Voice and compel our appreciation for the inherent instability and indeterminacy of all folkloric texts. We also come to appreciate the fluidity, creativity, and affective powers of the many poetic and prosimetric genres that lend themselves so well to oral and textual adaptations and transmissions—something easily forgotten by us decidedly prosaic postmoderns.

PART I

BALLADS FROM LATE-IMPERIAL CHINA

1

TREKKING TO THE WALL

YOUTH BOOKS, A GENRE OF BALLADRY, WERE POPULAR IN eighteenth- and nineteenth-century Beijing. The genre acquired its name because it was primarily the "sons and younger brothers of the members of the Eight Banners" (*baqi zidi*) who engaged in it. These Manchus insisted on being amateurs rather than professional entertainers. The genre achieved popularity by the middle of the eighteenth century and went out of fashion by the early years of the twentieth century, but many of its texts continued to be used by performers of other genres, such as the big-drum ballads.

Youth books are all in verse. The basic format is the seven-syllable line, which, because youth books were performed to very slow music, allowed for the inclusion of many additional syllables, and lines of up to thirteen syllables are not rare at all (this variation in line length in the original is reflected in the great variation in line length in the translation). Texts in this genre consist of one or more chapters, each about a hundred lines in length. As a rule, a chapter is introduced by an eight-line poem. Throughout one chapter, the same rhyme is maintained. Youth books are considered one of the most literary genres of popular balladry. Many derive their topics from popular novels and plays, and they were often composed by writers with considerable literary skills, some of whom are known by name. The texts of youth books circulated widely in written form, usually as manuscripts produced by specialized book-shops, but some youth books made it into print at a relatively early date. These texts served the needs of both singers and readers.

Weeping at the Wall is among the earliest preserved youth books. Lu Gong, who includes this text in his *Meng Jiangnü Travels for a Myriad of Miles to Find Her Husband* (Meng Jiangnü wanli xunfu ji), bases his edition on a printed edition that he dates to around 1750. The following translation is based on the edition provided by Lu Gong.[1] This version of the legend emphasizes the description of the hardships Meng Jiangnü endures on her trek through the desolate, late-fall landscape of northern China.

Anonymous

WEEPING AT THE WALL

CHAPTER 1

A fame of shame for all eternity for Lü Buwei,[2]
Lusting for wealth and power, he offered a beauty.
His crime of cupidity is hinted at by the historian;
The rumor of his parenthood is a wordless stele.[3]
Disaster reached the pond's fishes, creating later misery;
This child of disaster buried scholars and burned books.
Lü Buwei's wife carried the seed of lust, lusting for the realm of Qin;
This root of lust sired a seed of lust, who became a villain of lust!

Mencius said it well, "A country's security does not depend on mountains and
    ravines as bulwarks,"[4]
But the First Emperor of the Qin built the Long Wall, and white bones were
    piled up.
He utterly harmed the common people, horrifying all-under-heaven;
The poison spread throughout the world, saddening gods and ghosts.
    The Traditions harmed, the Classics destroyed—Transformation through
        Teaching was ruined;[5]

The state was divided, the nation in turmoil—norms and rules were annihilated.
There was only the wife of that Fan Qiliang, that Meng Jiangnü;
She was a beauty created by the whole nation's primordial right breath.[6]

Ever since her husband had taken his leave to work on the Wall,
That beauty, alas, had wasted away till her slim waist was worn and haggard.
In her eastern room she hung up the curtain hooks in the cold;
At the northern border her soul wandered till break of dawn.

Rouge and powder on purpose departed from her sorrowing face;
She had no heart to paint with green and black her furrowed brows.[7]
Her tears continued to fall until she was soaked all over her body;
Because of the bitter verses she wrote of longing for her husband, her brush was a mess.

She thought to herself, "In which place may my husband be suffering now?
He must be carrying those huge bricks on his back.
Who takes pity on him as his shoulders are worn?
His strength is limited, he'll be overcome by pain!

As a student of books you're so weak, but who cares for your suffering?
The officials in charge are cruel and mean, they will abuse their power.
Their cursing and beating is hard to bear—how can you stand it?
But how can I as your wife accompany you though our hearts are linked despite a myriad of miles?

You have left me here all alone with my shadow cast by the lamp;
Each night again, always until the disk of the moon is sinking.
As I gaze at the edge of the sky, I see scattered white clouds;
In the autumn wind on the old road red leaves are fluttering.

When will there ever come an end to this disconsolate sight?
Alas, when will my unfortunate husband ever come home?
I cannot but travel a myriad miles all by myself to find my husband;
Even if I die in that strange land, at least my soul will be with him!"

This beauty's heart as pure as ice was combined with a gall of steel;
She didn't consider her small curved shoes and socks,[8] bright teeth and curved brows.
A linen skirt and wooden hairpins hid and lessened her voluptuous charms—
In a wind-blown drizzling rain, under the slanting rays of a pale moon.

All alone she went to find her husband, her heart filled with fear;
She personally took him his winter clothes, the pack on her back.

TREKKING TO THE WALL

She noticed how in the frosty groves bereft of leaves the wind had turned
   chilly,
How lines of geese flew above the autumn shapes of river-maples.
   "Where in this boundless expanse of the wide world may my husband be?
I can rely only on my one gall of determination and my two heroic brows!"[9]
Alas, the beauty found it hard to move her lotus-steps—her feet were so
   painful!
Her willowy waist was so delicate, and her eyes were so dark!
   Her sleeves were incapable of protecting her apricot-cheeks against the
   dust storm,
And to her distress the hem of her skirt trailed through the mud—she fur-
   rowed her brows.
Her travel luggage and her umbrella became heavier and heavier,
While her meager strength gradually became less and less.
   As she shed pearly tears in the westerly wind, she complained to herself,
"Oh Heaven, when will I be able to return home together with my husband?
He once told me, 'It's hard to know when I will return from this myriad of
   miles,
But who dares disobey when he is sent away by order of the king?
   I, your husband, will only by my single death discard my white bones,
So do not hope that I will come back again to paint on your eyebrows.
So I urge you, my darling wife, not to be stubborn and obstinate;
Don't think that a mirror once broken one day will shine again!
   Even though my not inconsiderable property is enough to provide for you,
My wife, don't betray your verdant spring, as I will not be able to return.'
My husband, even though your words showed such deep concern for me,
You should also give some thought to how your wife has always behaved.
   You did not consider how we, united in love, were like fish and water—
How can you treat like ashes and mud this marriage that ties our hair?[10]
How could you know that my breast filled with hot blood harbors a deter-
   mined gall,
And that my heart as pure as ice is as white as an unblemished piece of jade!
   Because of my force and the affective power of my undiluted sincerity,
I will even be able to pull around the heart of Heaven itself!
Moreover, I, Meng Jiangnü, have received the instruction of my father,
And to this very day my whole heart is set on the rules for women.
   I have also received your teaching and tempering, my husband,

So how could I be willing to betray my father, forget my husband, and trample
      rites and righteousness?
So I will not shrink from traveling a thousand miles to find my husband,
I cannot but make the distant journey to the border regions!"

CHAPTER 2

"The leaves on the trees are rustling and swishing, my small feet are hurting;
Look how the autumn storm once again is sending off the setting sun!
Whose house tonight will hide this body of mine?
In strange lands one nowhere has a father or mother.
     Endlessly the wilting grass covers the whole wide world;
Chilly, oh so chilly, a cold haze envelops me, Meng Jiangnü.
Returning crows, dot upon dot, roost in the wood and caw,
Telling me here all alone, 'On an old road at dusk—please make haste!'
     Suddenly I heard from somewhere the endless tolling of a bell;
This means that on the road ahead there must be a village!
So I must follow the sound in order to find that place.
Through the wood I can vaguely make out the light of a lamp!"
     When our beauty arrived in the wood and wiped away her tears,
She saw a small temple—a well in front of the gate—dedicated to the Dragon
      King.
     "Let me rest for a while under the offering table;
I am so hungry the front of my stomach sticks to the back of my stomach.
Let me drink some cool water to suppress the fire in my heart—
Oops, there's no well-bucket here, so how can I fill my stomach?"
     The beauty who did not know what to do was awash in tears,
And she kowtowed before the god, as she begged the Dragon King,
"Please do not blame me, Jiangnü, for defiling your godhead;
I truly do not know where else I may take shelter from wind and frost."
     She put down her travel luggage and her umbrella, checked the dust,
Then lay down all curled up on the icy ground before the god's image.
She forced herself to gnash her teeth, and a haze came over her eyes,
As gust upon gust of autumn wind pierced her shift and skirt.
     When our beauty sat up, she saw the sickle of the sinking moon;
Its bright light shone on her creamy breast, as white as snow.
     Facing the Toad Palace, Meng Jiangnü heaved a heavy sigh,

Saying, "Your Majesty Chang'e, why don't you take pity on me?"[11]
You shine on the whole wide world, on all living creatures—
Where, oh where in the world is my Fan Qiliang?
    Three-inch feet and the world is so large;
I'm just one single body on this desolate road.
I beg you, Your Majesty, to be so kind as to send me an informative dream;
I am taking him his winter clothes to protect him from the freezing frost of
    the last month of autumn.
    If you only would take pity on him, that lonely fellow who met with
    disaster,
You also will commiserate with me, Meng Jiangnü, who treks a myriad of
    miles.
Even though I am suffering wind and dust, I'm barely nineteen years old;
I rely only on this spark in my heart, and tears course down without end."
    As soon as our exhausted beauty had closed her eyes,
She was overcome by sleep and entered the land of dreams.
There she saw the shape of a man, his brows in a frown, all awash in tears;
All his clothes were reduced to rags, and his face was vexed and troubled.
    He repeatedly bowed his head to her and heaved a heavy sigh,
Saying, "My wife, don't you recognize me anymore? I'm Fan Qiliang!
Many thanks for coming to find me despite a myriad of miles of wind and
    dust;
I will express my gratitude by pulverizing my body and bones!"
    In her dream the beauty said, "Husband, here you are!"
Both saddened and gladdened, it took her a while to react.
As she walked up to her husband and wished him well,
Autumn-sounds came from the trees, moon-shadows fell on the windows.
    When our beauty woke up with a start and opened her eyes,
The sky was full of stars, while the earth was covered with frost.
When Meng Jiangnü thought back upon her dream, she said,
"This really makes me afraid it may be very inauspicious!
    He said he will pulverize body and bones to pay me back;
Involuntarily this cuts up my nine-twisted guts inch by inch.
In case something 'as high as the mountains, as wide as the sea'[12] has hap-
    pened to him,
This 'three thousand miles of clouds and streams'[13] will not benefit at all our
    [love] 'as long and lasting as Heaven and Earth.'"[14]

Rationalizing, she said, "Dreams have always been the imaginations of the
    heart;
Usually our visions in dreams reflect our concerns.
Alas, because I am afraid that my husband may be suffering some illness,
That's why my dream is so upsetting with its evil premonition.
    So be it! Oh Heaven, this must mean I will find my husband below the
    earth!
If that is indeed to be my fate, I pray I may be buried alongside my husband.
But where will I, as his good wife, in this endless expanse find his corpse?
I worry no end that I, Meng Jiangnü, may die too quickly halfway on the road!
    How miserable I am! My whole body feels as if drenched in cold water,
And in the middle of the night I have no food to still my hunger.
Heaven should brightly display some more warming sun,
But it's the moisture of the earth that's turned into frost!"
    Hear, the crows in a ruckus start up from the branches of the pines,
And a storm fills the sky with brown dust by the ancient road.
The beauty rises to her feet and bids adieu to the minor ghosts,
And she next bows down before the Dragon King.
    Her jade-white fingers lightly so lightly pick up the umbrella,
And her fragrant shoulders slowly so slowly shoulder the luggage.
Sad at heart she says to herself, "Only now do I know the sufferings of
    travel,
But it's all because of this irrepressible marital affection!"

CHAPTER 3

The falling leaves are rustling and rustling, the whole world is autumn;
Clouds of dust come in, wave upon wave, the road to go is one of sorrow.
Jet and black aimlessly adrift, her brows tell her suffering;
Rouge and powder all alone, her figure shows her discomfort.
    The dew soaks her breast-wrap—delicate and diffident;
The wind buffets her body—wandering without end.
"I don't even know whether he is still alive or where he may be.
Ah! I don't know where my rotten bones will be buried either.
    I remember how he used to paint my eyebrows with his brush, those black
    cool curves;
How he played the zither below the flowers during moonlit autumn.

But where may he be now of the myriad of miles of the Long Wall?

The road enters the last month of autumn, the year has not yet passed.

How can we experience the day of his return so I may lift the tray again?[15]

Most likely there is no need as of today to ascend the tower once more.[16]

Alas! Husband, this must be due to the karma you and I created in an earlier life.

That's why we, husband and wife, in this life have to grind away this sorrow.

Alas, grinding away the soles of my feet, I've grown skinnier than those yellow flowers,[17]

As I load upon my shoulders that autumn of red leaves.

What troubles me is that I walk alone on this ancient road, no village in sight;

Deeply I enter into a hoary mist, into the darkness of rows of trees.

What disturbs me is 'the frost on the wooden bridge as yet untouched, the crowing rooster below the moon over the thatched inn.'[18]

When dogs bark, it's because of homing crows outside the gate on willow branches.

Of course I had thought of all these many sufferings beforehand,

But now I sorrow through each of these miseries one by one."

When the sun was already approaching noon, she still had had no food to eat,

But as a rule from early till late the village inns have gruel for sale.

Our beauty saw that there was yet another guesthouse,

So she hastened for an extra few steps across the wooden bridge.

The woman of the inn noticed that her travel gear might be poor,

But that her tender disposition was manifested in her behavior,

So she said, "Young lady, please take whatever you may want to eat!"

But the beauty said, "I'll have what's ready, some gruel from the pot is fine."

When the beauty had eaten her fill, she became active again;

With her handkerchief she wiped away the beads of sweat all over her head.

This showed off her two peach flowers, her pair of willow leaves,[19]

Her hundreds of graces, and her thousands of charms.

The woman of the inn said, "That's a fine young lady, of excellent bearing!

Full of right breath, her face is filled with sorrow."

So she asked her, "Where did you come from? And where are you going?"

Meng Jiangnü heaved a heavy sigh, and her tears coursed down.

She said, "Because my husband left his home village to build the Long Wall,

My heart has been filled with a myriad of miles of anxiety as I shed my tears
      in clear autumn.

The snowstorms of the border regions freeze the wide world;

The wild and chilly rains and mists make all the days cold.

   From far away I take these winter clothes to my husband;

Walking on foot, I am making my way to dissolve my worries.

When I get to the Long Wall and the truth comes out, my heart may die,

But it's better than being wrecked by sorrow, shedding tears of blood, doing
      nothing."

   The woman of the inn said, "Too bad! Too bad! That is impossible!

A journey of thousands of miles, and that in this late-autumn weather!

And that on such tiny feet! And also with such a delicate body!

Those bandits infesting the mountains! Those demons all around!

   On a southwesterly wind you, girl, have come to the northeast;

You left home in late summer, you're on the road late in fall.

What most can move one to sympathy, elicit one's concern,

Is that there are those ropes binding women, throats hit by a cudgel!"[20]

   The beauty said, "We, husband and wife, were like mandarin-ducks sport-
      ing together;

In life after life, despite death after death, we cannot be separated.

I have thought about all those dangers you were so kind as to point out to me,

But the tie that binds this little stupid heart will never be broken.

   Nobody wants to be a single shadow in the setting sun!

Shall I forget that our two souls are wrapped by white autumn?

Even if we meet each other below the earth on this trip,

The bond of love will tie together the intertwined branches on the mandarin-
      duck grave!"[21]

   When the woman of the inn heard the beauty speak these heartrending
      words,

She could not help but twist her face as her tears started to flow.

She observed that the beauty was filled completely with hot gall

And said, "That story moves you at once and continues to haunt one—it pulls
      at the strings of my heart!

   But now the matter has come this far, what can be done?

How could you go on? But it will also be hard to make you stay!

But if you don't stay, I'll risk my life to come along with you;

I may be just one person, but it beats being a woman alone!"

TREKKING TO THE WALL

The beauty was moved to sighs but said, "How could I dare
Without any reason to make such a demand—who'd take care of your house?
Auntie, I am deeply appreciative of your great love;
Later, when I return, I will express my gratitude."
    The woman of the inn could do nothing but prepare a room for her;
Raising the wick, the two of them talked together all through the night.
Alas, soon the call of the cock urged her on, as the watches ran out,
And our beauty packed her luggage and took to the road in haste.

CHAPTER 4

The autumn wind, gust after gust, is blowing in her face, the morning air is
    crisp,
The rustling leaves are falling down in a whirl, dew drops have coagulated.
The fading stars are disappearing from sight, casting only faint shadows;
The sun weakly shows itself from time to time through the transverse
    branches.
    Her tender body lost and forlorn—few people travel this ancient road;
Her thin shadow freezingly cold—in the westerly winds her tears are red.
Her oh so tight embroidered shoes make it hard to walk on that bitter road;
Her strength is getting less and less—how can she stand the pain in her bones?
    Alas, the beauty's fragrant body was already skinnier than a yellow flower.
How could she withstand the frost that blew in her face, the wind that pierced
    her bones?
As her two feet walked on through the freezing mist, she resembled a floating
    stick;[22]
As her single body ground down the autumn colors, she was like drifting
    tumbleweeds.
    Filled with sorrow, she feared to advance on the thousand-mile road;
Her gazing eyes were startled to see mountains in myriads of layers.
She said, "To whom can I tell the bitter vexations of my broken heart?
Oh Heaven, where on earth will I find that Long Wall?"
    There was nothing she could do but muster her energy and travel that
    ancient road;
As she wiped the tears from her eyes, she abandoned herself to the western
    winds.
All along the way she asked for information about her husband,

And so she heard, "Right now they are working at Mountain-Sea Pass."[23]
When our beauty heard this information, her mind was a little settled,
And she said, "Fortunately, now I know where I have to go.
If only I will be able to meet with my husband on the road ahead,
I will not have suffered in vain the bitter pain of this trekking, this endless
    travel!"
Now the First Emperor of the Qin wanted to build this Long Wall to defend
    the country against attacks
And had ordered Meng Tian to complete the construction within a day![24]
He wasted the people's resources, exhausted the people's strength,
Drained the blood from their bones, caused the deaths of millions!
The common laborers transported water and stones, crossing mountains
    and ridges;
Truly, even at night and under the stars, nobody ever dared to rest.
Those untold laborers who had died were bricked in all together.
Truly, bones piled up like mountains all over the roads.
The breath of their grievance filled heaven, broke into the blue firmament;
The cries of their anguish shook the earth and moved all human beings.
Once that Fan Qiliang as a conscript laborer had left his hometown,
He had entered the construction site and learned to do the work.
But alas, his physical constitution had never been used to such exertion,
And as a result he had fallen ill before the construction project was finished.
As a weak and skinny student he could not bear these torments,
And alas, his soul sank with the moon, his breath went with the wind!
There were some companions who, pitying him for his lonely suffering,
Buried his corpse in the gravel and shingle at the foot of the Wall.
This day happened to be Double Ninth, when the teams should have a
    rest,
And the imperial commissioner gave orders to halt all construction.
Right at this moment our beauty first reached the border region;
She saw how landscape and habitation were quite different.
That one girdle of the Long Wall continued across the steepest ridges;
As a mighty bulwark it rose up high from cloud-piercing peaks.
When the beauty had observed this scene, she sighed to herself,
"This can only have been accomplished by an effort that overturns oceans
    and moves mountains!

TREKKING TO THE WALL

If I had not been filled with this sincere desire that does not shirk from a
  thousand miles,
How could I all alone have accomplished this journey of a myriad of miles on
  foot?
But it is difficult to find out the whereabouts of my husband.
There's nowhere a road, so whom can I ask for information?"
As the beauty was standing there, doubting what to do next,
She suddenly saw a few laborers walking in a little group.

Each of them looked haggard and worn, their clothes were in tatters;
They carried paper money in their hands,²⁵ a sad expression on their faces.
Immediately she straightway walked toward the Pass, saying,
"Why shouldn't I ask them for some news? They are bound to know!"
Meng Jiangnü approached them and hastily greeted them, saying,
"I have a question to ask you, so please be so kind as to stop for a while!"
Those people stood still and answered her greeting,
Seeing that the beauty's expression was filled with sorrow.

Even though she wore a linen skirt and wooden hairpins and was covered
  with grime,
She still displayed an exceptional bearing, an uncommon radiance.
Her behavior was meticulous, her personality was tender,
She was all friendliness, her face was all mildness.
She asked them, "Among the conscript laborers on this project at this
  location—
Is there a Fan Qiliang? He is my husband and was conscripted for the Long
  Wall."
When they heard this question, they were all moved to sadness
And said, "Sister, so you have come here to look for brother Fan!

We are conscript laborers from different places, assigned to this stretch;
We left together, we traveled together, and worked together with brother Fan.
But because he was not used to heavy labor, he already has passed away.
As we could not bear to leave his body exposed, we buried his corpse in the
  Long Wall.
Because today is Double Ninth, we got double rations on this rest day,
And we decided to burn some sheets of paper money to express our
  friendship."
But even before the laborers had ended their litany of sorrow,
The beauty had already fainted and fallen, her almond-eyes closed!

CHAPTER 5

In this human life nothing is more bitter than parting;
Moreover the love of this couple was exceptionally affective.
As soon as Meng Jiangnü heard that her husband had passed away,
The soul of this beauty had already flown off to the ninth heaven.

She looked just like a flower that in the rain has suffered a blow to the head,
Like the moon that is covered by clouds and increasingly obscured.
Saying, "My husband!" she could hardly breathe as her throat was choked;
Her weak body collapsed on the ground, right in front of many watching
      eyes.

Only after quite a while did the beauty open her almond-eyes in a haze;
Her peach-like cheeks were torn as she opened her ruby-like lips.
Weeping, she cried, "My husband, you are causing my death!
Why does High Heaven make good people suffer so much?

You, my husband, observed the rites, studied the books, and understood
      principle;
You cultivated your person, waited for Fate, knew the rules and the norms.
I so much had hoped that you would return and make yourself illustrious.
Who could have known you would disappear without a trace, like a rock in
      the ocean?

I still remember how you, my husband, bid me adieu at the Long Pavilion;
The words you entrusted to me really moved my heart!
You said, 'Husband and wife are birds that share the same wood,
But once the Great Term comes, each goes its own way.

Of course I would love to live with you to a ripe old age in riches and glory,
But things don't depend on man when they are determined by prior karma.
I am afraid that I will not be able to return from this work on the Wall,
So, my wife, if you would want to see me again, it will have to be in a dream.'

Now today your words have come true, you have met with disaster.
So where at this edge of the sky do you want me to mourn for your soul?
As a result, there's no looking back in this endless expanse of the wide world!
To which family can I now entrust myself, all forsaken and forlorn?

Alas, unable to move either backward or forward, I only can die,
Ending up as a pile of white bones at the mercy of the westerly winds!"
When people saw Meng Jiangnü weeping in such a heartrending way,

They rushed forward and said, "Young lady, don't cry, first calm down a
   little!"
   The beauty forced herself to place her hands over her wounded heart and
   bow deeply,
Saying, "Gratitude for your kindness in burying my husband is engraved in
   my heart;
One word is unable to fully express the suffering in my heart.
Please show me the way so I can see my husband's grave."
   All people shed tears as they were equally moved,
And they said, "Please come along with us so we may mourn at your husband's
   grave."
Meng Jiangnü shouldered her travel luggage and grasped her umbrella—
Tears froze in her limpid eyes, her breath reached the azure vault.
   After a while they passed the Pass and arrived at the seaside—
The white-capped waves of the sea, the frosty chill of the woods.
The Long Wall reached all the way to the Eastern Ocean;
Its hundreds of battlements leaned on the North Star.
   Gravel and shingle formed piles, ashes and dust covered the earth,
Wind-blown smoke filled one's eyes, the cold pierced one's bones.
The beauty said, "How can anyone support such a wild and desolate location?
Alas, my husband, your one pile of yellow earth rests in autumn clouds."
   Meng Jiangnü looked at the laborers and asked them,
"Where in this desolate area do I find my husband's grave?"
These people heaved a sigh and said, "Young lady,
This is a strategic location for the state, who would dare erect a grave?
   Brother Fan's body has been temporarily buried at the foot of the Wall
As a slight expression of our sympathy for a fellow creature.
We put up a three-foot white stone so as to mark the spot.
Your husband's name is written on it, so it may serve as a stele."
   When our beauty heard this, her heart was deeply saddened;
Lightly she moved her lotus-steps, the almond-eyes clear.
The laborers pointed the stele out to her,
And the beauty saw a stone that was buried at the foot of the wall.
   The characters, she saw, had become so blurred they were hardly
   distinguishable,
Partly because of the storm and rain, partly because of the dust.

The beauty threw her weak body upon the ground at the foot of the wall,
And her breast felt like a pile of firewood burned by a raging fire.
    She said, "My husband, where has your little lonely soul gone off to?
For whom has your wife suffered all this hardship and pain?
I made this desolate journey of a myriad of miles to find you,
Foolishly still hoping that I could be reunited with you!
    Who could have known that you—a sunken pearl, a crushed jade—were
        buried among wild weeds?
This makes me a waning moon, a wilting flower entrusted to a drifting cloud!
From now on I am drifting tumbleweeds in the endless expanse of the wide
        world,
And even in dreams it will be impossible to meet with you again!"
    This beauty brought down the Long Wall by her weeping because she was
        looking for her husband's bones;
The startled imperial commissioner reported this event to the throne.
The Son of Heaven of the Qin summoned her, but she rejected his proposal;
With her husband's body in her arms, she jumped into the sea to display her
        pure chastity.
    The First Emperor of the Qin was moved by her chastity and admired her
        virtue;
Outside the Pass he erected a large temple, where Meng Jiangnü became a god.

2

GUIDING THE SOUL

IN SOUTHERN FUJIAN AND ON TAIWAN, THE MAJOR CHINESE
dialect is Minnanese (or Southern Min). From at least the sixteenth
century, the performance-related literature of this area, such as song,
drama, and ballads, has been written in the local dialect. In order to write
Minnanese words that had no obvious analogue in the Mandarin vernacular,
many rare characters were used for quite common Minnanese words, and the
resulting texts make no sense unless they are pronounced in Minnanese.[1]

The common name for Minnanese ballads on Taiwan is "ballad booklets"
(*gezai ce*). These ballad booklets are composed in lines of seven-syllable
verse that do not allow for additional syllables. The basic building block of
these ballads is a group of four lines, all of which rhyme. Originally the ballad booklets were printed in southern Fujian cities such as Quanzhou and
Xiamen (Amoy), but from the early twentieth century onward, they were also
printed on Taiwan. The emergence of a strong "Taiwan-consciousness" on
Taiwan in recent decades has resulted in a remarkable change of status of the
genre. Ballad booklets were long despised by intellectuals as vulgar literature,
but now, thanks to the efforts of Ong Sun Liong (Wang Shunlong), the Academia Sinica on Taiwan hosts an exhaustive selection of texts at its Web site

under "The Texts Database of Folk Songs in Southern Min Dialect." This translation of the *Song of Jiangnü* is based on the modern edition provided at the Web site.[2]

The *Song of Jiangnü* is one of the earliest preserved ballad booklets; the earliest known edition is a woodblock printing from 1836. This translation is based on Wang Shunlong's edition of that text, which is based on a later printing by the firm of Shang Zhihe Ji. The anonymous text was repeatedly reprinted throughout the nineteenth and also in the early years of the twentieth century. The language of this text is still very close to the common vernacular and does not show the peculiar rhyming scheme of later ballad booklets, so perhaps this ballad originated outside the Minnanese dialect area and happens to have been reprinted at Xiamen.[3] However, a lithographic edition of a "special, improved" version, *Song of Meng Jiangnü Who by Her Weeping Brought Down the Long Wall of a Myriad of Miles* (Meng Jiangnü kudao wanli Changcheng), by a certain Chitaoxian, was published in 1914 in Xiamen. It expands the text by almost a hundred lines and gives the language a much more Minnanese coloring, but it adheres closely to the plot as presented in the *Song of Jiangnü*. The *New Song of Meng Jiangnü Marrying a Husband* (Meng Jiangnü peifu xinge), which is almost three times as long, also maintains the basic outline of the plot. This version, by a certain Qiu Shou, was first printed in 1936, in Jiayi, Taiwan, and was reissued after World War II in a slightly abbreviated version by the Zhulin Bookstore in Xinzhu.[4]

In contrast to these later revisions, the *Song of Jiangnü*, to judge from its final section, was originally intended to be performed as part of funeral ceremonies. The text credits the invention of "spirit streamers" to Meng Jiangnü and spends a number of lines on their function in "summoning and guiding" the soul of the deceased back home from foreign lands and through the courts of the Underworld to the palaces of heaven. The construction of a spirit streamer symbolized the nature of human souls.[5] During funeral processions, the principal mourner carried the spirit streamer. The *Song of Jiangnü* and versions of the legend that are known from Guangxi share this focus on the spirit streamer. While the genre of ballad booklets as such is not linked to funeral rites, other parts of China, such as Hubei and Hunan, know ballad genres that are specifically tied to these ceremonies. In Hunan, for example, the legend of Meng Jiangnü is very much part of the repertoire of "mourning drumming" (*sanggu*), long ballads sung at nighttime in preparation for a funeral. In Taiwan, little skits on Meng Jiangnü could be part of nighttime funerary rituals too.

Whatever its origin, the text makes frequent references to the Sizhou Buddha, who enjoyed a special veneration in southeastern China. The figure of the Sizhou Buddha originated in a seventh-century holy monk who had come to China from India. He eventually died in Sizhou, at that time a major city on the Grand Canal, halfway between the Huai and the Yangzi. There he became widely venerated for his victories over demons that caused inundations (despite this victory, Sizhou was later swallowed by Hongze Lake, and its site was transferred to Sixian, in northern Anhui). Legend held that he had been a manifestation of the Bodhisattva (or Mahasattva) Guanyin. In Fujian and Guangdong, however, the Sizhou Buddha was widely venerated as a patron saint of lovers. Meng Jiangnü's vow that she will marry any man who sees her naked body was already a part of at least one early play (as discussed in "Meng Jiangnü: The Development of a Legend," in this volume).

Anonymous

THE SONG OF JIANGNÜ

Stop playing the gongs and drums, and stop making noise,
And I will tell the story of how Tripitaka left to fetch the sutras.[6]
Xuanzang fetched the sutras and returned from the Western Paradise;
Mulian saved his mother, so she could ascend to the Western Paradise.[7]

Meng Zong wept over bamboos, and in winter they produced shoots;
His mother suffered from an illness, which then improved by itself.[8]
Wang Xiang practiced filial piety, and fishes jumped from the river;[9]
When burying his son, Guo Ju discovered the Heaven-sent gold.[10]

When Dong Yong sold his body to benefit his father and mother,
Heaven dispatched the Weaving Maid to become his wedded wife.[11]
Ding Lan carved wood into the likeness of his father and mother,
And later Heaven and Earth imbued these statues with true feeling.[12]

The black crows practice filial piety together with the hundred birds;
The hundred birds in the forest all tie the knot and form couples.
Let me not tell the stories of all these sages of ancient times,
But let me tell the story of Jiangnü delivering winter clothes.

This happened because the First Emperor of the Qin dynasty

Issued an edict to all-under-heaven to build the Long Wall!
Of every three men in a house one was drafted, of every five two;
Those who were single and those without support all had to go.

Mr. Fan in Huazhou had only been blessed with a single son,
Who went by the name of Fan Qilang, his childhood name.
Fan Qilang at that time was just fifteen years of age;
Every morning and every day he spent studying the books.

But all of a sudden one day they heard the edict, which said
That he was to be taken to Chang'an to build the Long Wall.
The trip there and back would take only five or six months;
Even if it took longer, he'd be back home after one year.

Mr. Fan then told his son how depressed he was at heart, saying,
"Once you have left, we will have no one here at home!"
He urged Qilang time and again to take good care of himself
And to come back home as soon as the Wall had been built.

Young Fan took his leave of his father and mother and left,
So now let us talk about the circumstances of Jiangnü.

Jiangnü was living in the prefecture of Wuzhou;
Piles of gold and heaps of jade—she was quite charming.
Elder brother and younger sister shared paper and brush,
But her brother had left for other lands to seek an office.

The fifteenth of the First Month is the feast of First Night;[13]
Jiangnü dressed herself up to watch the festive lanterns.
The main hall was decorated with balloon-shaped lanterns;
The brilliant light illuminated her, this divine immortal.

Her ten fingers were long and tapering like bamboo shoots,
Her lips were as red as the pomegranate flower in bloom,
Her face and fine figure were truly stunningly beautiful—
She looked exactly like Guanyin of the Southern Sea![14]

The second day of the Second Month is the Day of Flowers;
Jiangnü dressed herself up and went into the flower garden.
The swallows were now returning to the beams in couples,
While pairs of bees and butterflies buzzed and flew about.

The seasonal feast of the Third Month is Clear and Bright;[15]
Jiangnü dressed herself up—she really was someone!

Her hair she had done up in a bun of coiling dragons;
Her feet were shod in curved shoes with mandarin-ducks.

The gauze skirt she was wearing was as clear as water—
She wore a blazingly red shirt and a green gauze skirt.
No time of the year can beat the third month of spring;
On lotus-steps she walked in the garden to enjoy spring.

"When the hundred flowers open, they then set fruit—[16]
When oh when will I succeed in becoming a couple?"

In the Fourth Month, early summer, days grow longer;
Rice sprouts, and all kinds of grain fill the farming fields.
Jiangnü at that time wanted to go out and have some fun.
"Sizhou is efficacious—I should burn him some incense!"

So she raised her feet and entered the hall of Sizhou,
Where powdered butterflies fluttered across high walls.
Paired branches of pinkwort produced paired flowers—
"When oh when will I succeed in becoming a couple?"

Holding the incense stick with both hands she prayed,
"Devoutly I make a vow in order to find a good match.
The first of my vows is that when I am taking a bath
And at the foot of the poplar have taken off my clothes—

The second vow is that when I am upstairs in the tower,
Combing my hair and dressing myself in the tower—
The third vow is that when I am in my orchid room
And with needle and thread do a couple of mandarin-ducks—

If there is any young man who comes and sees me then,
Whether rich or poor, I'll tie the knot to become a couple!
These three vows I pronounce here in front of the Buddha—
I'll lift the tray as high as my brows to be the bride!"[17]

Jiangnü then bowed deeply in front of the Buddha;
She bowed down deeply there in the hall of Sizhou.

The festival of the Fifth Month comes at midyear;
Gongs are beaten, drums are beaten, a deafening noise!
Every family quaffs and drinks sweet-flag wine, and
On every river and lake dragon-boat races take place.

"The dragon-boats race in pairs to the Eastern Sea,
But I am sitting here all alone on the river's bank."

Jiangnü thought of the three vows she had made.
"If only I too could quickly become a couple!"

The stifling heat of the Sixth Month is hard to bear;
The sun is like a fire, the rivers seem to be boiling!
Jiangnü went into the flower garden all by herself
And hastily took off all her clothes to take a bath.

Her shirt and skirt she hung on the poplar tree;
Lightly she splashed water over her lovely body.
But when she saw that someone was watching her,
She fled with lotus-steps to put on her clothes.

She grabbed her clothes to put them on again;
She put on the blue, the purple, and the yellow!
When she was dressed again, she looked up the tree,
And saw that someone was hiding up in the tree.

Jiangnü promptly asked him, "Where are you from?
From which prefecture? And from which county?"
Fan Qilang addressed her in the following manner,
"I, a young student, hail from a village in Huazhou.

The lord of Qin in the Western Capital is bereft of reason.
From each three men one is drafted to build the Wall;
During daytime we carry the loam, at night we pound it.
The extreme hardship of this work was too hard to bear.

So all by myself, without any help, I decided to flee.
At night I walk on the road, during daytime I hide—
Please oh please, young lady, please help me out;
When the sun sets in the west, I'll head for home!"

Jiangnü at that moment immediately thought,
"Today indeed I have met with my lover and lord!"
She ordered Fan Qilang to come down from the tree,
"You and I will tie the knot to become a couple!"

Fan Qilang immediately answered her as follows,
"Young lady, please listen to what I have to say.
I am a deserter threatened by the death penalty;
Even if we would get married, it couldn't last long.

Please oh please, young lady, please help me out;

When the sun sets in the west, I'll head for home!"
Jiangnü lifted her head and laughed out loudly,
And that Fan Qilang almost died on the spot—

"If you, Fan Qilang, do not come down from that tree,
I will call all the neighbors and have you arrested!
We'll take you to the official, who'll have you beaten,
Because you are a deserter on the run from Chang'an!"

When Fan Qilang heard this, he was scared out of his wits;
His hands were trembling with fright like shaking bells.
"If you, young lady, are willing to take me in and keep me,
I will never forget that favor till the day I am buried!"

Jiangnü then asked him, "Are you willing or not?"
At the foot of the poplar tree they became a couple.

"From now on, you will be my husband and lord,
And as of now I will be your loving wife.
Now I have met today with you, Qilang,
I will inform my parents so they can take charge."

Jiangnü took Qilang with her to the main hall,
And there they bowed as a couple to her parents.
"Father and mother, please bring out the tablets;
We want to bow to the divinities as a couple!"

First they bowed to Heaven and the Three Jewels,[18]
Secondly they bowed to the gods and the ghosts,
Thirdly they bowed to her parents and uncles,
Fourthly they bowed to father- and mother-in-law.

Jiangnü and her lover bowed to each other;
They resembled Chang'e confronting a phoenix![19]
Husband and wife were like fish and water,
As they prayed to be together for all eternity!

Jiangnü and her husband entered her orchid chamber,
Where red lanterns and wax candles shone brilliantly.
Red gowns, gauze skirts, gold-rimmed bed curtains,
Crystal and amber sparkled on the ivory couch.

Husband and wife slept together, sharing a cushion,
Only fearing that night is short and dawn will break.

Her father and mother were truly filled with joy

And ordered a pig and a goat to be slaughtered.
To the east they killed the pig and set out wine;
To the west they set out wine and tea and soup.
   The next day at dawn as the sky brightened,
The husband and wife emerged from her room.
But let's not tell about the pleasures of Fan Qilang;
We'll have to return to the First Emperor of the Qin.

When General Meng Tian was checking the teams,
He found out Fan Qilang from Huazhou had fled.
The Third Son of the Li family issued an order,[20]
Promptly dispatching a soldier to his village.
   When he arrived in Huazhou's Xuguang county,
Nobody there knew where Fan Qilang could be.
So the soldier asked all travelers coming and going
About that Fan Qilang from Huazhou who had fled.
   The travelers then immediately reported to him,
"Fan Qilang is currently at Meng Family Village.
There he met with Meng Jiangnü, who is so young;
Every day and every night he spends in her room.
   Fan Qilang right now is only fifteen years of age;
The Meng family took him in as their son-in-law."
When the soldier heard this, he was filled with joy,
"Tomorrow I will go to Meng Family Village!"
   When the Golden Rooster crowed before break of dawn,
Black crows were cawing all around the house.
Halfway through the fifth watch, at break of dawn,
Lucky magpies repeatedly called in front of the gate.
   Fan Qilang thereupon said to Jiangnü, his wife,
"Indeed they have come from Chang'an to fetch me.
For three days here we could be husband and wife,
But I am afraid our marriage is not intended to last."
   Jiangnü thereupon stealthily conceived an idea,
Hastily got up, combed her hair, and got dressed.
Before the Three Jewels, the Buddha, she made a vow;
She made a vow to all the gods and to all the ghosts,
   "If you ensure that Fan Qilang will have no worry,

I will redeem my vow—so please see to his safety!"
But even before Jiangnü had finished her vow,
She already heard the dogs, which were barking loudly.

   In front and in back the house was thrice encircled;
Loudly they shouted, "We've got a warrant for Fan Qilang!"
Fan Qilang was immediately taken and arrested;
His body all tied up with iron shackles and chains.

   Jiangnü thereupon stealthily conceived an idea;
She brought out gold and silver to change their minds.

   "Whatever gold and silver you bring, I will not accept;
Here on an official mission I don't dare let him go.
It is essential that Fan Qilang arrives there in person.
It's part of our job—we cannot accommodate you."

   Fan Qilang thereupon bowed to her father and mother,
"Now I have to leave today, don't think of me anymore.
I am afraid that once I have left, I am bound to die;
Your daughter should make other plans for her future."

   Her father and mother answered him as follows,
"You should consider things well while on the road.
We here will be at peace if you travel with care
And return as soon as the Wall has been built!"

   When Fan Qilang thereupon said adieu to his wife,
His tears fell so profusely they wetted his breast.
"Once I have left, there's no chance I'll return;
On leaving home, my heart is filled with anxiety!"

   Jiangnü escorted her lover beyond the gate,
"My dear husband, when will you be able to return?
Qilang, you are leaving, you are the one flying off,
Leaving me here all alone for god knows how long!"

   For every ten steps he went, he nine times looked back;
The two of them watched each other, unable to part.
Tears flowed from his eyes like a copious spring rain,
As Fan Qilang kept longing for his wife without end.

   Jiangnü accompanied her lover till beyond the gate;
She stood looking till he had disappeared from sight.
"You have plucked and taken away the finest flower.
Who'll pick up the tattered flower fallen to the ground?"

GUIDING THE SOUL

When she returned to her room and the double cushion,
She saw only the cushion but not the man anymore.
"Yesterday I spent here chatting with you, but today
We have been ripped apart and have been separated!

I have gold and silver aplenty, but it is of no use,
As a thousand gold cannot buy my husband's return.
Every day and every night I long for your return—
I've waited till today and still not seen you come home.

While I am here at home, my tears keep coming down,
While you out on the road must be all down and out.
Down and out you may be, there all by yourself—
You've also left me here all alone in an empty room.

You must be suffering terrible hardship on the road.
When will I be able to see my husband's body again?"
Let's not talk about the many vexations of Jiangnü,
But let's tell of Fan Qilang's arrival at the Wall.

General Meng Tian came out and interrogated him,
"Fan Qilang, where did you go after you fled?"
Fan Qilang immediately replied in the following way,
"Fifteen years old, I spent all my days in my study!

I am capable only of essays and of policy papers;
I am unfit for carrying earth and building the Wall.
By day we carry the earth, and at night we pound it;
That hardship and suffering are impossible to bear!

My father and mother at home are advanced in years,
So I implore you to allow me to return and see them.
I hope with all my heart you will pardon my crime,
That you'll set me free as I am a student of books."

The general upon these words exploded with rage
And shouted and cursed, "Fan Qilang, you are dead!
Fan Qilang merits the death penalty for his desertion;
Soon he'll be a person awakened from his dream!

Of all the millions of conscript laborers at Chang'an
We will not forgive that one person Fan Qilang!
Immediately execute Fan Qilang by beheading;
Wrap his bones in loam and bury him in the Wall!"

But Fan Qilang's heart did not accept his death;
His soul did not disperse and returned to the village.

At that time it changed into the shape of a phoenix
With a bright-colored crest, all dressed in white.[21]
It flew to the poplar tree of the Meng family,
Carrying in its beak a letter for Meng Jiangnü.
    "On the seventh of the Seventh Month, the autumn wind rises;
The Oxherd and the Weaving Maid visit the moon.[22]
They can see each other at least one time every year,
But now your husband has gone, the river remains silent."
    When the phoenix had dropped the letter, it flew off again,
But Jiangnü picked it up and opened it and read it.
"The letter does not say anything else, but urges me
With each and every word to marry someone else!"
    Jiangnü thereupon suddenly conceived of an idea,
Even as tears flowed down her cheeks in profusion.
She got her key and opened her boxes and chests
And took out silk and gauze to make him some clothes.
    When she had taken out the silk, she had to cut it—
"But I do not know the size of my lover anymore!"
Jiangnü thereupon suddenly conceived of an idea
And took some of his old clothes from the chest.
    "By these measurements he was seven feet tall!"
Tears coursed down from her eyes in great profusion,
"I see here only the clothes, but I do not see the man—
When will I ever be able to see my lover's body?"
    Her aunts in the upper rooms helped with the cutting,
Her sister in the lower room helped with the sewing,
And in only a few days the clothes were finished.
The winter clothes were done—who could take them?
    Jiangnü then conceived of a plan in her heart.
Hastily she went to her parents and told them,
"A few days ago my husband sent me a letter.
In his letter he speaks of his lonely misery.
    His letter did not contain any empty verbiage;
With every word he told me to send him winter clothes.

GUIDING THE SOUL

These last few days I have finished making those clothes,
And now I will deliver them to Fan Qilang to wear!"
    Her parents cursed her, "You are out of your mind!
The road to Chang'an is long—to the edge of the sky!
For a man it takes two months to make the journey;
For you as a woman the trip would take half a year!

    There are all those dark woods with their robbers!
There are all those mountain ridges that rise to the sky!
There are all those deep ravines without any bridges!
There are all those river fords without a ferry or boat!

    There are all those mountain forests without any inns!
There are all those hungry tigers by the side of the road!
Of the ten people who make the trip, only a few survive!
You must want to end your life and go to the Springs!"[23]

    In the hall Jiangnü bowed to her father and mother,
"Dear father and mother, please listen to my words.
Because we have been married as husband and wife,
I have to come to his aid now he needs me most.

    I want to go, and I don't fear how long the road may be;
If one's heart is strong enough, a rock will be pierced.
If there is no inn, I will sleep in the mountain forest,
And if there is not a mat, I will slumber on the grass.

    Please, father and mother, please do not worry;
Tomorrow at break of dawn I will leave on my trip."
On the first day of the Eighth Month she left her home—
The water of the brook before the gate was white as sand.

    Her serving maid carried the load and walked on ahead,
While Jiangnü followed behind her, trekking on foot.
She carried an umbrella to protect her against the sun,
Afraid that the sun might do damage to her body.

As they were walking, they first came to a hermitage;
A priest consulted the hexagrams for sorrowing souls.
Jiangnü paid him money to consult the hexagrams
Concerning her search for her husband Fan Qilang.

    The priest thereupon said to the young woman,
"The hexagram I have found tells death and disaster.

I'm afraid that your husband must already have died,
So I urge you, young lady, go back to your hometown."

"Only last month Fan Qilang sent me a letter;
I'm afraid that your predictions are none too accurate!"
When Jiangnü heard his tale, she did not say a word;
As she traveled on, she cursed him, "That priest is dead!

When I've found Fan Qilang, and we come back this way,
We will return and put your little temple to the torch.
Then I will be dressed in quite a different manner,
And you will use all your fine words to praise me!"

Secondly she arrived on her trip at a Sizhou hall—
"Sizhou is quite efficacious; let's burn some incense!"
She lifted the incense stick in her hands and bowed down,
"I am on my way to find my husband Fan Qilang!

If Fan Qilang is still alive, let me throw three Sages;
If Fan Qilang has died, let me throw three negatives!"[24]
She threw three negatives and not one single Sage—
Jiangnü was awash in tears and did not say a word.

"When I've found Fan Qilang, and we come back this way,
We will gild the statue of the Sizhou Buddha with gold."

Thirdly she arrived at the village of huge snakes;
The huge snakes blocked the road in great profusion.
She prayed to the mountain god and the god of the soil,
"Please remove these huge snakes so I can travel on!"

Fourthly she arrived at the village of hungry tigers;
These tigers blocked the road and wanted to kill her.
She ran to the Mountain King's temple in the village
And prayed, "May your Royal Majesty save my life!"

The hungry tigers immediately let her go unharmed,
And Jiangnü bowed down to thank the divinity.

Fifthly she arrived at the Village in the Snow, where
There were no inns where she could stay for the night.
Jiangnü had to spend the night out on the road, and
She slept with a stone as cushion and grass as her mat.

When she had slept till the fifth watch and dawn broke,
She shouldered her luggage once again and went on.

Sixthly she arrived in a mountain forest, where

The general in charge of the lair blocked her road.
Alas, that still so very young Meng Jiangnü was
Hindered from traveling on in search of her husband!

 "Take that young lady back to the camp for this night—
Tomorrow I will see you off as you leave our lair!"
When Jiangnü heard this, she replied to the general,
"The red disk of the sun sinks behind the western hills.

 If I spent the night with you inside gauze bed curtains,
I am afraid that that would give strangers cause to gossip."
When the lord of the lair heard this, his lust was aroused,
And he wanted to tie the marriage knot with Jiangnü.

 "I will now become your husband and lord,
And you will now become my wedded wife."
When Jiangnü heard this, she immediately refused,
"Do not lust and scheme for the wife of someone else!

 Can you shoot two arrows at once with one bow?
Did you ever see a single horse carry two saddles?
It does happen that one man marries two women,
But one woman never marries a couple of men.

 A pair of arrows shot by one bow doesn't get far;
A horse carrying two saddles cannot travel at all.
The world may be full of women with two men—
I for one definitely am not that kind of person!"

 When the lord of the lair saw she would not obey,
He drew his sharp sword and wanted to kill her.
When Jiangnü heard this, she said, "I am happy to die,
But I will not be your person inside the bed curtains!"

 When the lord of the lair saw this, he felt remorse,
"Where in the world does one find this kind of person?
You go on to Chang'an to look for your husband;
When you come back, we'll become sworn brothers!"

 When Jiangnü arrived at Plum Blossom Village,
The first inn refused to provide lodging to women.
The second inn refused to provide lodging to women,
So the two women set out again and promptly returned.

 Passing the mountain forest, they arrived at Rage Village,
And they arrived for the night at the Xiaoxiang Pond.

At Xiaoxiang Pond there was no boat to be found,
So she prayed to the Dragon King to show his power
And to bring into being either a bridge or a boat—
The Dragon King of the Four Seas can work miracles.

   That very night he turned the pond into a ford;
Working the oars of a boat, he became a ferryman.
He ferried Jiangnü across the river in his boat,
With palms pressed together she bowed deeply to the sky.

Jiangnü went on and arrived at Sandy Fields county,
Where she saw the soldiers busily building the Wall.
She stepped forward and asked them for information,
"I came here looking for Fan Qilang from Huazhou."

   The troops told her, "Young lady, now listen,
Fan Qilang is working in the southern section."
So Jiangnü immediately went to the southern section
To go and look there for her husband Fan Qilang.

   East, west, south, north, she could not find him,
And when she asked again, she learned he had died.
Loudly she wept for seven days and seven nights,
Bringing down Chang'an's Wall of a Myriad of Miles.

   Her weeping brought it down for eight hundred miles;
The bones of the skeletons were as white as silver.
The bones at the foot of the Wall came in millions;
She had no idea which ones were her husband's.

   Jiangnü's filial piety moved Heaven and Earth;
It moved the Star of the Great White atop his cloud.[25]
The Star Lord of the Great White appeared on his cloud;
He descended to the mortal world to instruct Jiangnü.

   "If you bite on your fingers till blood flows from them,
The bones that take the blood are those of your husband."
When Jiangnü had been told this, she bit her fingers;
Awash in tears, she dripped the blood on the bones.

   She picked up all of the bones that took the blood,
Just as tenderly as if Fan Qilang were still alive.
She detached her breast lapel to wrap the bones,
And of three feet of white gauze she made a streamer.

GUIDING THE SOUL

With this streamer she guided his soul in leaving Chang'an,
And by doing so moved numberless people to sadness;
She guided his soul to go out of the gates of the city,
And by doing so moved old and young to sore distress.

The general reported this matter to the local government;
The local government reported this to their lord and king.
Halfway through the fifth watch the king ascended the hall;
Civil officials and military officers were arranged in rows.
    "If you nobles have any business, report now to the king;
If there's no business, don't dare bother your lord and king!"
First of all General Meng Tian of the southern section
Stepped before the steps of the hall, reporting to his king.
    "Meng Jiangnü, unshakable in determination and courage,
Came here to look for her husband, named Fan Qilang.
Eight hundred miles of the Wall collapsed for her weeping,
Causing the death of quite a number of excellent workmen!"
    On his throne the lord and king agreed to the proposal
To promptly dispatch runners to arrest Meng Jiangnü.
When Meng Jiangnü was arrested and came before the throne,
She bowed before the emperor, wishing him a myriad of years.
    "My husband was assigned to the southern section for labor,
But Meng Tian had him beheaded without any clear reason."
The king was unhappy her weeping had brought down the Wall,
But all he said was that he wanted to be married to her,
    "I have no need anymore for the thirty-six palaces,
And those seventy-two consorts now all are dead.
I'll appoint you as the empress in charge of the palace,
So you can rule the realm and establish Great Peace."
    Jiangnü addressed her lord and king as follows,
"I came here despite the long distance to find my husband.
If you want me to become your wife and empress,
You must behead Meng Tian to avenge my husband!"
    The emperor on his throne promptly agreed to her wish;
Immediately he dispatched officers to arrest Meng Tian.
Meng Tian was taken to the market and promptly executed;
Beheaded with one cut of the sword, he went to the Springs.

Jiangnü then told the emperor, "The rank of empress
Is far too lofty for such a mean and lowly person as me!"
    The king of Qin on his throne answered her as follows,
"Young lady, please listen to what I now have to say.
I want to marry you because of your exceptional beauty,
Without any regard at all for nobility or low-caste status."
    Jiangnü thereupon addressed the emperor as follows,
"I came here despite the long distance to find my husband.
If you really want me to become the empress, you will have
To organize a vegetarian feast for the benefit of his ghost.
    Five hundred priests will have to invite and guide his soul;
Five hundred monks will have to guide him through hell."
As soon as the emperor had heard her make this request,
He ordered Buddhist monks to perform the relevant rituals.
    When the five hundred priests had all been assembled,
They performed their services for the release of Fan Qilang.[26]
Jiangnü then came before the emperor and bowed to him,
"I must make an offering of wine and greens to Fan Qilang.
    When I will have seen Fan Qilang off returning to the river,
I'll come back here and obediently serve my lord and king."
Holding a stick of incense in her hands, Meng Jiang prayed
As she offered sacrifice to Fan Qilang at the bank of the river.
    "If your soul has consciousness, manifest your divine power!
If your soul has no consciousness, I'll marry our lord and king!"
Even before Jiangnü had finished speaking this prayer,
Fan Qilang addressed her from a cloud in the following way,
    "My darling, I am grateful for your virtuous fidelity.
Jiangnü, I am grateful for you bringing me my winter clothes,
Grateful for your undiminished love in the world of mortals,
Even when the emperor wants to marry you as his wife."
    One brown cloud arrived at the bank of the river;
A second black cloud arrived at the side of the river.
The brown cloud carried Meng Jiangnü away;
The black cloud carried Fan Qilang away.
    The officer who escorted her was completely at a loss,
"Today my life is bound to sink to the Yellow Springs!"

GUIDING THE SOUL

Jiangnü thereupon told the general the following,
"I am the Weaving Maid from the celestial palace.

Because of my earthly longings, I was set to suffer.
The emperor of the Qin is actually the planet Mars,
General Meng Tian is actually the planet Mercury,
And Fan Qilang is actually the planet Venus."

When men listen to the story of Meng Jiangnü,
Its many ups and downs fill them with vexation;
When women listen to the story of Meng Jiangnü,
Husband and wife will live their life in mutual love.

Fan Qilang and Meng Jiangnü returned to heaven;
The emperor of the Qin never came to the steppe.[27]
Earlier people loved to tell the events of the past,
And so I can now eventually narrate it to all of you.

I have told to the end the story of Meng Jiangnü,
With its vexations and troubles and more vexations,
Meng Jiang nü weeping and crying by the river
Or trekking to find her husband Fan Qilang.

For men we summon and guide Liang Shanbo;
For women we summon and guide Meng Jiangnü.[28]
Patriarch Peng reached the high age of eight hundred,
But Fan Qilang returned to heaven fifteen years old.

If there's a bond, you'll meet, irrespective of distance;
If there's no bond, you won't, even when face-to-face.
The colored streamer was originally invented by Jiangnü,
The colored streamer that guides the soul of the departed.

I don't fear that people may condemn this as hearsay;
Husband and wife together rose to heaven as a couple.

I urge you, all young women before the hall,
Don't go wash clothes on the bank of the river!
During daytime you soil the water of the river;
At night you pollute the dragon king of the sea.[29]

May all guests now return to their inn for the night;
We have guided the soul of the dead up to heaven.

End of the Song of Jiangnü

3

RETRIEVING A FAN

*T*HE REVISED VERSION OF THE COMPLETE STORY OF THE *Steadfast Chastity of the Maiden Meng Jiang, Who, Searching for Her Husband, Brought Down the Long Wall by Her Weeping* (Chongbian Meng Jiangnü xunfu kudao wanli Changcheng zhenjie quanzhuan) is from the Jiangnan region. It is a rewriting of an earlier text titled simply *Meng Jiangnü Travels a Myriad of Miles to Find Her Husband* (Meng Jiangnü wanli xunfu). The earliest known copy of *Meng Jiangnü Travels a Myriad of Miles to Find Her Husband* is a printed version of 1868. Ch'iu-kuei Wang points out that this text shares one hundred lines and vocabulary items in another one hundred lines with the *Precious Scroll of the Immortal Maiden Meng Jiang* (Meng Jiang xiannü baojuan). He concludes therefore that *Meng Jiangnü Travels a Myriad of Miles to Find Her Husband* derives from that precious scroll, as our earliest known printing of this particular precious scroll dates from 1854.[1] But as the earliest preserved printings of a text do not necessarily reflect the date of origin in the field of popular literature, it is equally possible that the precious scroll borrowed from the ballad. The precious scroll offers a rather idiosyncratic version of the legend (see chapter 4) that is not reflected in the ballad at all, which in many ways stays remarkably close to the legend's

Tang-dynasty version. While the text presented in translation here is a later rewriting of *Meng Jiangnü Travels a Myriad of Miles to Find Her Husband*, I prefer it to the earlier version because it presents a much smoother narrative. Both this text and the text on which it is based would appear to have enjoyed a tremendous popularity in the late nineteenth and early twentieth centuries. According to Gu Jiegang, hundreds of thousands of copies had been printed by the 1920s. This ballad also provided the basis for George Carter Stent's Victorian rendition in rhyming verse.

This translation of *The Revised Version of the Complete Story of the Steadfast Chastity of the Maiden Meng Jiang, Who, Searching for Her Husband, Brought Down the Long Wall by Her Weeping* is based on Lu Gong's *Meng Jiangnü Travels a Myriad of Miles to Find Her Husband*.[2] Lu Gong states that his edition is based on the lithographic edition by the Huaiyin Shufang in Shanghai of around 1920. In his compilation, Lu Gong classifies this ballad and its predecessor as southern ballads, or *nanci*. The term "southern ballad" is occasionally used as a general designation for "string ballads" (*tanci*), the overall classification for long prosimetric ballads from the Jiangnan region; the same term is also used more specifically for prosimetric ballads from Zhejiang. Ch'iu-kuei Wang questions whether these texts should be classified as southern ballads, as they are not divided into chapters, and prefers to call them simply "ballads."[3] The texts are written throughout in rhyming lines of seven syllables. This has been by far the most common form of verse employed in popular verse and prosimetric narrative since the ninth and tenth centuries.

The text translated here contains one passage written in ten-syllable verse. Whereas seven-syllable verse has a caesura following the fourth syllable, lines of ten syllables fall apart either in two groups of three syllables followed by one group of four syllables or in one group of three syllables followed by another of four syllables and yet another of three. In my translation I have tried to show this tripartite structure of the line on the page by typographic means. The text maintains the same rhyme (-*en*) throughout, up to the section in ten-syllable lines. When the seven-syllable lines resume, the rhyme shifts (-*ang*). The text also incorporates folksongs, such as "Weeping for the Seven Sevens" and "Singing the Names of the Flowers," and is introduced and concluded with a four-line poem.

Anonymous

THE REVISED VERSION OF THE COMPLETE STORY OF THE STEADFAST CHASTITY OF THE MAIDEN MENG JIANG, WHO, SEARCHING FOR HER HUSBAND, BROUGHT DOWN THE LONG WALL BY HER WEEPING

A poem reads:

> *For delivering his winter clothes, she arrived in the border regions.*
> *How could she know her husband had left for the Yellow Springs?*[4]
> *The Long Wall was brought down by her weeping: in vain her grief,*
> *And for all eternity her remaining lament is entrusted to the cuckoo.*[5]

Now I've recited a poem, I will tell you the main narrative
Of a wife who's listed in *Biographies of Exemplary Women*.
Do you want to know the name of this virtuous woman?
She was called Meng Jiang, a rare female beauty indeed.

She hailed from Songjiang prefecture in the Jiangnan region;
Her family had its house within the borders of Huating district.[6]
Her father was called by the name of Meng Longde,
And her mother was a virtuous and very good person.

The family was very rich and exceedingly powerful,
But they lacked a son to carry on the ancestral rites.

The couple of husband and wife did many good deeds,
And eventually they were blessed with the birth of a girl.

After the soup-and-cake party on the third day,
They promptly gave the little girl a nursing name.
The name they chose to call her by was Meng Jiang;
As she grew up, till her dying day, it was not changed.

Her first and second year she spent in her mother's lap,
And her parents loved her like a pearl in one's palm.
In her third and fourth year she was able to play,
And once she was five, she knew to obey her parents.

When the little girl had reached the age of six,
The family invited a tutor to teach her to read.
The first book she read was the *Classic for Girls*;[7]
The characters she wrote had two or three strokes.

Four Books for Women, Biographies of Exemplary Women:[8]
Her teacher explained them to her in great detail.
Meng Jiang was smart and intelligent from birth;
She memorized these books after a single reading.

At thirteen and fourteen she learned to do needlework,
And an embroidery teacher was hired to instruct her.
Flying birds, running beasts, dragons and phoenixes,
Human beings, flowers and plants: she did them well.

When Meng Jiang had reached the age of sixteen,
Her moon- and flower-like face was oh so lovely!
Her father's and mother's hearts were filled with joy;
They spoke to her, "Little darling, please listen to us!

It is too bad that you are a girl in hairpins and skirt,
So there's no one to manage this property of millions.
We want to bring home a dragon-riding groom,
So he may as a son carry on the ancestral rites."

Upon these words Meng Jiang replied as follows,
"Dear father and mother, please listen to me!
Your child may be a girl in hairpins and skirt,
But in filial piety toward my parents I'm the same!

If you would want me to marry in haste and hurry,
How on earth can you know the mind of that man?"

Upon these words her parents praised her, "Right!
Dear child, what you said makes really great sense."
  Now we will leave Meng Jiang aside for a while,
Take up a different subject, talk about someone else.

In Suzhou there lived a certain Squire Wan,
And his only son was living with him at home.
The boy was called Qiliang and was quite renowned—
His wet nurse held him in her arms at all times.
  When Qiliang had reached the age of five or six,
A teacher was hired to teach him reading and writing.
Once he was done with the Four Books and the Five Classics,
He deeply studied each one of the Hundred Philosophers.
  But let's not talk of Qiliang and his scholastic abilities;
Let me tell of the First Emperor, that ruler without the Way!
  He did not practice love and virtue, so the borders rebelled;
He wanted to build a long wall to block the foreign troops.
This Long Wall of a Myriad of Miles was a huge project,
On which who knows how many myriads of people died!
  One fiendish villain, only too eager to harm the people,
Wanted to murder Qiliang so sent up a report to the king,
"In Suzhou may be found a certain Wan Qiliang,
Who all by himself can do the work of a myriad!"[9]
  Upon this report, the emperor's heart was filled with joy,
And an imperial edict was brought to the city of Suzhou,
"On all streets and markets a placard will be displayed
For the arrest of Qiliang, who will build the Long Wall!"
  The prefectural and county officials were in a panic,
And posters were put up in layers on top of each other.
"Anyone acquainted with the whereabouts of Wan Qiliang
And reports them is rewarded a thousand ounces of silver.
  Anyone who arrests this aforementioned Wan Qiliang
Is appointed to highest office, half as high as the emperor.
But if one hides this Wan Qiliang from the authorities—
A major crime—one's whole family will be killed."
  They also ordered the yamen runners and ward officers
To inspect and search every house, without any delay.

看書寫字

長城的蓽里

千銀

RETRIEVING A FAN

All these runners behaved like wolves and tigers,
And they extorted lots of money from every family.
   If you did not give them the money they demanded,
They would say that you were hiding Wan Qiliang.
They would take you away to be condemned to death,
And how would you ever be able to right that wrong?
   The poor and destitute people without any money
Sold their sons and daughters just to have some cash.
Suzhou prefecture seemed to have risen in open revolt;
The pestered common people were not left in any peace.

When the squire learned about this state of affairs,
He was so scared he broke into a sweat all over his body.
   And when his wife heard about it, she wept and wailed,
"Our family only has this one single son and heir!
In case something bad and untoward happens,
On whom would we be able to rely in old age?"
   So the squire came up with a plan in his heart:
He would send his son away to escape certain death.
He ordered his son to go and take a bath
And then to don a disguise and flee for his life.
   He bowed to the ancestors and to Heaven and Earth,
"May you divinities protect and guard our only son!"
Following his prayer, he ordered his son to leave home,
"First of all, most importantly, be very careful!
   When you have managed to escape from Suzhou,
Find a place where you can safely settle down.
And then write us a letter and have it delivered,
So your father and mother won't have to worry."
   After Qiliang had taken his leave of his parents,
Weeping and crying, he went out of the gate.
Even though he had escaped from the house,
He had no idea what his future would bring.
   In case he indeed ends up being arrested,
He would die on the Long Wall and never return.
His father and mother were advanced in years—
On whom could they rely for care in their old age?

He wept for a while and then walked for a while,
He wept for a stretch and he walked for a stretch,
And while on the road he heard people talking
Of catching Qiliang, who would build the Long Wall.

    Qiliang was so scared his heart was aflutter,
And as fast as he could, he pursued his journey.
After being on the run for some days and nights
On a stretch, he arrived in the city of Songjiang.

    When he lifted his head and looked around him,
It turned out he stood before a flower garden.
He saw that the garden's gate was half opened,
So he sneaked through the gate, into the garden!

    He hastily closed the gate behind his back
And walked farther on as quickly as he could.
After he had passed below a parasol-tree,
He decided to hide himself under a palm tree.[10]

    "Today I will spend the night at this place;
Tomorrow, as soon as it's light, I'll go on."

But let's leave aside Qiliang for a while
And return to the subject of Meng Jiang.

    She was sitting quietly in her embroidery room,
Spending her day embroidering flowers and figures.
When she had finished embroidering a baby carrier,
The red sun was already about to set in the west.

    She took a fan of light gauze in her hand
And went into the flower garden for distraction.
The garden's flowering shrubs were elegant,
And the cool air permeated her jacket-front.

    The lovely sun-bathed lotus flowers seemed about to talk;
The breeze-tossed pine and bamboo sounded like music.
The birds' chatter and the flowers' fragrance were lovely,
As fragrant herbs covered the courtyard with their green.

    She could not look at the hundred flowers one by one:
A thousand of reds and myriads of purple vied in beauty.
The red balustrade and stone bridge curving and winding—
Meng Jiang walked to the pavilion for taking in the cool.

RETRIEVING A FAN

Playing fishes made the new lotus flowers tremble and shake,
And leaning on the balustrade, she counted their kinds:
Black carp and white carp stayed at the bottom;
While flounder and turtle swam near the surface.[11]

Frogs bumped into the stems of the lotus flowers
And then in one jump dived deep into the water.
But most adorable of all were the goldfish
As they blew their bubbles in shimmering colors.

While Meng Jiang was looking at the joyful fish,
A sudden gust of wind passed through the flowers.
Meng Jiang was caught up in watching the fishes,
And so her fan was suddenly blown into the pond!

Meng Jiang thereupon was at a loss as to what to do;
She called for a maid to fetch the fan from the water.
She called a number of times but nobody answered,
So the only solution was to step into the pond herself.

She took off all of her outer and inner garments:
Her naked body was as white as if made from powder!
Slowly and carefully she stepped down into the pond
And with her hand retrieved the fan from the bottom.

But when she turned around, she saw the young man
Who all the while had been leaning against the palm tree.
Overcome by shame, Meng Jiang now had nowhere to hide;
She could only step out of the pond and put on her clothes!

Qiliang addressed her softly in the following words,
"Who are you, beautiful girl, and what is your name?
Today I have truly been blessed by good fortune
As I could see you take off all of your garments."

While Meng Jiang was hastily putting on her clothes,
She silently thought as she blushed even behind her ears,
"I have only myself to blame for this stupid mistake,
To blame myself for acting in such a reckless manner!

I am only a virgin, so how could I be so unthinking
As to take off my clothes here in the flower garden?
What on earth is the value of a single palace-style fan?
But this body bequeathed by my parents is priceless!

A girl should guard her body unblemished like jade;

Every hour of the day, every minute she should be alert.
A girl cannot take off her garments at random;
She can do so only in front of her wedded husband.

Now that I have taken off my clothes before this person,
It is impossible for me to marry anyone else.
In case this man is still without a wife,
I am his for the rest of my life as his spouse!"

Gathering courage, she addressed him as follows,
"Where do you hail from? Where do you live?
To judge from your appearance, you're a student
And not some criminal out to commit a crime.

So what is the reason you entered this garden?
So please explain to me what is behind this."
Questioned like this, Qiliang started to cry,
"Dear young lady, please allow me to explain!

If you ask for my home, my home is not far;
I'm not a person from a family without renown.
I hail from Yuanhe county in Suzhou prefecture,
And our address is on the inside of Changhe Gate.

My father is known to all people as Squire Wan,
And I am the only, the single son born to him.
When a teacher was hired for me when I turned six,
The name that was chosen for me was Wan Qiliang.

But alas, our befuddled ruler is without the Way
And wants me to work on the border's Long Wall.
But how can I, a student used to reading books,
Supervise the work of building the Long Wall?

Once I get to the Long Wall, I am bound to die—
On whom then will my parents rely in old age?
In this extremity there was no other solution
But to flee from death, and so I got to this place.

I pray you, dear young lady, to show kindness
And on no account to divulge my presence.
Let me stay in this garden for a single night,
And tomorrow at dawn I'll be gone, having fled."

Hearing his words, Meng Jiang heaved a sigh,
And she asked the man who was fleeing disaster,

RETRIEVING A FAN

"You still must be young, so what is your age?
Did you already find a fitting marriage partner?"

    Qiliang thereupon replied to her as follows,
"Dear young lady, please allow me to explain.
This year I've reached the age of eighteen;
I do not yet have a fitting marriage partner.

    And may I dare ask your name and surname?
Please also inform me of your father's name.
If by any chance I escape with my life, I hope
To visit your family later to express my thanks."

    The young lady said, "Don't be so formal!
There's no need to talk about 'expressing thanks.'
My father is called by the name of Meng Longde,
And the name I am called by is Meng Jiang.

    Today I stepped into the pond to retrieve my fan,
And so I took off my clothes in the garden pavilion.
I had no idea you were resting below the palm tree
And would be in a position to have a good look.

    But a girl's naked body is to be seen by no one,
Except that it may be seen by her husband.
Because my body now has been seen by you,
I entrust myself to you for the rest of my life!"

    Qiliang addressed her as follows, "Dear young lady,
Consider the matter of your marriage with care!
I have arrived at this spot while fleeing danger,
And I do not know whether I will live or die.

    If something untoward were to happen,
Wouldn't that mess up the rest of your life?"

    Meng Jiang addressed the young man as follows,
"You may have read books but lack understanding.
You were born in the prefecture of Suzhou,
And I grew up here in the city of Songjiang.

    You arrived here while fleeing for your life;
As chance would have it, you sneaked into this garden.
I came to the pavilion and looked at the fish,
But was there no purpose to that gust of wind?

    It blew my fan straight into the water of the pond,

And when I called for a maid, there was no reaction.
Only because as a rule no one comes to this garden
Did I dare take off my clothes and step into the pool.

    When I turned around, I saw you under the palm tree,
So I blushed for shame and turned red behind my ears.
It's not that I willfully entrust myself to you—it rather is
A karmic connection that conspires to make us a couple.

    Let the two of us first swear an oath of eternal love
And then go to the high hall and see my parents."
They then swore an oath with Heaven their witness,
"The sea will run dry before we change our hearts!"

Meng Jiang took Young Master Wan along
To the high hall, where he met with her parents.
She told them the story from the very beginning,
And both her parents beamed with joy at this story.

    And they said to the young man, "Please sit down,
And listen carefully to what this old man will say.
I am an old man and have only this one daughter,
And she has not yet found a fitting marriage partner.

    If you do not despise her for being too ugly,
I will take you into my home as her husband.
First of all, you will escape from danger and disaster;
Secondly, you will take care of the family for me.

    When this storm is over, you will go back home,
And the two families will be united into one."
Upon these words Qiliang replied as follows,
"Dear sir, allow me to explain my situation.

    I am a fugitive who is fleeing for his life,
So how can I be a mate for your lovely daughter?
If the authorities were to get wind of this,
Even your family would be involved in my crime."

    The squire then said, "That is no problem at all!
Young man, all you'll have to do is just relax.
As long as you stay here in our inner apartments,
Who on the outside will ever know this secret?"

RETRIEVING A FAN

He ordered lanterns and decorations hung up,
While Meng Jiang was dressed up as the bride.
But alas, happy events are beset by tribulations,
And in a moment the rumor had spread outside.

In layer upon layer the gate was encircled:
The runners arrived to arrest Wan Qiliang!
They searched everywhere but without result,
Until they caught him in the firewood shed.

In his upper body they pierced his collar bone;
His lower body was tied up as tightly as could be.
Moreover, his hands and feet were bound together
In such a way that he looked like a meat-filled dumpling.

A carrying pole that went through was put through,
And two people carried him, panting and grunting.
So they carried him bodily to the high hall—
At this sight the squire was quite distressed.

He called out loudly, "Young man, what now?
You, two mandarin-ducks, are cruelly torn apart!
Once at the Long Wall you'll be gone forever,
So on whom can the two of us rely in old age?"

As his tears coursed down, Qiliang replied,
"Dear sir, you should not overly be distressed!
Luckily your darling daughter is still a virgin,
So find her another husband to run your estate."

Following these words, he said to the young girl,
"I urge you, darling, not to be overly distressed!

Even though you and I are man and wife in name,
In fact the marriage has not yet been consummated.
If the marriage indeed had been consummated,
I would really have ruined and wrecked your life.

Once at the Long Wall I am bound to die, so
On no account should you keep thinking of me.
You are a perfectly pure and undefiled virgin;
Please find yourself a spouse and get married."

When Meng Jiang heard these words, she cried,
"My husband, what you say is not fit to be heard!

The marriage of man and wife is not a charade;
Once one has said 'yes,' one's future is settled.
   Even though you and I have not slept together,
I belong, in life and in death, to the Wan family.
Never in all my life will I marry somebody else!
The future, my husband, will prove my resolve!
   Lucky people enjoy the protection of Heaven;
I'm looking forward to your speedy return."

As husband and wife were in the throes of grief,
The imperial commissioner ordered departure.
Qiliang was carried away and aboard a ship, and
Meng Jiang, in tears, turned back and went inside.
   Let's not narrate how Meng Jiang went home,
But let me tell again of Qiliang's sadness and grief.
   "I now will be put on transport to the Long Wall,
But my parents back home will have no idea.
How could I know, when I fled and took to the road,
I'd end up in the City of Those Who Unjustly Died?[12]
   My parents will lean at the gate, eagerly waiting,
Waiting for their darling son to come back home.
Please, I pray, let my parents not be filled with hope;
In vain they have raised me, their son, to no result.
   If I die, it will be just the end of a single life, but
On whom will my parents be able to rely in old age?"
Qiliang wept till his guts and innards were sundered,
And it turned out he had arrived at the Long Wall.
   Once he had arrived at the Long Wall, he fell ill,
And after three days of work on the Wall he died.

Let's not talk of the manner of death of Qiliang;
Let's return to the subject of the beauty Meng Jiang.
Ever since the moment Qiliang was arrested,
She thought of him every single minute of the day.
   She dispatched Meng Xing to gather information,[13]
And he found out that Qiliang had passed away.

RETRIEVING A FAN

When Meng Xing came home, he didn't dare tell,
And so he kept the truth hidden from Meng Jiang
By saying only, "The climate doesn't suit him well,
And his three daily meals he eats without gusto."

When she heard these words, her heart felt as if pierced,
And with tears in her eyes she implored her parents,
"Qiliang is currently suffering some illness,
But ill as he is, he still has to work on the Wall.

Soon the season will be winter with its bitter cold,
The cold of the north that freezes people to death.
So I want to go and bring him winter clothes—
Would you, my parents, give me your permission?"

When her parents heard this, their tears flowed down,
Out of attachment for their son-in-law Qiliang.
"Alas, this befuddled ruler is bereft of reason;
He cruelly destroys the life of this young man!

But you, darling daughter, are a girl in skirts.
How could you go to the Long Wall, all alone?
The best is still to send Meng Xing once again
And provide him with more money for his trip."

Meng Jiang obeyed her parents' instruction
And quickly prepared a set of winter clothes.
She also took out one hundred ounces of silver
For Meng Xing, who was ordered to go.

As soon as Meng Xing had walked out of the gate,
He lowered his head and thought to himself,
"Qiliang has been dead now for quite a while,
So why take these winter clothes to the Wall?

Far better I should go to Suzhou and stay there,
Have fun for a while, and then return home.
I will say I delivered these winter clothes.
How are these people ever going to find out?"

Having made up his mind, he sold the winter clothes
And bought himself a fancy set of fashionable gear.
"As I to this very day am still without a wife,
I will first go to a brothel to break my fast!"

As the prostitute saw that he was a country yokel,
She demanded an extraordinary amount of silver.
Meng Xing, concerned about having a good time,
Did not care at all how much money she wanted.

When the money was spent, his clothes pawned,
He traveled back home, shod in straw sandals.
"Young lady, I have delivered the winter clothes,
And your husband asked me to convey his thanks."

But that very night Meng Jiang had a dream
In which her husband said to her, "Darling,
Meng Xing never delivered those winter clothes;
He sold all of them in the city of Suzhou.

With the money he got, he went to a brothel;
Only when the money was spent did he go home.
I lost my life a long time ago at the Long Wall,
So I urge you to marry another man soon.

I hope you also will kindly inform my parents,
So they will not continue to hope for my return.
They should select a son and heir and adopt him,
So he can assure the continuation of the ancestral rites."

When the beauty woke, it was only a dream—
Weeping, she went to the hall and informed her parents.
Her parents immediately summoned Meng Xing,
But Meng Xing had fled without leaving a trace!

Meng Jiang once again implored her parents,
"Your child wants to go to the Long Wall in person.
First of all, I can deliver a set of winter clothes;
Secondly, I want to see for myself what is true."

Her parents replied, "Absolutely impossible!
How could you as a girl make such a far journey?
There are no suitable places for you to lodge at night;
You couldn't stand the wind and dew, the rain and frost!"

Hearing this, Meng Jiang implored her parents,
"I'll risk death and brave danger to make that journey!
This married life of husband and wife is finished already,
So allow me at least to express my deepest devotion!

RETRIEVING A FAN

Starting from today, I will count the first of the Sevens;
I will erect a tablet for his soul and burn paper money."[14]
    In front of the tablet she offered lots of soup and rice;
She wept till her eyes were as red as peach blossom petals.

When the first Seven arrived, / how grieved she was!
Meng Jiang, just a girl, arranged the offerings.
In front of the tablet she poured out a cup of wine,
But she did not see her husband taste it in person!

When the second Seven arrived, / how sad she was!
Meng Jiang thought to herself in her heart,
"I only hope this dream will turn out to be false,
That I'll be able to meet my man at the Long Wall!"

When the third Seven arrived, / her tears flowed down!
Weeping she called out, "My husband! My Heaven!
Before we were married, you'd already passed away;
You have no one to burn paper money on your behalf."

When the fourth Seven arrived, / her tears had run dry,
And a weeping Meng Jiang collapsed in her room.
"Nobody's suffering has ever been as much as mine;
Married for a lifetime, we never shared a single night!"

When the fifth Seven arrived, / how sad she was!
Monks were invited to recite the Buddhist sutras.
"May my husband, freed from the sea of suffering,
Soon be reborn in heaven, so I may be at peace."

When the sixth Seven arrived, / she wept to her parents,
"Quickly make winter clothes I can take to the Wall!
I'll risk death and brave danger to deliver them there
And also find out whether my husband is still alive."

When the seventh Seven arrived, / her pain was too much!
About to depart she took her leave of her parents,

"Your child now is leaving, but please do not worry;
Make sure, my dear parents, to take care of yourselves."

When her parents heard this, their hearts were broken;
Wailing and weeping, they were overcome by grief.
     "Darling daughter, you have grown up to this age
Without ever leaving your parents' side for an instant.
We have raised you with our own hands from infancy
And treated you as our priceless jewel and treasure.
     We, husband and wife, never were blessed with a son;
We hoped to bring in a son-in-law to manage our estate.
By good fortune we brought Wan Qiliang into our house,
So we all might spend our days at ease and with comfort.
     Who could have known that before you were married,
He would be arrested and sent to work on the Long Wall?
If you, our child, now are taking him his winter clothes,
How would it be possible for us not to worry and fret?
     You, a tender maiden who never left the inner apartments—
How can you make that journey of thousands of miles?
Fierce animals roam the wild mountains and wastelands,
While bandits and robbers infest the roads in the north.
     Our child, your face is as beautiful as a flower,
So we fear that you may be kidnapped and raped.
In case something untoward happens,
On whom can the two of us rely in old age?
     Please do not go, our child, oh please do not go,
On no account can you go to that Long Wall.
Whenever people dream, it reflects their concerns,
So you cannot take these signs in dreams for truth.
     If our son-in-law has the good fortune to recover,
He'll come home once the Long Wall is completed.
But in case our son-in-law has already passed away,
You can't bring him back to life even if you go."
     Meng Jiang felt in her heart as if knifed and strangled,
So she knelt down in the dust and implored her parents,
     "No matter whether Wan Qiliang is dead or alive,
I want to live up to the conjugal love in my heart.

RETRIEVING A FAN

For better or worse, I'll journey to the Great Wall—
Once I am back, I'll serve you, my dear parents!"

Her parents shed tears as they heard these words
And said, "Darling daughter, the apple of our eye!
If you insist on going, we will not stop you,
But please be careful when you are on the road!

When evening comes, don't stay in derelict temples,
As these may be infested by monsters and ghosts.
Inns and hostels also are not suitable for you;
It is best to seek lodging in private homes."

Meng Jiang replied in tears, "I will do as you say!"
Then shouldered the winter clothes and departed.
In the high hall she took her leave of her parents—
They staying, she leaving: all equally brokenhearted.

Meng Jiang was dressed in a white skirt and
Carried her luggage and umbrella on her person.
As Meng Jiang set out on the road to Yang Pass,[15]
Her father and mother wept in one unending wail.

Meng Jiang's heart felt as if stabbed with a knife,
As she stiffened her courage and forged on ahead.
She was not riding a cart, not borne in a sedan chair—
Her two legs carried her till their strength gave out.

She struggled on for one mile, and then for another,
And soon the Chang Gate appeared before her.
She had no desire at all to see the sights of Suzhou,
And soon the Hushu Pass appeared before her.

As she arrived in front of the pass, the sky grew dark,
And a new moon appeared with the evening dusk.
Meng Jiang's only desire was to cross the pass,
But the guard wanted money to buy some wine.

"If you give me some money, I'll allow you to pass,
But if you don't, just forget about passing the gate!"
Meng Jiang was in a fix because she had no money,
So she took off her skirt as a substitute for cash.

When the officer in his room heard about this,
He sent someone over to learn more about her case:

"Ask her from which prefecture she hails and which county,
And why she as a woman is traveling all by herself."
    Meng Jiang, just a girl, piteously stated,
"I was born and raised in the county of Huating.
My father is known by the name of Meng Longde,
And Meng Jiang is the name by which I am called.
    The name of my husband is Wan Qiliang;
He was arrested by the emperor to work on the Wall.
Because I have had no news from him since he left,
I am now on my way to the Wall to find my husband."
    The officer ordered her to sing the names of flowers:
"Sing the names of the flowers and I'll let you go."
So for a weeping Meng Jiang there was no way out
But to enumerate the names of the hundred flowers.

百花

"In the First Month the winter plum takes first place,
While every home and family celebrates the New Year.
In other families husband and wife are united and happy,
But the bright moon and I—we miss one half of ourselves!

In the Second Month spring returns in willows' fresh color;
Herbs and grasses sprout forth, turning the whole earth green.
In the rain young apricot flowers shed red tears, as you too
Must be grieved to the core on account of Meng Jiang!

In the Third Month peach blossoms mark Clear and Bright;
In pairs and couples the swallows return to look for their nests.
Hither and thither in pairs and couples—they're filled with joy,
While I, Meng Jiang, have to make my journey all alone.

In the Fourth Month roses fill gardens with their fragrance,
As I, Meng Jiang, travel a thousand miles to find my husband.
Of my husband at the Long Wall I have had no news, so
I do not know whether he is still alive or may have died.

In the Fifth Month the pomegranate tree is a riot of red.
Everywhere the dragon-boats compete at Double Fifth.

RETRIEVING A FAN

The crowds that are watching are coming and going, but
Nowhere do I see my darling husband Wan Qiliang!

In the Sixth Month the lotus flowers are bathing in sunlight,
And I am reminded of how I met with Qiliang in the garden:
As soon as he and I had become a couple of mandarin-ducks,
He was arrested by the agents and taken away without trace.

In the Seventh Month the water chestnut wafts its fragrance
And the mosquitoes are raising a din like a rumbling thunder.
I would rather they bite me and suck my blood
Than that they go to the Wall and bite my husband.

In the Eighth Month the cassia flowers fill the gardens
And a lonely goose brings along the frost on its head.
That lonely goose and I are suffering the same pain because
A happy pair of mandarin-ducks has been separated and parted.

In the Ninth Month / the weather starts getting cooler,
But the chrysanthemums by the hedge defy the autumn frost.
If only I would be able to find my darling loving husband,
We'd together drink our dogwood-wine on Double Ninth.

In the Tenth Month / the northern winds are high
And the reed-flowers, white like snow, rustle in the wind.
At the Long Wall the weather must have turned to freezing;
Without his clothes my husband's not able to stand the cold.

In the Eleventh Month / the snowflakes swirl about—
My husband, once departed, has still not returned.
I am therefore taking him his winter clothes in person;
Never in my life will I go back unless I have seen him!

In the Twelfth Month / the narcissus is fragrant;
It brings back memories of my parents at home.

Last year on New Year's Eve it was the three of us,
But this year the two of them will be without me."

When she had sung "the flowers of the twelve months,"
Even the officer who had been listening was affected.
"Quickly allow her to go through the pass,
And return that skirt to little Meng Jiang!"
    After crossing the pass, she forged on ahead,
And soon Wangting appeared before her.
    After passing by Wangting and Zhoujinggang,
She arrived at the city of Wuxi.
Shitang, Luoshe, and the town of Henglin,
By way of Qishu and Dingyan to Changzhou.
    When people saw how beautiful Meng Jiang was,
They all flocked together to have a look at the girl.
Watched from afar, she resembled a heavenly fairy;
Seen from close by, she looked like a living Guanyin.[16]
    When the girl Meng Jiang arrived at the southern gate,
She rested for the night at the Qingliang convent.
And when the eastern sky turned white with dawn,
She collected her luggage and set off once again.
    Our maiden Meng Jiang was overcome by grief,
Weeping and crying, she forged on ahead.
After passing by Danyang, she arrived in Zhenjiang,
Where her way was blocked by the Long River.[17]
    The river's waters reached to heaven in one color
As the expanse of waves churned up dark clouds.
Our maiden Meng Jiang wept and wailed as she stared
In the direction of the Long Wall, crying, "My husband!"
    Just as Meng Jiang was perplexed by this quandary,
A fishing boat approached from the middle of the river,
And someone called out, "Dear girl, do not weep,
I will ferry you across the river to Guazhou!"
    At these words Meng Jiang was filled with joy;
She boarded the fishing boat and arrived in Guazhou.
    "May I ask you, dear uncle, your name and surname?
I will remember them carefully in my heart, and when

RETRIEVING A FAN

I have found my darling husband at the Long Wall,
I will not, dear uncle, forget the favor you've shown me."

Upon these words the old man smiled broadly and said,
"I was out fishing on the river, so I threw out my net.
When I saw you, this beautiful girl, overcome by grief,
I hauled in my net, and I beamed you across the river.

How is it possible to speak of any favor shown!"
Meng Jiang knelt down in the middle of the place,
With her hands in her sleeves she made four bows,
Then raised herself again and hastened to Yangzhou.

By way of Wantou and Shaobo to the town of Cheluo,
By way of Gaoyou and Baoying she arrived in Jingjiang.
After passing through Jingjiang, she forged on ahead
Until she arrived at a stretch of the wide Yellow River!

To the east the river reached to the Eastern Ocean;
To the west it stretched as far as the Great Western Waste.[18]
Its waves and billows were raging like a cooking kettle,
And no fishing boat was to be seen on its surface.

"This is a disaster, this truly is a disaster,
This is the place where I am bound to die!"

Meng Jiang wept till she was overcome by grief,
But then the wife of a peasant approached.
She called out to the beauty, "Why do you weep?
Please be so good as to tell me your story!"

Meng Jiang then promptly called out to the woman,
"If you ask for my story, it will afflict you with grief!
I am on my way to the Wall to look for my husband,
But my road now is blocked by the Yellow River."

When the woman heard her, she laughed heartily,
"You beautiful girl, you don't understand!
What you see are waves and billows mightily surging,
But the water's so shallow it doesn't cover your instep.

I myself, I live on the northern bank of the river;
I wade through the water, I don't need a boat.
All you have to do is close your eyes firmly, and
I'll carry you on my back across the Yellow River!"

Having said this, she took the girl on her back,
And with her hands she supported her behind.
Meng Jiang, who had closed her tear-filled eyes,
Only heard the wind as it whistled past her ears.

    After the time it would take to drink a cup of tea,
The woman put the girl down again on the ground
And said to her, "Darling girl, now walk slowly,
In a moment's notice you'll arrive at the Long Wall."

    Meng Jiang lowered her head and thought to herself:
"This woman is trying to fool me!

    After I left the Qingliang convent in Changzhou,
It took me ten days of walking to reach Huaicheng.
So how can I now, in the time of drinking a cup of tea,
All of a sudden already have arrived at the Long Wall?"

    But when she lifted her head again to have a look,
The woman had disappeared without leaving a trace.
Meng Jiang first made four bows toward Heaven,
Then turned around and rushed off to the Long Wall.

When Meng Jiang reached the region of the Long Wall,
Her haggard face was so emaciated she didn't look human.
Nowhere on the road was any decent food to be had,
So suppressing her hunger, she forged on ahead.

    When hungry she just pulled her belt somewhat tighter;
When thirsty she moistened her heart with icy water.
While on her way and out on the road she ran into a rainstorm,
And her clothes were soaked through over all of her body.

    After the rain the road turned to mud and was hard to walk on,
As if you needed a thousand pounds[19] to pull out one rusty nail.
When evening fell, there was no place to seek lodging,
So she took shelter in the hole of a pond near the river.

    Not alone did she fear for wolves and tigers;
She was also afraid for bandits, monsters, and goblins.
Shivering all over, beset by fear, never closing her eyes—
Startled even more as soon as the wind moved the grass!

    The tears from her eyes dropped down on her jacket

RETRIEVING A FAN

And turned to ice in the freezing cold of the local clime.
When, at the end of the night as the sky became bright,
She set out, she first had to shake the frost from her clothes.

The skin of her feet had turned callous from walking;
Her embroidered shoes had no soles left, no heels.
A young lady like a branch of gold, a leaf of jade—
Her bitter sufferings this time were truly grievous!

She hoped that once she arrived at the Great Wall,
She would find her husband and tell him her woes.
Meng Jiang, just a girl, was awash in tears, and our tale
Shifts to ten-syllable lines when she saw the Long Wall.

When the maiden Meng Jiang
    Arrived at the Long Wall
        And lifted her head to observe it,
She saw the Long Wall
    Had been built in such a way that
        It was as impregnable as an iron bucket.
The outside, with the use
    Of button-style tenons,
        Had been constructed of smooth stones;
With the use of starch
    And the use of lime
        These had been tightly cemented together.
The inside had been built
    Using yellow loess
        More than twenty meters thick,
And the heavy stone slabs
    On the outside
        Had been cast in molten iron.
The watchtowers
    Had all been built
        With bronze and iron walls,
Able to withstand
    Those barbarian troops
        Like a river, like a flood!
This Long Wall

From east to west
    Measured a full ten thousand miles,
So this construction project
    Was truly enormous—
        Wasting money, exhausting the people!
Of the black-headed people
    And simple commoners,
        How many lost their lives?
Their corpses and bones
    Were piled up high
        Into mountains and hills.
In the high halls
    They had left behind
        Their white-haired fathers and mothers;
In the inner apartments
    They had abandoned
        Their brides in the prime of their youth.
Their wives and children
    Back at home
        Hoped all day for their return.
How could they know
    That not even their bones
        Would return to their villages?
But when later
    The people at home
        Eventually were informed,
The son wept for his father,
    The mother wept for her son,
        The wife wept for her husband.
Then you also would have
    White-haired people
        With only one single child,
Who would have lost
    Their son and heir—
        How truly distressing!
This was all due to
    The First Emperor of the Qin's
        Policies that harmed the people!
Just have a look:

RETRIEVING A FAN

How could his empire
    Ever last long and forever?
As to those orphaned souls and wronged ghosts
    Who had lost their lives
        While working on the Long Wall—
When would there be anyone
    Who in front of their graves
        Would burn a single sheet of paper money?
"I have no clue
    To which section
        My husband may have been assigned.
If I do not find him,
    How do I know
        Whether he is alive or dead?
I only thought
    That once I arrived at the Long Wall,
        It would be easy to find my husband.
How could I know
    That this one wall
        Would be more than a myriad miles long?
If I go to the east,
    I have to fear
        That he may not be found in the east;
If I go to the west,
    I have to fear
        That he may not be found in the west.
If I have to visit
    Each and every place
        Along this wall,
Then even one year
    May not be sufficient
        To find my husband!
This place is so big,
    The people so many.
        So whom should I ask?
Because of this matter
    I really am
        At a loss as to what to do!"
When the maiden Meng Jiang

Had reached this conclusion,
    Her head was dizzy, her eyes turned black,
Her legs gave way,
    And she collapsed
       There on the ground!

Meng Jiang then sat down on the ground and dozed off
And in her dream saw her darling husband Wan Qiliang.
Before he had spoken a word, his tears coursed down,
But then he said, "My virtuous wife Meng Jiang!
    I recall how we swore our oath in the flower garden,
Hoping our love would last as long as Heaven and Earth!
Who could know that even before the marriage took place,
The two mandarin-ducks would be torn apart without reason!
    When I had been at the Long Wall for just three days,
I, your husband, caught an illness and passed away.
My corpse was thrown down at the foot of the wall, and
The Hexagonal Pavilion was erected on top of my bones.
    You have been so kind as to come here out of devotion,
And I am deeply grieved by your sufferings on the road.
So I have appeared in your dream for the very purpose
Of urging you to go home and find yourself a fitting spouse.
    You are the only child of your father and mother, so
It will not do to guard the lonely lamp in an empty room."
    When Meng Jiang woke with a start from her dream,
She did not see her husband Wan Qiliang anymore.
She felt like a mule that is running in circles and
By running in circles digs itself a deep hole.
    "This day I rushed forward, and that day I ran,
Ran to the Long Wall to meet with my husband.
But now I have arrived at the Long Wall's location;
I've hauled up water in a bamboo basket—all in vain!"

A weeping Meng Jiang came to the Hexagonal Pavilion,
And at the foot of the pavilion she wept for her husband.

RETRIEVING A FAN

"All I desire is to collect your corpse and your bones.
Why are they buried below this Hexagonal Pavilion?
If Heaven and Earth indeed have numinous power,
May they bring down this wall, overturn the pavilion!"
She wept loudly three times, and heaven darkened;
She wept softly three times, and earth turned to dusk.
Heaven and earth enveloped in darkness: somber clouds arose—
She wept until in the four directions a sad fog developed!
When the laborers on the Long Wall heard her weep,
They recalled their homes, and their tears coursed down.
As she voiced her plaint, all was suffused by sadness—
She wept until the Giant Tortoise reversed his body![20]
With a thunderous sound the Wall collapsed, and
The Hexagonal Pavilion came tumbling down!
When Meng Jiang now saw the bones of the corpses,
She wept her heart out, while fainting again and again.
She bit on each of her ten slender fingers till they bled,
Checking the identity of the bones by dripping blood.
"If these are indeed the true bones of my husband,
This pearl of blood will not change in the slightest!"
There was one drop of blood that congealed, so she
Clasped the skeleton to her breast and wept till dazed:
    "My dear husband,[21]
Ever since the moment you and I swore that oath,
    I truly hoped that
You and I would live our lives in perfect harmony,
That we would enjoy the pleasures of the nuptial couch,
And that I would give birth to a son to continue the rites.
    Who could know that
A marriage meant for a hundred years was not meant to be?
We were incapable of even a single bout of spring romance!
    I recall how
That day you were arrested and taken away by the agents,
    My heart
Traveled with you, my dear husband, to the Long Wall.

You, my husband, were a student who reads his books,
So how could you supervise the work of building the Wall?
      I was afraid that
The northern water and soil might not suit you well,
Was afraid that disaster and misfortune might hurt you.
Land and people were strange to you, you must have felt lonely,
Each hour of the day and each minute longing for home.
      I was afraid that as the winter season was approaching,
You did not have the right gear to withstand the cold.
So we dispatched Meng Xing to bring you the clothes,
But who could have known that he was a scoundrel!
      He sold the winter clothes and wasted the money in
Eating, drinking, whoring, gambling, having a good time.
And when he came home, he told us that you were ill,
So I in my heart felt as if scorched with fire.
      Not afraid of hundreds of mountains, thousands of rivers,
I came to find you, my darling husband Wan Qiliang.
But now I have arrived here today at the Long Wall,
      All I see is
This pile of white bones at the foot of the wall.
      It was your fate to leave home, not to return
To your parents back home who are worried to death.
      I remember
The words you spoke as final parting when you left,
Urging me to find someone else as my husband.
      But I am a woman who is steadfast in virtue, so
All my life I will not seek another marriage partner.
Even if we in life never shared the marriage bed,
In death you and I will share one grave and tomb!"

Then she cursed, "This befuddled ruler, bereft of reason,
Caused the death of my husband, Wan Qiliang!"
      The official patrolling the wall shouted loudly,
"Cursing our lord and king is a major crime!
I have to arrest you and take you to the palace;
You will be immediately condemned to death."
      He ordered his underlings to take action, and

RETRIEVING A FAN

With chains and ropes they tied Meng Jiang up.
They brought her in front of the gate of the palace;
The official entered to report to his lord and king.

    When the First Emperor heard this, he was furious,
"Who is so brazen as to dare curse the emperor?
Bring her inside this golden palace hall, so We
May have a look at this maiden Meng Jiang."

    The guards in the palace hall acted promptly;
They brought in Meng Jiang, this virtuous woman.
As soon as the First Emperor saw Meng Jiang,
He was smitten by her unmatched fine qualities.

    "People all say that Xi Shi is so beautiful,
But she surpasses Xi Shi by a hundred percent![22]
We may have seventy-two high-ranking concubines,
But none can compare with her outstanding features."

    When the First Emperor saw her, he was filled with joy,
And he told the civil officials and military officers,

    "If Meng Jiang is willing to become Our spouse,
I will appoint her as the Number One of the palace.
I will not condemn her for the crime of cursing her lord
But grant her a full and complete pardon for her sin."

    Meng Jiang immediately came up with a clever plan,
"If you agree to three conditions, I'll accept your offer.

    First I want a piece of land three miles square,
Which may serve as a tomb and grave for my husband.
In the second place I want you to build me a bridge
Twenty yards high, close by the side of the grave.

    In the third place I want you to wear heavy mourning
To go to that Long Wall grave and offer sacrifice in person!
If you're willing to accept my three conditions, I'll be
Happy to enter the palace as Your Majesty's spouse."

Hearing this, the First Emperor was filled with joy;
His imperial order was transmitted to the Long Wall.
When his officers and officials received this command,
They promptly started this huge construction project.

    Within a short time, all construction was finished,

And they invited their lord and king to come and visit.
The civil and military officials all followed His Majesty
To the Long Wall, and there they saw clearly

That the high bridge had been constructed very well,
That the tomb and the grave pit had been built with care.
A sacrificial banquet for the deceased had been laid out,
And the civil and military officials stood in two rows.

At this moment the First Emperor thought to himself,
"How can a lord and king bow before a mere commoner?

But if I do not bow before the grave of Qiliang,
Meng Jiang is bound to refuse to become my wife,
And as I desire to have Meng Jiang for my wife, I
Cannot but lower my head and bow before a commoner."

He ordered the musicians on both sides to perform,
"We, emperor, bow and bring offerings to Wan Qiliang!"
With the gait of dragon and tiger he performed the ritual;
With both his hands he offered up one stick of incense.

In person the emperor poured out the three cups of wine,
Then he turned his head around and said to Meng Jiang,
"We have fulfilled each and every condition that you set,
So now come with Us to the palace so we may be married."

Meng Jiang, hearing this, exploded with rage, and she cursed,
"You befuddled king, you are a ruler without the Way!
You are not an emperor who has received the true Mandate;
Lasciviously lusting for wine and sex, you are truly a beast!

You do not teach loyalty and filial piety, chastity and duty,
But rather build this Long Wall to block barbarian armies.
        Understand that
The world's submission to civilization depends on virtue;
Even the highest wall cannot stop those invading troops.

The money that's wasted is the common man's blood;
You exhaust the people and waste their riches—a crime!
You have killed my husband, now threaten my virtue—
There never has been such a befuddled ruler before!

Once I'm dead, I'll lodge a plaint in the world of shades
To ensure that your empire will not last for long!"

RETRIEVING A FAN

Having said this, she jumped from the bridge—
Alas, this was the end of the life of Meng Jiang!

The First Emperor heaved a sigh, returned to the palace,
And there told the empress what had happened.
      The empress spoke,
"He who protects a woman's chastity is a sage lord,
But a befuddled ruler ruins a person's reputation.
    You are the lord of all the officers at court; you
Had no right to force a widow to forget her virtue.
Because you have caused the death of Meng Jiang,
You will be an object of vilification for all eternity!"
    A furious First Emperor, upon hearing this, ordered
The empress shackled and taken to the South Gate.
But Her Majesty the empress-dowager,[23] highly upset,
Commanded that she be spared from execution.
    The pardoned empress returned to the palace.
She also ordered a proper burial for Meng Jiang.
She had husband and wife now buried together—
Alive they never shared a couch, in death they shared a tomb.
    Her chastity was recognized, a temple was erected,
With spring and autumn offerings for Meng Jiang.
Meng Jiang was recognized as a heavenly immortal,
And an honorific arch was built before her temple.
    So now I have composed this Tale of Chaste Virtue,
So her name may be transmitted through all ages.

A poem reads:

    The woman Meng Jiang: a thousand miles to find her husband—
    Clear as ice and pure as jade, her determination was like frost.
    Her chaste heart never once betrayed her earlier commitment,
    Leaving a fragrant reputation that will endure through the ages.

4

BORN FROM A GOURD

T HE *PRECIOUS SCROLL OF THE IMMORTAL MAIDEN MENG Jiang* (Meng Jiang xiannü baojuan) enjoyed considerable popularity from the middle of the nineteenth century onward. The text was published repeatedly in woodblock editions and lithographic printings. At least two manuscript versions are known. In the one that dates to 1854, the text is said to have been compiled by the Master of Breeze and Moonlight (Fengyue Zhuren) of Yunshan, but this is such a generic pseudonym that no further identification is possible. The text most likely hails from Suzhou or its surroundings, as the author's knowledge of geography beyond the Suzhou region is quite shaky. The following translation is based on an undated lithographic edition from the early decades of the twentieth century in the collection of the Harvard-Yenching Library.[1]

The genre of precious scrolls originated probably as early as the twelfth or thirteenth century, and the earliest scrolls preached Buddhist piety through narrative. One of the earliest and most popular precious scrolls tells the legend of the princess Miaoshan, who adamantly refuses to marry and eventually achieves Buddhahood, manifesting herself as the Bodhisattva Guanyin.

The Bodhisattva Guanyin, who, from the time of the Song dynasty, was widely venerated in female form, was one of the most popular deities of the popular Chinese pantheon. She also makes an appearance in the *Precious Scroll of the Immortal Maiden Meng Jiang* together with other characters from Chinese mythology such as the Queen-Mother of the West (ruler of all female immortals, who treats her fellow divinities to the peaches of immortality), the Jade Emperor (the highest authority in heaven), and the Star of the Great White.[2] In the Ming and early Qing dynasties, the new and sectarian religions often made use of the precious-scroll format to spread their teachings, which focus on the Eternal Mother. By the nineteenth century, however, "precious scroll" had become the general designation for pious and didactic tales of any denomination. Quite often the specifically Buddhist nature of the genre is reduced to a short invocation at the beginning of a text and a final prayer at its end for the continued protection of the audience by the buddhas and bodhisattvas. Although the actual performance of precious scrolls could still have a strongly ritual character, many of the texts were printed and distributed as popular reading materials.

The *Precious Scroll of the Immortal Maiden Meng Jiang* clearly belongs to this late phase in the development of the genre. The text is written in alternating prose and verse. The most common form of verse is the seven-syllable line, but the text also contains two sections in ten-syllable verse. As is quite common in nineteenth-century precious scrolls, the text incorporates two sets of songs for the five watches of the night. The inclusion of a number of formal documents such as placards, letters, memorials, and sacrificial texts, is a special feature of these prose sections.

In many ways, the *Precious Scroll of the Immortal Maiden Meng Jiang* presents the most idiosyncratic version of the legend. Ch'iu-kuei Wang notes that this precious scroll completely ignores or hardly deals with many plot elements that are found in most versions.[3] In contrast to other versions of the legend, both Meng Jiang and Wan Xiliang are now introduced as denizens of heaven: the later Meng Jiang is a manifestation of Seventh Sister (the Weaving Maid of ancient lore), and the future Wan Xiliang makes his first appearance as Sprout Lad.[4] Sprout Lad descends to earth on his own initiative when the First Emperor, who is building the Long Wall of a Myriad of Miles, intends to bury ten thousand men (one for each mile) in the foundation of the wall as human sacrifices in order to ensure its stability. As *wan* also has the meaning "ten thousand," Wan Xiliang alone will be able to substitute for all these innocent victims. Once Sprout Lad has descended to earth and is reborn as Wan Xi-liang, he apparently forgets his original intention. Seventh Sister, who follows Sprout Lad down to earth, maintains her awareness because she opts for a pure mode of birth—from a gourd.

The Master of Breeze and Moonlight

THE PRECIOUS SCROLL OF THE

IMMORTAL MAIDEN MENG JIANG

Once deluded, now enlightened—blazingly clear!
The Three Jewels are the Compassionate Ferry.
With a single stick of holy incense
I devoutly revere the Dharma King.[5]

Now the precious scroll of Meng Jiang has been opened,
I'll again expound the roots and tell of ancient emotions.
You, good men and faithful women, listen attentively, as
It increases good luck, extends one's life, and averts disaster.

Reverently I open the book of the Maiden Meng Jiang. The story took place in the days when the First Emperor of the Qin was building the Long Wall of a Myriad of Miles, leaving behind this tale of ancient times. The construction projects of the First Emperor were without equal in past and present. In building the Epang Palace and in constructing the Long Wall of a Myriad of Miles, he alarmed and shook Heaven and Earth, he wearied the people and destroyed their wealth, and the people could not live in peace.

Now let me tell that in the palace of heaven that day winter solstice was festively celebrated. The gate of heaven had been opened widely, and all gods came to court to offer their congratulations. The great immortals of the ten continents and the three isles all arrived at the Jade Portal and offered homage to the Jade Emperor. Once the immortals had all been received in audience, the perfected beings of the three heavens also retired, and the pearly screen was lowered again.[6] Because of this festive occasion the immortal officers and clerks all went off to roam through the three realms. We'll leave that topic and only tell of the Seventh Sister Star of the Palace of Immortal Beauties. She was one of the Seven Immortal Beauties, who are in charge of sericulture in the world of men.[7] There also was the immortal officer Sprout Lad of the Cockfighting Palace, who was in charge of farmers' sowing and irrigating. While walking about, he arrived before the southern gate of heaven. It just so happened that Seventh Sister had also arrived there, and together they gazed on the world below. From inside the houses an aura of death rose up to heaven, as the people were suffering great harm. Sprout Lad thereupon said to Seventh Sister, "So be it! I see that in the world below an aura of death rises to heaven. It is because the First Emperor of the Qin wants to build his Long Wall of a Myriad of Miles, killing a myriad of men. Together with you I want to go down and save these myriad men from disaster. Immortal Sister, what about it?"

The immortal beauty replied, "Immortal officer, this is a mistaken idea!

You don't know how evil the people are in the world below;
If you go, the harm you will suffer will be anything but slight.
This is an affair decided on in the Purple Tenuity Enclosure;[8]
Do not treat its power over life and death as a minor affair.

You and I are in charge of the Heavenly Market Enclosure;
There is no need for us to take on any more responsibilities!"
"Immortal beauty, please do not argue that I make a mistake!
A myriad of men suffer misfortune; that's not a minor affair!

If we just sit and watch and don't care about human affairs,
See them die but do not save them, we lack Heaven's heart.
To carry their disaster and misfortune is the heart of compassion!
I've made up my mind to go down to earth this one time."

The immortal beauty did not know how to answer his words;
This journey of his clearly would be beset by many problems.

BORN FROM A GOURD

The immortal lad straightaway descended to the mortal world
In order to be reborn as a human being in Suzhou prefecture.
 The immortal beauty was filled with worries in her breast,
Because she worried the immortal lad would now be in danger.
She found out he had descended to the mortal world and
Was about to be born at the term of his mother's pregnancy!
 He was born as the only son of the Wan family
And was called Xiliang for a very good reason.
His father the squire was called Wang Tianxin,
Whose wife, Lady Zheng, was of the same age, so
 When late in life they obtained this son, it was a treasure;
They were overjoyed (xi) as if Heaven had bestowed a treasure.
He was as perfect (liang) as a fine jade without any blemish,
So they called him Xiliang, to be the Wan family's son and heir.
 His impressive appearance was divinely sculpted—
A flat crown, a broad forehead, a mouth like a water chestnut,
Ears hanging down on his shoulders,[9] the Five Mounts aligned,[10]
Eyebrows clear, pupils bright, the three parts were equal.[11]
 With his white teeth and red lips his appearance was extraordinary;
He looked just like an immortal child come down to earth.
No less than two wet nurses were engaged to take care of him,
And a servant girl always carried him, never leaving him alone.
 But let's not tell anymore of the immortal lad Xiliang
And tell again of the immortal beauty and her loyal heart.

Now let's tell that the immortal beauty had seen with her own eyes that the immortal lad had descended to the mortal world. On this journey he was bound to meet with untoward events. Even though it might be said that as man and woman they had to maintain distance, they still were "ministers serving in the same palace" up in heaven. Now he suddenly had conceived the mind of compassion and wanted to save a myriad of men and carry their disaster and misfortune. "I cannot bear just to sit and watch! I'll have to descend to the mortal world and go ahead and save him! In the event I can avert this *kalpic* ordeal,[12] it will display to some extent my natural goodness, and perhaps I can return together with him to the heavenly palace." The immortal beauty immediately left for the mortal world, and riding a cloud she departed toward the north.

She went out of heaven's gate and promptly rose on a cloud;
  All she saw was
Millions of tiles, arranged like fish scales, thickly covering earth.
The clouds served as her horses, the wind as her chariot,
And the myriads of miles through the clouds were an instant.
  Having left the gate of heaven, she arrived in the mortal world;
In less than a moment she had arrived in the city of Songjiang.
Traveling on from there, she arrived in the county of Huating,
Which was filled with a miasma of evil, an unbearable stench!

  This miasma of hatred wafted upward to the highest skies,
And clouds of red dust surged forward in billowing waves.
When would this ocean of suffering ever come to an end?
White-capped its waves—how deep is that river of lust!
    "I do not want
To be born as a baby so messily on a river of blood;[13]
I'll come up with some trick to be born in the mortal world."
As she looked all around from the edge of her cloud,
She saw the gourd vines spreading in Meng Family Village.
  On one of these vines a gargantuan wax gourd was growing,
"I will have to make use of this gourd to be reborn on earth!"
On her cloud she silently considered all the details and
Figured out that the gourd belonged to water and wood.[14]
  She made use of water and wood to sneak into the gourd
And once in the gourd seated herself in the lotus position.
  Let's not tell about the immortal maiden seated in her gourd,
But we will narrate of the owner of the field, the local squire.
This squire was none other than Meng Longde, a man so rich
One could never list his fields and gardens and village farms.
  Everybody therefore called him Millionaire Meng;
Throughout the county he was known for his wealth.
In Huating county he was considered the number one;
The only thing he lacked was a son playing in his lap.
  His relatives and neighbors were only distantly related,
But even though not close kin, they acted like close kin.
Every day they came to ask for loans or ask for gifts,
And he lacked someone to keep the accounts in order.
  When Magnate Meng felt deeply vexed by this,

BORN FROM A GOURD

His wife comforted him in the following words,
"Having this money but no son does us no good,
So let's do good deeds to prepare for our next life!"

Lacking a son or a daughter, she suffered greatly,
So his wife Lady Li was moved to deeds of charity.

Every fifth and tenth day she fed Buddhist monks,
Every third and ninth days she fed men of the Way,
Piously kept to the fasts, recited the name of the Buddha,
Asked permission to buy living beings and set them free.

The story continues that in Meng Family Village there also lived an Auntie Jiang. Almost eighty, she had neither son nor daughter and lived in abject poverty. She repeatedly had borrowed money from Squire Meng, but she still was not satisfied. When we come to speak of this gourd today, it was the case that the seed had been planted by Squire Meng's servant Meng Xing, but because the vines had extended up to the foundation of Auntie Jiang's house and had produced this gargantuan gourd there, she had long harbored the intention of picking this gourd. But before she had done so, Meng Xing came by to pick this wax gourd. Auntie Jiang ran outside to assert her ownership, "It's only because I took care of this gourd for many days that it could grow to this size! How can you just come by and pick this gourd without spending any effort?"

Meng Xing replied, "Slowly, slowly! Old woman, you talk without rhyme or reason! I, Meng Xing, planted this gourd with my own hands, so how could you think of grabbing this gourd? You are really bereft of reason!"

A furious Auntie Jiang started to beat Meng Xing, and Meng Xing, who could not accept defeat, promptly went to report her to that star of disaster, the village head.[15] The latter said, "How can you, Mrs. Jiang, make free to pick a wax gourd from the vine that has been planted by Meng Xing?"

Auntie Jiang replied, "The vine may have been planted by Mr. Meng, but the gourd grew on my property, and I have taken care of it for quite some days, so why should I not be allowed to pick this gourd?"

The star of disaster said, "The two sides both have a reasonable case. OK! According to my judgment, the two of you should divide this gourd in two. Is that acceptable?"

Meng Xing thought to himself, "This is only a trifling matter, so I better take my loss," and he promptly got out his knife. Who could have known that the immortal maiden, seated in the gourd, had not anticipated this and pan-

119

icked, loudly shouting from inside the gourd, "Please, Mr. Star of Disaster, slice the gourd open from the top and allow me to climb out of the gourd before you cut it to pieces!" It was not only the star of disaster who was scared out of his wits when he heard her screaming like this; all three of them were so scared that they scurried away in all directions.

But the village head steeled his courage and asked, "What kind of demon are you in truth? Tell me immediately!"

The immortal maiden answered his question as follows:
"Mr. Star of Disaster, please listen to my full statement.
    I most definitely am not what you perhaps think I am,
And I certainly am not some monster or some evil sprite.
I am Seventh Sister from the Palace of Immortal Beauties;
Among the Seven Sister Stars I am counted number seven.
    I have now descended to this mortal world only because
My brother will meet with misfortune on earth here below.
I wanted to come to his rescue and rise to heaven together—
People have always needed other people for their deliverance.
    For this reason I came to the east to descend to this world,
        But I did not want
To be born as a baby so messily on a river of blood.
So I borrowed this gourd to serve as my birth mother,
And later I will find some patron who will raise me."
    When the star of disaster heard this unbelievable tale,
He immediately opened the gourd to see for himself.
When he opened the gourd with the knife and looked,
He indeed found a baby girl seated in lotus position.
    Seated cross-legged in meditation just like a buddha,
White teeth and red lips, without peer in this world!
Eyebrows clear, pupils bright, hard to find on earth,
Her imposing mien was yet full of elegance and grace.
    When Auntie Jiang saw her, she clasped her in her arms,
And filled with joy she expressed her thanks to the gods.
When Meng Xing saw her, he was flurried and flustered,
And he ran off to report this piece of news to the squire.
    The squire and his lady both came over to have a look

BORN FROM A GOURD

And saw that this baby girl was like a precious pearl.
Heaven bestowed this baby child on the Meng family!
 So they told the servants,
"Now take this baby and quickly bring it to our place!"
 Auntie Jiang got so angry she didn't know what to do;
She kicked and cursed without ever shutting her mouth.
Auntie Jiang raged on and on, but nobody cared at all,
So she ran to the district office and urgently beat the drum.[16]
 When the district magistrate promptly questioned her,
Auntie Jiang lodged an accusation, word for word true.
When the district magistrate heard this unbelievable case,
He immediately summoned Mr. Meng to appear in court.
 His careful inquiry into the Meng and Jiang families
Revealed that both families were without any children.
 Mrs. Jiang had almost reached the age of eighty years;
Not only did she have no relatives, she was also poor.
Mr. Meng's possessions were counted in millions, but
As he had neither son nor daughter, he wanted the child.
 "This immortal maiden who has descended to earth
Has been born in a gourd that served as her mother.
The vine was planted in the land of the Meng family,
But the gourd lodged on the land of Mrs. Jiang to grow.
 The house of Mr. Meng is therefore the place of birth;
Auntie Jiang qualifies only as a 'temporary lodging.'
But as her name I choose the name of Meng Jiang—
From this date onward, the two families will rest their claims!
 The judgment of this magistrate is fair and impartial;
As justice is done, both parties should now be at ease."
Mr. Meng and Auntie Jiang knelt down on their knees
And expressed their thanks for the magistrate's grace.

The district magistrate then closed the session, and of him no more. Our story goes that Mr. Meng took Auntie Jiang into his home as a member of the family. They all loved and cherished Meng Jiang as a precious pearl, and from that moment onward, the two families lived in harmony. Auntie Jiang reached the age of eighty-five and then passed away. Meng Jiang was six years old at the time. Everything for the coffining and burial of Auntie Jiang was provided for by Squire Meng.

In the wink of an eye, light and shade quickly passed by;
At the age of six she excelled in all kinds of needlework.
Her superior intelligence had been given to her by birth;
Her exceptional dexterity was without equal in this world.
　　Once she had grown up and reached the age of fifteen,
She managed all household affairs with great expertise.
No need to tell that since Auntie Jiang had passed away,
All her needs were taken care of by Mr. Meng.
　　He wanted his daughter to marry an in-living son-in-law
Who could continue the Meng family as its son and heir.
So he ordered her servant girl to tell the young mistress,
"Her ladyship has some matter she wants to discuss."
　　When the young lady learned her parents had called for her,
She lightly moved her lotus-feet and left her chamber, and
When she arrived in front of the hall, she greeted her parents,
Calling out to them, "My parents, your daughter is here."

When the young lady arrived in front of the hall, she bowed in greeting, "My dear parents, your daughter wishes you all happiness. What instructions do you have for me now that you have asked me to come here?"

　　The squire said, "Daughter, you have reached the age of fifteen, so we want to select for you a fine husband, who upon marriage can continue the ancestral sacrifices of the Meng family, and for this reason we have asked you to come here to discuss this matter."

The young lady immediately replied in this manner,
"My dear parents, please allow me to answer as follows.
Your child is still very young of age, so I urge you,
Father and mother, to postpone this issue for a while.
　　Moreover, both of you are followers of the Buddha,
And I have been a strict vegetarian for all of my life.
I'd rather practice the way of immortality in my room,
Share in your religious exercises for as long as I live.
　　This is actually your daughter's greatest desire.

There is no need for you, my parents, to worry!
I desire to practice religion, recite the name of the Buddha,
And continuously refine my breath and my essence.
    Early and late I 'revert the light' and 'reverse the glare,'[17]
Always turning the Wheel of the Law, without stopping!
Each day I eat the Crow's liver and the Hare's marrow;[18]
The 'joined pear' and 'fiery jujube' are immortal dishes.[19]
    Heavenly nectar and ambrosia I imbibe in each season;
I subdue both dragon and tiger by my own numinosity.[20]
May the three of us together penetrate the Way and
Ascend to heaven's palace to venerate the Three Purities![21]
    Your little daughter originally is not of mortal stock;
She descended to the world of dust for a higher cause.
If you, my parents, are willing to grant me my wish,
I will never seek a husband until the end of time!"

The squire laughed heartily and said, "My child, you are mistaken! Lord and
vassal, father and son, and husband and wife are the great principles of social
relations. What need is there to practice immortality and study the Way? My
child, go back to your room, and your father will make arrangements."

The daughter took her leave and returned to her room,
"How could my parents understand my immortal motives!
The reason the immortal lad descended to the mortal world
Was his earnest desire to rescue from death a myriad of men!
    This vow of compassion is not some trifling matter;
By carrying disaster and misfortune, his sin is dissolved.
On his own initiative he carries away their misfortune, so
I figure luck will be scarce in this matter, adversities many.
    The immortal lad wanted to carry away their suffering;
        My determination
To descend to the mortal world then arose as a reaction.
Long ago he invited me to descend to the mortal world,
So we could together take on the people's kalpic disaster.
        I only thought that
    The unfathomable decisions of the Purple Tenuity Palace
        Were of no concern

To our deep passion in the Heavenly Market Enclosure.
    Who could have known
That the vow of the immortal lad was so extensive that
He would disregard his own safety to substitute for the people?
    I realized adversities would be many, luck would be scarce,
But despite my pleading he did not change his mind at all.
Risking his life and fate, he descended to the mortal world,
Without any concern for the root of his nature and fate.
    At this moment I cannot bear to sit idly by and watch,
        Filled with fear that ·
His one spiritual true nature may be unable to return to heaven.
No one else knows he sacrifices his body to save the world.
Who will witness his merit if he kills himself by himself?
        Because you, immortal lad,
Sacrifice yourself in order to save the lives of a myriad of men,
I too therefore will sacrifice myself in tandem with you.
    Common mortals do not understand the affairs of immortals—
Vulgar words and vulgar phrases of messy misunderstanding!
My parents only understand the affairs of this world;
They can't know the subtle causes hidden in darkness."
    When her sighs reached this point, she melted in tears;
Behind the closed door of her room, she cried without end.
Let's not tell of the sufferings in Meng Jiang's heart
But narrate again of new developments in heaven.

On this day the Jade Emperor, the Highest God, ascended the throne and
summoned the civil and military immortal dignitaries in order to scrutinize
the rewards for virtue and punishments for evil in heaven and on earth. The
multitude of functionaries of all the offices of city god, earth god, and stove
god presented their reports. As the Jade Emperor was carefully reading these
with his dragon eyes, he came to the report submitted by the chief immortal
official in charge of the Heavenly Market Enclosure, which read:

> The First Emperor of the Qin of the northern extremity of the southern
> continent of Jambudvipa,[22] upon the completion of the conquest of the six
> kingdoms, exhausted the people in building his capital. Recently he has
> started the construction of the Long Wall of a Myriad of Miles, and for every

mile he intends to bury one subject in the foundation for the wall, because only in that way will the construction be solid. Because of this he will secretly kill a myriad of persons—a cruelty beyond words!

I hereby report that Sprout Lad, one of the twelve Sprout Gods of the Cockfighting Palace who each year in turn serve at the Beginning of Spring, and the Seventh Sister Star in charge of sericulture of the Palace of Immortal Beauties, last year, following the completion of the court audience on the occasion of the winter solstice festival, together visited the southern gate of heaven and, observing a miasma of death rising to heaven from the northern extremity, became aware of the disaster awaiting a myriad of people. The immortal lad wished to save these myriad of people, and Seventh Sister tried to dissuade him, but without success, and the immortal lad stealthily went out of the gate of heaven. When Seventh Sister saw that he had descended to the mortal world, she could not bear to sit idly by and watch, so she also went out of the gate of heaven. I am not acquainted with the later developments.

Your servant does not dare not report this matter to Your Majesty, and I await your disposition.

When the Jade Emperor read this report, he said angrily, "This rascal dared to stealthily go out of the gate of heaven without reporting to Us! He should be punished for such rash behavior. Even though his compassionate wish to save the world is a meritorious affair, he still should have reported to Us, so the immortal ministries might have discussed the matter. Now he has already descended to the mortal world, so we can only bring his mission to fruition."

He thereupon commanded the Metal Star of the Great White to descend to the mortal world and quickly spread a children's ditty, so it would come to the knowledge of the First Emperor—and he was not allowed to make any mistake! The Metal Star kowtowed to express his gratitude, left the palace, and went out through the southern gate of heaven. When the Jade Emperor had finished reading all the reports, the rewards and punishments were all clearly allotted. When all decisions had been taken, all the officials expressed their gratitude and left the palace. The golden bell resounded thrice, the pearly curtain was lowered, and the Jade Emperor returned to his private apartments in his dragon conveyance, but enough of that.

When the Metal Star arrived in the kingdom of Qin, he spread and taught the following children's ditty:

> *In Suzhou lives a person by the name of Wan Xiliang,*
> *Who all alone can take the place of this myriad of men.*
> *Ennoble him quickly as the Great King of the Long Wall,*
> *And the Long Wall of a Myriad of Miles is forever secure.*

Within ten days all the children of the capital were singing this song, and it also became known inside the palace of the First Emperor of the Qin. The First Emperor then summoned Prime Minister Li Si to court, to question him about the meaning of this ditty. The prime minister came to the palace as soon as he received the summons and said, "As this ditty exists, this person must also exist. Your Majesty should issue a placard for his arrest." The First Emperor followed the prime minister's advice, and an imperial placard was immediately posted in the city of Suzhou, and imperial guardsmen were posted beside it. The placard read:

A placard issued by the reigning emperor

Re: The construction of the Long Wall of a Myriad of Miles for the protection of the security of the imperial line and of the national prosperity and the people's welfare.

Heaven and men are all filled with joy, and therefore Heaven has sent down a popular ditty that can ensure the wall's lasting solidity. We hereby instruct the military and civilian population as follows,

Whoever hides Wan Xiliang and does not report him will immediately be beheaded;

Whoever knows the whereabouts of Wan Xiliang and comes forward with that information will receive a reward of one thousand ounces of silver;

Whoever arrests Wan Xiliang will be ennobled for three generations.

In each prefecture and county this placard was posted;
The imperial placards were posted all over the place.
People in every village and hamlet knew its contents;
The population of the whole empire knew about it.
If one would dare conceal or hide this Wan Xiliang,
One would immediately be beheaded, without mercy!
If one's most remote relatives would conceal him,
The whole family would be exterminated for sure.
If one did know the whereabouts of Wan Xiliang,

The reward for that lead was one thousand silver.
And if one took the yamen runners to Wan Xiliang,
Three generations of the family would be ennobled!

City and village, township and hamlet were in an uproar;
Squire Wan was so frightened he was shaking all over.
The squire and his wife discussed the matter together;
That very night they told their son to flee for his life!

The squire wept to such a degree his heart was wounded;
His wife fainted from weeping but eventually recovered.
Xiliang comforted his parents in the following manner,
"It is not a big deal that I will be out on the road.

From my earliest youth I have never gone outside,
So there is nobody there able to recognize your child.
I will flee to a faraway place to escape this danger,
To escape and survive this evil day and evil hour.

After a full year or six months I will return home,
And I will come back again to serve my parents.
Dear parents, please take good care of yourselves,
Do not worry too much on behalf of your son!"

The squire urged him repeatedly not to linger and tarry;
With all speed he sent off his son to flee for his life.
There was no need to carry another set of clothes;
He only needed to carry some extra loose silver.

He bowed to Heaven and Earth and the ancestors,
Then turned around and also bowed to his parents.
He forced himself to let go of his parents' hands;
His tears coursed down, and his heart was grieved.

"I know that the sins of my previous life are many,
And that thus I am punished by this evil retribution.
May the gods and ancestors offer me their protection
As I accumulate merit in preparation for my next life!"

Risking his life, fleeing from danger, he ran all night,
And he kept on running all night till break of dawn.
Now running, now walking—the sky turned to dusk,
And the golden crow was slowly sinking in the west.[23]

In a grove of trees there appeared a large mansion—
He had already arrived at the city of Songjiang.

When he entered the city and looked around him,
He noticed a flower garden thickly planted with trees.

By chance the gate of the garden had not been closed,
So he sneaked inside the garden to rest for a while.
Let's not tell about Xiliang standing in the garden,
But let's speak of the immortal maiden Meng Jiang.

Burning incense, she chanted the name of the Buddha;
Having recited the *Yellow Court*, she went for a walk.[24]
By the shortest route she went to the flower garden
With its myriad kinds of elegant flowers and shrubs.

The white plum displays its oh so pure jade bones;
The orchid raises its elegant fragrance of kingly allure;
The camellia welcomes pure guests with graceful mien;
The pink plum in gorgeous toilette is especially lavish.

The blooming apricot's charming colors delight in a drizzle;
The chrysanthemum by braving frost increases in spirit;
The narcissus's icy skin reveals a heart of iron and stone;
The peony is famed as national beauty, heavenly fragrance.

The jade trees rise tall and erect on the steps of the stairs;
The golden lotuses sway languorously in the garden pond;
The herbaceous peony's fragrant form is truly without equal;
The pomegranate's beautiful substance is famed as unique.

The precious pearls of camellia flowers are famed as noble;
The fragrance of the winter plum flower tastes very intense.
The crab apple puts forth the figure of a divine immortal;
The Lucky Scent flower opens strings of dripping gold.

Top-Graduate's Red grows opposite Golden Lion,[25]
While golden carp sport and frolic in the lily pond.
Embroidered-ball flowers bloom like the full moon,
While lush tulips cover the ground, white like clouds.

The roses when in bloom fill the yard with fragrance,
The azalea's refined fragrance is also oh so lovely—
There's no end to enjoying all those thousands of flowers;
No one can list these myriad kinds of blooming fragrance.

As she lifted her head, she saw the west garden's sights,
With its banana trees and parasol-trees in layer upon layer.

BORN FROM A GOURD

As she left the eastern garden to go to the western garden,
She had to walk across a winding bridge over the pond.
    Suddenly a fierce whirlwind arose out of nowhere,
Swept her off her feet and made her fall into the water.
Meng Jiang shouted for help again and again, and this
Aroused the young gentleman Xiliang to action.
    As soon as Xiliang saw the situation, he didn't wait
But hastily ran from the grove to come to her rescue.
When he had sprinted to the winding bridge to look,
He discerned the young lady who had fallen into the pond.
    Xiliang immediately grasped her by both her hands
And pulled her out of the water and up onto the bridge.
The squire and the maids had also heard her shouts,
And all arrived, together with her mother, on the scene.
    "My child, how could you be so stupid as to go off
To the garden without maids all by yourself for a stroll?
And from where does this young gentleman come?
What on earth is he doing here in our flower garden?"
    The squire in his heart was filled with suspicions,
And the young lady also found it difficult to speak,
So the squire now addressed his question to Xiliang,
"Where do you come from, from which county?
    If you tell me the facts from the very beginning,
I will forgive you, not blame you, and let you go."

Our story goes that Xiliang could do little else but step forward, greet the
squire with a bow, and say, "Please allow me, sir, to explain the situation."

Xiliang explained his situation to the squire,
"I am a person from the prefecture of Suzhou.
My family is settled in Suzhou's Yuanhe county;
The Wan family of the Chang Gate is well known.
    My father is called by the name of Wan Xinde,
And I, dear sir, go by the name of Xiliang.
It is all because this muddle-headed emperor
Wants to arrest me to build his Long Wall.

Without any cause or reason he wants to kill me,
So my parents sent me away to flee for my life.
Day and night I fled for my life—what suffering!
I was just trying to get some rest in this garden.

   When I had sneaked my way into the garden,
I heard someone shouting for help from the pond.
I hurried to the winding bridge to have a look
And was able to save your daughter from drowning.

   This, sir, is the true story of my circumstances;
I would not dare lie to you, not even half a word.
If you are willing, sir, to save my life, I will never
To the day of my death forget your great favor."

   The immortal maiden Meng Jiang heard his tale;
It was as if a drop of cold water fell into her heart,

   "This man turns out to be the immortal Sprout Lad;
It must be preordained we meet each other here.
I descended to the mortal world only because
I wanted to save and deliver this Sprout Lad.

   It must be fate that we meet each other here today;
The Lord of Heaven truly completes our destiny,
But I have to keep this as a secret in my heart;
I may know, but I cannot divulge it by speaking.

   Only because the Long Wall brings such adversity,
We arrived here, truly 'shadow following form.'"

   Let's not talk of Meng Jiang's affairs of the heart,
But return to the squire, who urged Wan to stay,
"As you are Young Master Wan from Suzhou,
Your father is indeed an old friend of mine.

   As karma has brought you to our house today,
I have something I would like to say to you.
If I do not save your life, I am not a good friend,
So I will manifest the full extent of our relation.

   You are the only child born to your father;
We have only one daughter—a perfect match.
Both families are of equal standing and status;
Today's a lucky day, so let's have a wedding!"

The young man said, "Dear sir, you are mistaken! I am a man who is beset by danger, so how does it make sense to have your daughter marry me? The imperial court, moreover, is making such a great effort to have me arrested that I would not dare stay in your mansion for a marriage out of fear that you too would be implicated!"

The squire said, "Young Master Wan, don't worry! If you are staying in the inner apartments of my mansion, how could outsiders know about it? There truly will be nobody who will kill you."

Xiliang thought to himself, "At this moment I really do not know where to run. If I were able to escape here from my evil day and evil hour, I may yet have a chance to live." So he forced himself to comply, "But might I know what is the young lady's opinion?"

Once the young lady heard this, she thought to herself, "I'd better adapt my plans to circumstance." And she immediately answered, "It was actually my original intention to practice religious exercises and recite the name of the Buddha, and I had no desire whatsoever for marriage. But the ancients have said, 'While one is still at home, one obeys one's father; once one is married, one obeys one's husband.' As my father and mother are present here, I obey the decision of my parents."

When he had heard this reply from the young lady,
Xiliang kept silent once he had heard her words.
The squire that very moment promptly gave orders
To light the lanterns, decorate the house—all at once!

The whole family, old and young, was busily occupied;
In a flash—flower and candle—she played the bride.
But unexpectedly this happy event ran into trouble,
Because people outside immediately were informed.

The Meng family mansion was tightly surrounded;
They came to arrest Young Master Wan Xiliang!
Xiliang was that very instant arrested and shackled,
To be put on transport leaving without any delay.

All of a sudden he was trussed up in the high hall,
And the squire at that sight was moved to tears.
"What crime indeed has the young man committed?
What is the need to truss him up tighter than tight?

It is not that he is a highway robber or river pirate,
But even those are not arrested so ferociously!
Where is your human conscience in this moment?
It is not that he is your long-standing archenemy!
    You arrest him without any proof or evidence!
Tell me, imperial commissioner, what is his crime?"
The imperial commissioner also was moved to tears,
"Of course I do not have any old feud with him!
    I fully realize the young master is without crime;
The emperor wants him arrested to build the Wall.
We act according to an edict of the present emperor;
It's not the case that I am acting too ferociously!"

The squire said, "As you obey the imperial edict, you know very well that the young master is without crime. It is all the fault of this muddle-headed emperor bereft of reason! May I bother you gentlemen to take good care of the young master while on the road? I will definitely make up for your trouble."

    The government agents said, "We wouldn't dare take your money! Sir, there is no need to worry!"

Xiliang spoke to the squire in the following manner,
"Sir, please listen to what I have to say.
Once I have left, I most likely will lose my life,
So let your daughter find another marriage partner."
    Xiliang also spoke to the young lady as follows,
"Once I have left, I am bound to lose my life.
In this life I'll have no chance to reverse my fate,
So there's no need at all to keep longing for me."
    A crying Meng Jiang answered him as follows,
"Young man, please listen to what I have to say.
Even if you will never be able to reverse your fate,
I will never consider marrying another husband.
    The marriage may not yet have been consummated,
But we have been engaged, and I will not remarry.
If today you do not give credence to my word,
The future, my husband, will manifest my heart!"
    As the couple was sadly taking leave of each other,

The imperial commissioner urged him on to depart.
Xiliang, tied up and in shackles, went into the boat,
While Meng Jiang wept in a heartrending way.

Each and every one was moved to tears at this sight;
Everybody loudly cursed the muddle-headed emperor.

Without delay he was transported to the Long Wall—
And what, you may wonder, was his final fate there?
Let's not discuss Xiliang and the building of the Wall,
But let us first narrate again about the Wan family.

Ever since the day Xiliang had departed from home,
They had not received any news or letter from him.
Day and night they were worried by the lack of news;
They sadly thought of their son—it broke their hearts!

"If our son is able to return home safely,
We will repair temples and donate golden images!
If our son survives to live a life without worry,
We will keep to the fasts to repay Heaven's grace!

If our son is able to come back home to us,
We'll thank Heaven and Earth and all the gods!
But if our son never comes back home again,
On whom are the two of us to rely in old age?

If our son really never returns home again,
To whom should we then entrust our millions?
What evil karma did he create in an earlier life?
For no reason that stupid emperor had him arrested!

Day and night there is no end to our sad tears, as
We cannot forget about him for even a minute.
If only our son could escape from this dire disaster,
We'd light red lamps on a thousand-story pagoda!"

Let's not discuss how Squire Wan and his wife were day and night overcome
by sadness. Now Squire Meng of Songjiang actually was the best friend of
Squire Wan from Suzhou. When Wan Xiliang, fleeing from danger, ended up
in Squire Meng's flower garden, Squire Meng discovered by his interroga-
tion that Xiliang was the son of Squire Wan, but the muddle-headed ruler had
issued a placard for his arrest, and he was fleeing from danger. When Squire
Meng saw that Xiliang was both smart and handsome, he was filled with joy,

"I was looking for just such a well-educated sophisticated fellow, and they are not easy to find! It must be that Heaven today bestows this match! He is a perfect partner for my darling daughter—a couple of mandarin-ducks! Squire Wan and I will be tied not only by the bonds of friendship but also by those of marriage!" But who could have known that even before the wedding took place, misfortune would strike! Xiliang was arrested by the imperial commissioner and taken away—how saddening! "As an added aggravation to my misery, I now have to write a letter to Suzhou in order to inform Squire Wan of what has happened. That's the only right thing to do!" The letter read,

To the most honorable Wan, Esquire

My dearest elder brother and relative by marriage Tianxin,

You and I have always been linked by an unshakable friendship, but separated by mountains and passes we have long been unable to meet, to my most intense regret! Now I can inform you that on the third day of the first month of fall, your son took refuge in our flower garden. Only when I met him and questioned him did I learn that he was your son, so my heart was filled with joy, and I treated him with greatest concern, as if he were my own child. I then married my daughter to your son, and the wedding took place that same day. My private hope was to keep him at my place and inform you later, so I might perhaps persuade you to move to my place and we could form one united family. In that way both you and your wife and my wife and I would have someone to rely on in our old age. That would have been my greatest joy!

But who could have known that Heaven does not always grant people's wishes! Even before the marriage was consummated, our house was ever so tightly surrounded by an imperial commissioner, who arrested your son and put him on transport to the Long Wall. There was then no possibility of saving him. How saddening indeed! All my efforts had been expended in vain and turned into a yellow-millet dream.[26]

For this reason I make free to send you this letter to inform you of the urgency of the situation. Would you perhaps know of some Heaven-reaching stratagem that might rescue your son from this fatal danger?

Overcome by sorrow and emotion, I respectfully submit this.

I hope the season finds you well and beg for your indulgence.

BORN FROM A GOURD

Squire Wan received this letter, opened it, and read it. Realizing that with the arrest of his son the ancestral sacrifices of the Wan family had come to an end, he beat his breast, stamped his feet, and loudly wept, "Heaven, oh Heaven!

August Heaven does not protect us from bitter suffering.
On whom does he want the two of us to rely in old age?
The Long Wall of a Myriad of Miles is the emperor's project.
Why on earth does he need our son to build the Long Wall?
    All the many other sons and daughters are not arrested;
The one and only person to be arrested is our son alone.
What crime did our son Xiliang ever commit in his life?
Without rhyme or reason our lord kills an innocent man.
    When I, this old man, will appear before King Yama,[27]
I will accuse that muddle-headed emperor of murder!"

His wife Lady Zheng advised him, "Now that our son has been arrested by that muddle-headed emperor, he will have no chance to survive. It must be because you and I grew too little good karma in our earlier existence, and that is why we are punished in this life by having no children. What use are all our possessions to us now? Much better we assist the needy, support those in danger, repair bridges, pave roads, feed monks, make donations, distribute money, and donate clothes, so as to grow good karma for a future life."

    The squire replied, "My wife, your words make perfect sense." From this moment on, Squire Wan realized the vanity of the red dust,[28] kept to a vegetarian diet, and recited the name of the Buddha; he refrained from slaughtering sentient beings and freed captured animals—he engaged in all kinds of good deeds and truly displayed sincere piety. Thus it is said, While secret dealings and vile deception may eventually lead to glory and luxury, such prosperity will not last; despite practicing goodness and accumulating virtue, one may remain without a son, but upon death one will become a god. Squire Wan and his wife, pained in their hearts right to their marrow, had realized the vanity of possessions and devoted themselves to doing good in order to grow good karma for a future life—but no more of that.

Let's talk of Xiliang, who was transported to the Wall;
Once he arrived there, his body was wrecked by illness.

Both the imperial inspector-in-chief Cheng Liangyu
And the imperial supervisor of construction Wei Zonglin,
Upon being informed of the arrival of Wan Xiliang,
Thanked Heaven and Earth and thanked all divinities.

"Otherwise we
Would have had to kill common people without number!
We were truly scared when we received the secret edict.
Without making any distinction, we were making arrests;
To see those people die would be truly heartrending!

Even though we acted obeying the emperor's edict,
We still remain human beings and have consciences.
Wan Xiliang also may have committed no crime at all,
But his surname makes him a substitute for a myriad.

And even though he will soon die a most cruel death,
Upon his death he will become a god for all eternity!"
The two commissioners knelt down to welcome him,
A plate of incense on their heads, with utmost respect.

They respectfully welcomed him to the building site;
The two commissioners treated him most solicitously.
They also immediately informed the prime minister,
And the prime minister then reported to the emperor.

Your servant Li Si reports to Your Majesty,

Because of the construction of the Long Wall of a Myriad of Miles, Your
merit will last a myriad of generations, and Your virtue moves the nine
heavens. For this reason Heaven bestowed on us a children's ditty. Wan
Xiliang was indeed located in Suzhou, which proves that songs and ditties
do not lie and that they are called forth by the superior virtue of Your Majesty. Yesterday the imperial commissioners reported that Wan Xiliang has
been arrested and is being kept at the construction site, and they request
Your decision in this matter.

Your servant would propose that Your Majesty should first offer sacrifice
to Heaven and Earth, make offerings to the gods of the mountains and rivers, and then comfort Wang Xiliang by sacrificing to him, so he will forever
enjoy Your Majesty's grace and will never forget, even after his death, to
exert himself to provide divine assistance. May you bestow on him the gown

and cap befitting a king and ennoble him as the Lord of the Long Wall of a Myriad of Miles, the High God King Wan, so he may forever ensure the stability of the Long Wall, the prosperity of the nation, and the peace of the people. Let him enjoy the gift of Your Majesty's grace and rejoice in sacrificial offerings in spring and autumn.

Prostrating myself, I request Your Majesty's decision, so an edict may be promulgated.

After the First Emperor had read this report, he agreed with all of its recommendations and issued an edict that they should be put into practice—promptly! The officials at court expressed their gratitude for his grace. The edict was immediately promulgated, and orders were given to the hundred civil and military officials to assemble for departure at the palace gate. That very day the emperor departed for Mountain-Sea Pass in order to offer sacrifice there,[29] and the civil and military officials followed in an endless stream. When the emperor arrived at Mountain-Sea Pass, the high official Wei Zongmin, the imperial commissioner in charge of construction of the Long Wall, and the high official Cheng Liangyu, the imperial inspector-in-chief, welcomed the emperor, who said, "We will in person offer sacrifice to the mountains and rivers and command you to make the suitable preparations."

The two imperial commissioners replied, "Your servants have been awaiting Your Majesty's arrival already for some time." The First Emperor stepped down from his conveyance and sat down behind the dragon desk, and the civil and military officials arranged themselves in rows to his east and west—quite an imposing sight! The prime minister then stepped forward from the ranks and said, "May Your Majesty offer sacrifice on the Altar of Heaven!" The First Emperor promptly rose from his seat, the musicians played their instruments in unison, and the eunuchs to his right and left adjusted the emperor's cap and waited on him in front of the altar. The official cantor chanted out the rites and respectfully offered three libations, prostrated himself, and read aloud the sacrificial text,

On the tenth day (a *jiawu* day), of the Seventh Month (which started on a *yiyou* day) of the tenth year of Correct Succession (a *gengzi* year),[30] your son and servant, correctly governing the thirty-six prefectures and leading all officials of the palace, offers sacrifice to Heaven and Earth, the sun and moon, the mountains and rivers, and the Five Marchmounts; the Four Canals and the Ten Continents, the Three Isles and Seventy-two Grottoes, the Thirty-eight Sources, and the immortals and perfected ones of the various heavens; the refined spirits of the various mountains, the divine gods of the hundred streams, and the dragon kings of the four seas, for their boundless grace of "covering and carrying," for their great merit of universal illumination, for their bounteous favor of cyclical movement, and the affective response of the various immortals.

Because we are now constructing the Long Wall of a Myriad of Miles, we dare pray for the protection of the gods. Our gratitude will be without bounds!

Respectfully we lay out a meager repast and beg you to partake of it.

While the instruments were played again, the emperor performed the ritual of the nine prostrations and poured out a libation. And when the gods had been sent off, the eunuchs assisted the emperor as he took his seat behind the dragon desk and respectfully presented some lychees to him. The prime minister then again stepped forward to report, "Your servant reports that the man named Wan Xiliang from Suzhou will be able by his might to stabilize the Long Wall of a Myriad of Miles so it will be strong and sturdy for a myriad of generations. May Your Majesty bestow on him one python-gown, one king's cap, and one pair of court boots. I also implore Your Majesty to ennoble him as a king in order to placate the popular feeling." The First Emperor accepted his proposal and ennobled Wan Xiliang as the Revered God King Wan, Lord of the Long Wall of a Myriad of Miles. Immediately the order was given to eunuchs and guardsmen to bring Wan Xiliang forward so he might show his gratitude for the imperial grace by kowtowing. On his journey Wan Xiliang had suffered all kinds of alarms, and he had been ill for more than half a month, so by this time his soul had left his body and he looked like a wooden puppet. The cantor expressed gratitude for the imperial grace on his behalf by shouting, "May the emperor live a myriad years, a myriad times a myriad years!" The emperor bestowed on Wan Xiliang one python-gown, one king's cap, and one pair of court boots, and he expressed his gratitude, "A myriad years, a myriad times a myriad years!" After he had expressed his gratitude . . .

BORN FROM A GOURD

Once he expressed his gratitude for the imperial grace,
His body truly resembled a puppet carved from wood.
Hovering on the verge of death, he still was breathing,
But bereft of consciousness he was a man in a dream.

    Next the eunuchs and guardsmen were given the order
To promptly dress Wan Xiliang in his new set of clothes.
And when he was properly dressed in the python-gown,
He was carried into the Long Wall's foundation pit.

    From all sides he was covered with clay and earth,
And so, alas, he lost his life in this heartrending way.
His single soul made the endless journey back home;
He was followed on this trip by a couple of servants.

    The Long Wall was secured by the King of a Myriad of Miles—
Even though he had to die, Xiliang most willingly did so.
When he arrived in Suzhou where he had been born,
A chilly wind whirled around the gate of the mansion.

    Let's not talk about how Xiliang returned back home,
Quietly listen to his parents weeping through the night.
His father and mother kept on weeping day and night,
Each and every instant concerned about his life and death.

Now let us tell how [his parents], the squire and lady Zheng, kept thinking of
their darling son, piteously weeping in a heartrending way.

    His mother lady Zheng
        Wept for Xiliang
            In a most heartrending way;
    Each time she wept,
        Each time she wailed,
            Her tears came down like a rain,
"I raised you, my son,
        Till the age of sixteen,
            Like a jewel, like a treasure,
There was not a moment
        I was not concerned—
            Sleeping or eating, never at rest!
Whenever there was food,

Your mother would first
    Call for you to eat your fill;
Before the weather turned cold,
    I would make sure
        Your winter clothes were made.
When you started to study,
    I wanted you to work hard
        All twelve hours of the day;
It was my hope that you
    Would pass the examinations
        And bring glory to our house.
Who could have known
    You would leave us midway
        And suffer this fatal disaster!
On this day today
    We, your parents,
        Are left orphaned and alone,
And not knowing whether
    You are dead or alive
        We constantly think of you.
We may never be able
    To see you again
        And tell you our worries.
Not knowing the day,
    Not knowing the night—
        Dusk is falling at sunset;
Not knowing hunger,
    Not knowing cold,
        We abandon sleep and food."

Who doesn't understand how Squire Wan and his wife day and night were filled with the most heartrending sadness? One night, as they could not get any sleep even in the fifth watch,[31] they dreamt of their son.

When the drum of the first watch came,
The son heard his darling mother weep piteously.
Even though yin and yang are securely separated,
Xiliang still was secretly deeply hurt in his heart.

BORN FROM A GOURD

When the drum of the second watch was beaten,
The son heard his mother as she loudly wept and wailed.
The mother didn't see her son, but the son saw his mother,
Who could not know that her child was crying even more.

When the drum of the third watch arrived,
The mother so wept for her child that all skies were darkened,
But how could she know he was watching her by her very side,
So moved by the sight of his parents that his tears coursed down?

When the drum of the fourth watch boomed,
She was so tired from weeping that she sank into a dream.
Xiliang entrusted himself to her dream to tell his suffering,
And his mother saw her child while dead as if he were alive.

When the drum of the fifth watch resounded,
The Cock crowed three times and called forth the dawn.
"Now your child cannot stay here any longer anymore,
So I take my leave of my parents as the sky brightens."

Mr. Wan and his wife saw their son return home in their dreams. The squire
told his dream to his wife. "If we have seen the same dream, it must mean that
our son has died!" They had seen him in a court gown, wearing a royal cap,
and accompanied by a pair of servants. They had seen their son kneeling
down and urging his parents not to be wounded by grief, "Your son has been
appointed as the Lord of the Myriad of Miles of the Long Wall, the divinity
King Wan. Even though I had to die, I willingly did so. But I have not yet
repaid the grace of your feeding and raising, and I have brought suffering to
my parents. So how can I be at peace in the world of darkness when suffering
this pain?" Such a dream could not be false!

All of a sudden they saw their son returning home;
At this time it was the third watch, and in a dream.
Both together, she tightly embraced her son and wept;
Embracing her child, she wailed without any restraint.
    "My son, today you have returned home and come back;
My son, so please explain how you managed to escape!

Tell everything to your mother, from beginning to end;
My son, let me hear all the sufferings you had to endure!

My son, from the moment you went out of the gate,
Your mother has been filled with worries without end.
My son, now I suddenly see you here kneeling down,
Expressing your thanks to your parents for raising you.

'I have been appointed as the Lord of a Myriad of Miles,
I may have died at the Long Wall, but I willingly did so.
From now on there's no need to worry about me, as I
In the land of darkness will support and assist my parents.'

When all of sudden I woke up, it turned out to be a dream,
But this dream most definitely must have some cause!"

But let's not talk about these sad affairs of the Wans,
And narrate again for a while about the Meng family.
Once Xiliang was put on transport to the Long Wall,
All of the Meng family was overcome with worry.

They promptly dispatched a servant to make inquiries,
The servant Meng Xing, to find out the state of affairs.
When he knew what had happened, he returned home,
And he reported to the squire in the following words,

"Xiliang was taken to the Long Wall straightaway,
And while on the road he fell ill of sorrow and fright.
Once he arrived at the Great Wall, he was hospitalized—
People who are ill cannot work on building the Wall."

The squire, when he heard this, was grieved at heart;
His daughter fainted from weeping and then recovered.
As autumn passed and winter came, the weather got cooler,
And they decided to send winter clothes to the Long Wall.

The immortal maiden Meng Jiang wanted to go herself
As a small expression of her wifely love and devotion,
But the squire refused to accept this when she told him;
He insisted on dispatching Meng Xing to the Great Wall.

This servant Meng Xing was secretly filled with joy;
Taking the winter clothes, he immediately set out.
But once on the road Meng Xing started thinking,
As he clearly knew that Xiliang had already died.

"There is no need at all for me to go to the Long Wall.

Why don't I go to Suzhou and have a good time?"
So he went, and sold and pawned the winter clothes,
And he spent all that money whoring and gambling.

Let's not narrate Meng Xing's whoring and gambling;
Let's tell how Xiliang appeared once more in a dream.

As a gust of chilly wind he arrived at the Meng mansion
And straightaway went to Meng Jiang's private chamber.
There he heard Meng Jiang weeping most copiously,
And each word as she wept was truly heartrending!

"Long ago I urged you not to descend to the mortal world,
But you had made up your mind to save a myriad of people.
And ever since you descended to the mortal world,
I too have been bereft of peace each minute of the day!"

She did not long for tea, and she did not long for rice;
Weeping and crying, she never had a moment of peace.
Throughout the five watches of the night she never slept
And kept on lamenting from the first watch to the fifth.

How could she know Xiliang was listening in the air
And was overcome by grief because of his fine wife?

"At the drum of the first watch / my heart is filled with suffering,[32]
As I think back on our common life in the palaces of heaven.
Why did you have to descend to earth to suffer this suffering?
Because of your action I too / knew no peace in my heart,
So I accompanied you to suffer this greatest of sufferings!

At the drum of the second watch / I recall how long ago
You watched the eastern lands from heaven's southern gate;
An aura of death rose up and up as misfortune was manifest.
In your compassion you decided / to save a myriad of men;
Disregarding your own safety, you chose the path of death.

At the drum of the third watch / filled with even more sadness—
When disaster struck, who was there to take pity on you?
You have died while I still live, without any love or concern!
Who could have known / that you out of your conscience
Would carry all this disaster single-handedly and all alone?"

At the drum of the fourth watch / her spirit was muddied;
In darkness and silence it was bereft of all possible energy.
In a dream Xiliang manifested his might and numinosity,
"My darling wife, your words / are each and every one true;
In your love you descended to earth to embody my person."

At the drum of the fifth watch, / when the sky was turning bright,
Xiliang entrusted the following words to his darling wife,
"I need you to go in person to the Long Wall and
Request the First Emperor / to order a temple built,
So the divine sacrifices to King Wan may last forever!"

(The above five songs are to the tune of "Ancient Zither Chant")

The immortal maiden Meng Jiang awoke with a start from her dream. "Clear
as day I saw my husband come back, and he entrusted a task to me as his wife,
requesting that I go in person to the Long Wall of a Myriad of Miles and
request the First Emperor to order the building of a temple for King Wan. This
task really is not easy, but as my husband manifests his numinosity like this
and orders me, I definitely will go to the Long Wall. I'll act according to circumstance, and perhaps this temple can be built. This also will manifest my
conscience as his wife!"

    The maiden Meng Jiang
        Reported to her parents
            The events in her dream,
    "In my dream I saw
        My husband,
            Who gave me an order;
    He requested me
        To go in person to
            The Long Wall of a Myriad of Miles,
    To confront the First Emperor
        And request the construction
            Of a fitting palace,
    Have him build

A temple to King Wan,
　　Ensuring his fame for all eternity.
I, your daughter, believe
　　That if my husband
　　　　Manifested such might and numinosity
By appearing in a dream,
　　He must have died
　　　　And is informing me in this manner.
So I wept and cried,
　　'My dear husband,
　　　　You are truly breaking my heart!'
I definitely want
　　To go to the Long Wall
　　　　And find my husband's bones,
And if I cannot find
　　My husband's remains,
　　　　I'll die weeping by the Long Wall!"
Once she had taken
　　This unshakable decision,
　　　　She made ready to depart.
Squire Meng and his wife
　　Tried by all means
　　　　To change their daughter's mind,
As they called out, "Dear daughter,
　　You've been pampered and raised
　　　　In the inner apartments,
So you have never once
　　Gone out of the gate—
　　　　So how can you make such a long trek?"
Her parents tried desperately
　　To make her stay at home,
　　　　But their daughter refused—
"How can the two of us
　　Not be worried
　　　　If you leave this house?
It is even inappropriate
　　For a little girl
　　　　To walk in the street,

So how could you travel
    Over thousands of miles
        Through cities and towns?"
The maiden Meng Jiang
    Replied to her parents
        In the following words,
"My parents, in my heart
    My true heart has
        A divine god's understanding.
As my husband
    Manifests such numinosity
        By appearing in a dream,
He certainly will ensure my safety
    By offering his protection
        As I travel on the road.
So I hope that the two of you
    Will not try in any way
        To stop me, your daughter, from going.
In my heart
    I've made up my mind to go to
        The Long Wall of a Myriad of Miles."
Before she had finished speaking,
    There also arrived
        A guest from afar who came to visit.
This turned out to be
    Squire Wan, who came
        To visit his relatives by marriage,
So Squire Meng hurried
    To greet his old friend
        At the gate of the mansion.
"It hurts my heart to speak of
    What has happened to
        My dear son Xiliang!
Dear elder brother,
    When earlier we received the letter
        You were so kind to send us,
The two of us
    Were awash with tears
        Once I had read it.

We are indebted to you
    For dearly loving our son
        And giving yourself so much trouble,
And we feel sorry for
    Your lovely daughter,
        This treasure from the inner chambers!
It is not fair
    That your lovely daughter's
        Entire life should be ruined,
And for that reason
    I have come to your house
        To discuss this matter.
It would be much better
    If she would marry
        The son of some fine family,
Because last night
    The two of us
        Saw our son in a dream.
In deepest darkness
    He sharply and clearly
        Appeared to us in a dream,
Followed behind
    By two servants
        And dressed in a dragon-robe.
He urged the two of us,
    Time and again,
        Not to grieve for him,
'Your son has been appointed
    As Lord of a Myriad of Miles;
        My might secures the Long Wall.
I may have died, but I
    Substituted for a myriad of men,
        So I have no regrets whatsoever!'
From this dream it is clear
    That our son definitely
        Has gone to the realm of shade,
So you should not ruin
    Your lovely daughter's
        Entire future existence!"

Squire Meng
      And his wife—
            Their tears coursed down,
"Just to mention what happened
      To your fine son
            Really hurts the heart.
Call the young lady
      So she may offer respect
            To her father-in-law!"
The maiden Meng Jiang
      Left her room
            And knelt in the dust,
And as she called out,
      "My father-in-law!"
            Her tears fell down.
Choked by grief,
      She closed her eyes
            And could not utter a word.
When Squire Wan saw
      This precious beauty,
            He was even more pained at heart.
The maiden Meng Jiang
      Addressed her father-in-law
            In the following words,
"Since ancient times
      A man's guidelines
            Are the marital rites.
Your daughter-in-law
      May be young in years
            But will never remarry.
Wait till I've come back
      From the Long Wall
            To settle on a solution.
If I can succeed
      In coming back home,
            We may practice religion together."
Once she had spoken
      These few words,
            She told him she would leave.

BORN FROM A GOURD

The maiden Meng Jiang had made up her mind to set out that very day. The whole household surrounded her and wept, and Squire Meng said, "My child, as you definitely want to set out, let me make the proper preparations. Let me select two capable servants and also choose two smart serving women, so you may travel by boat and carriage, and this very day we will see you off!"

Let me not discuss the wind and frost of the whole trip;
I will again discuss the two families, truly heartbroken!
Once they had seen off the young lady as she departed,
The families wept so much that they were awash in tears.
  "My daughter, now that you have left, what will happen to you?
And on whom are we, your two old parents, later to rely?"
A deeply moved Squire Meng wept till he fainted and recovered,
While his wife wept in an even more heartrending way.
  Eyes shedding tears looked at eyes shedding tears, as
Brokenhearted persons saw off a person also heartbroken.
Squire Wan addressed them, trying to offer some comfort,
"My dear brother, I urge you, please, be not so heartbroken!
    The four of us parents,
  Sharing sorrow and sickness, should grow old together!
    By far the best
Would be to combine our two households into one house.
My dear brother, please, let me know how you feel about it;
In that way the four of us can practice religion together.
  I only regret I didn't grow blessings in an earlier life, but
At least we should now prepare for our next existence."
As soon as he heard this, Squire Meng was filled with joy,
"Your proposal exactly conforms to my deepest wish!
  So why, my dear sir, do you not go home to Suzhou
To discuss this matter in detail with the lady your wife?
And when my daughter returns later from the Long Wall,
We all will be one family and practice religion together."

Squire Wan said, "Dear brother, your advice is very sound. I leave it up to you to decide whether your family should be united with mine, or whether my family should be united with yours. And when the young lady returns, we can discuss this further." After this, Squire Wan took his leave—but let's not talk about that.

Let's talk instead of the young lady now at the Long Wall—
Once she had arrived at Tong Pass, where should she look?
As she wept for one stretch, she walked one stretch, and
Each time she wept, she wept in a most heartrending way!

When she wept loudly three times, heaven had darkened;
When she wept softly three times, earth too had darkened.
A black sky, a darkened earth, nothing could be distinguished,
So Xiliang immediately manifested his mighty numinosity,

"Do you see that distant pavilion? Rest there for a while.
That pavilion is the Pavilion for the Reception of Officials."
A weeping Meng Jiang had come to the Long Wall's site;
Endlessly weeping she fainted, but she also recovered.

When she wept loudly but once, the wall tumbled down;
Where she wept for one stretch, that section collapsed.
This was because Xiliang manifested his numinosity;
The collapsing wall bared the body and bones of Xiliang.

Meng Jiang stepped forward to test their authenticity;
Dripping blood on the bare bones, each drop congealed!
"The true bones of my husband indeed have appeared!"
Meng Jiang fainted for weeping and did not recover.

She wept loudly just once, then collapsed in fainting,
And alas, she stopped breathing for more than half an hour!
The two serving women called out repeatedly to her,
"Young lady, young lady, please, please, wake up!"

Unseen by all, Xiliang supported and protected her,
And after an endless time the young lady recovered.

Soldiers guarding the wall absolutely lost not a moment
In reporting this incident to the commander of Tong Pass.
And when he came in person to inspect, he discovered
Meng Jiang indeed had crumbled the wall by her weeping.

When the commander reported this matter to the throne,
The First Emperor flew into a rage at this information.
And Meng Jiang, quickly arrested in order to be sentenced,
Was brought to the golden palace, before the emperor.

BORN FROM A GOURD

As soon as His Majesty saw her, his face showed his joy,
"This woman's beauty really surpasses that of all others!"
Meng Jiang prostrated herself in the golden palace,
And she reported to His Majesty the full state of affairs.
    "Xiliang was my darling husband, but without reason
He died a wrongful death to build this Long Wall.
I wept for a myriad of miles to come and find him;
My husband displayed his power by toppling the wall.
    It bared his body and bones, which I inspected in person,
And each drop of blood proved them indeed to be true.
This is the full account of the true facts of my case;
I will abide by Your Majesty's decision on what to do."

The First Emperor said, "Maiden Meng Jiang, you indeed know love and duty!
But in my eyes you are still beautiful and dignified. If you agree to remarry
and become Our wife, We will ennoble you as the empress of the land. What
would you think of that?"

Meng Jiang addressed His Majesty the emperor as follows,
"If you want me to become your wife, there is no problem.
As long as you are willing to meet my few conditions,
I will be more than happy to enter the palace as your wife.
    But if Your Majesty does not meet these few conditions,
No way even if you'd pound my body into a myriad of pieces."

The First Emperor asked, "Which conditions do I have to meet? Please tell
them quickly!"

Meng Jiang addressed His Majesty the emperor as follows,
"In the region of the Long Bridge is found the Long Wall. (?)
Ten miles long and ten miles wide, a square of ten miles,
Such should be the size of the grave mount to be constructed.
    In front of the grave should be built a temple to King Wan,
Where sacrifices will be offered in spring and fall, forever!
Once the grave has been built and the king's temple too,
Your Majesty will offer sacrifice in person at the grave!"
    The First Emperor agreed to each and all of these conditions;

He even was happy to offer sacrifice at the grave in person!
Immediately that very moment he issued an edict, ordering
That the construction be completed within one single month.
    First the grave was to be built and next the king's temple—
Construction had to be started that very day, as fast as a fire!

When all civil and military officials at court heard that the edict had been issued, they each went out to take the action required of them in the edict, and none of them dared disobey! First they built Xiliang's grave, and next they erected the temple for King Wan. That very day an imperial placard was posted, which read,

> By imperial command the *si* hour of the third day of the Eighth Month has been selected as an auspicious time to initiate construction for the royal grave of the Lord of the Long Wall of a Myriad of Miles Xiliang and for the temple to King Wan, where sacrifices will be offered in spring and fall. May all local officials, soldiers, and common people be unified in understanding wherever this placard is posted!

Let's not narrate this building of a temple at the capital;
Let's return to the subject of the Meng and Wan families.
After Squire Wan had taken his leave and returned home,
He and his wife discussed the matter and liked the idea.
    "In Changzhou there is a Monastery of Cool Purity;
Let's donate our house and goods to that monastery.
Our fields and gardens we'll entrust to our clansmen,
So we may devote ourselves to practicing religion."
    As for all the many laborers and serving women—
All were dismissed and sent back to their homes.
Together the couple traveled to Songjiang prefecture;
They wanted to settle permanently in Huating county.
    As soon as Meng De saw the squire and his wife,
He was overjoyed and came out to greet them.
Squire Meng and his wife both welcomed them;
The four of them, one of heart, lived in harmony.
    One of virtue and heart, they practiced religion;
They became the closest of kin in spiritual matters.

BORN FROM A GOURD

Hoping for the return home of the young lady,
The four of them always were filled with worries.
　　Let's not talk about the four parents back at home;
　　Let's narrate how the bodhisattva delivers mortals.

Let's tell about the Mahasattva of the Southern Sea, who follows the voices
to save us mortals from suffering. "I now see that Wan Xin and his wife have
both taken the decision to practice religion. The two of them have gone to
Huating county in Songjiang to join the family of Meng Longde. The four of
them all together have devoted their hearts to the Way, so I cannot but go
and deliver them so they will achieve success. The common mortals of this
world do not understand how these two immortals out of compassion sacri-
ficed themselves to save others. Wan Xiliang was originally the immortal
official Sprout Lad from the heavenly palace. When he saw that in the world
below a myriad of men were being harmed without cause, he could not but
descend to earth and sacrifice himself in order to save them—he substituted
for their disaster and calamity. Such was his vow from before his birth; his
fate was not due to some sin from a previous life! Meng Jiang was originally
the Seventh Sister Star; she is the seventh immortal maiden and also was
never born from a womb. But because she saw the immortal lad descending
to earth, and was unable to dissuade him, she feared that he might lose the
way in the world below, and considering that in the heavenly palace they were
servants in the same palace hall, she came down on purpose to join up with
him. And it is certainly not the case, as the vulgar rumor has it, that they
truly were man and wife. I am Guanyin of the Southern Sea. Standing here,
fully manifest and overjoyed, under the brilliant sky and its bright sun, I
cannot but disclose these background circumstances so as to clarify the
intent of the immortals."

The mahasattva descended directly to the world below
And arrived at the Meng mansion, begging for alms.
There the squire asked her what she was begging for,
"Please tell me, and I will listen most reverentially."
　　The bodhisattva promptly spoke in the following way,
　　"I'm not begging for rice or food, nor begging for money.
What I am begging for, dear squire, is your sincere heart;
What I am begging for, dear squire, is your devout mind.

Reciting the sutras and the name of the Buddha is common.
What I am begging for, dear squire, is your buddhahood!"
Upon hearing this, the squire's heart was filled with joy,
And he asked the teacher where she was staying, saying,
    "Please allow me my wish to serve you as my teacher!"
The four of them all came to the gate to welcome her.
Kneeling down in front of her, they begged her instruction,
Her instruction on the process of practicing religion.

    When the bodhisattva was asked for guidance, she said,
"Practicing religion all depends on the decision to do so.
Building bridges, paving roads brings worldly blessings;
Reciting the name of the Buddha and sutras dispels vengeful ghosts.

    But if you want to break free from the cycle of samsara,[33]
Find yourself an enlightened teacher and join the right path.
By practicing meditation, you will brighten heart and nature;
Time and again you'll see the emptiness of the five skandhas.[34]

    As soon as the sarira is formed,[35] you'll achieve buddhahood;
Free from birth and decay, you obtain eternal transcendence.
And once you have transcended the three types of world,
You'll never again be trapped in the created five elements.[36]

    Returning to root and source, you reach the Non-Ultimate,[37]
And nine generations of ancestors achieve transcendence."

    The two ladies and also the two squires, their husbands,
Bowed before their teacher, thanking her for her lesson,
But when they rose up, the teacher was nowhere to be seen;
The bodhisattva had risen to the clouds of highest heaven!

    "If you wonder who I am, I am nobody else—
I am the Bodhisattva Guanyin of the Southern Sea."

    She also spoke to them, "You ladies and you gentlemen,
Devote all your effort to your religion and never slacken!
Then divine immortals will come and welcome you home—
Hear the Way in the morning, and when you die that night,
    you will go up to the palaces of heaven!"

    Let's not tell how these four people practiced their religion;
Let's return to the topic of Meng Jiang at the Long Wall.

    The grave mount for Xiliang was quickly completed,
And the temple for King Wan was also constructed.

BORN FROM A GOURD

Inside the temple an image of Xiliang was erected,
And all of the myriad of men revered him as a god.

Devoutly they burned their incense and bowed,
Bowed to thank the god for saving a myriad of men.
And the inspector-general reported to the throne,
"The construction of the royal temple is finished."

Upon reading this, the First Emperor was filled with joy;
He issued an edict to offer sacrifice at the royal grave.
He issued an edict ordering the Court of Imperial Banquets
To prepare the sacrificial foods, and he promptly set out.

The beautiful maiden Meng Jiang was summoned,
And a smiling First Emperor then asked the beauty,
"As everything has been built according to your wishes,
You, beauty, must be willing to comply with my desire?"

Meng Jiang addressed him in the following manner,
"Your Majesty, many thanks for building the temple!
But Your Majesty still has to offer sacrifice in person;
Following that, I will of course be at your disposal."

Upon these words the First Emperor was filled with joy,
"Of course We will comply with Our darling's desire!"
But in her heart Meng Jiang was secretly thinking,
"How I hate that deluded ruler, that lust-besotted lout!

Fortunately the temple for King Wan is now completed,
So I'm satisfied that this wish of mine has been fulfilled."
She inspected the temple that had been built by imperial order;
To the left and the right the personnel was arrayed in rows.

First of all, the building inspired awe and reverence;
Secondly, he had been ennobled as Lord of a Myriad of Miles;
Thirdly, sacrifices would be offered in spring and fall;
And fourthly, he had been raised to the rank of king.

Eight runners in black stood arrayed on both sides,
And a pair of servants stood to his left and his right.
These ten people
All earlier had died in the building of the Long Wall;
Now they had been ennobled together with Xiliang.

Xiliang had of all of them the greatest foundation, as
In his compassion he wanted to save a myriad of men.

Don't think such divine fortune is easily enjoyed—
His great accomplishment startled Heaven and Earth!

His deed had been enabled by the Jade Emperor's grace;
Without the children's ditty it could not have happened.
But if the immortal maiden Meng Jiang had not helped,
How could the temple to King Wan have been built?

The officials on duty approached the emperor, saying,
"The sacrificial offerings have all been duly prepared,
So we pray Your Majesty to present these offerings."
The First Emperor, properly attired, bowed before the grave.

After bowing before the grave, he also bowed in the temple,
To the great consternation of the public, who remarked,
"A lord does not bow to his subject, that's the ancient rule,
But now, against all precedent, the lord bows to a subject!"

But who of the great ministers at court dared to protest?
The emperor's lust was overwhelming; reason was lost!

Following the sacrifice he burned silk and paper money,
No less than forty-eight boxes of great ingots of silver!
As all this burned, it looked like a mountain on fire;
The flames leapt up to the sky, terrifying each and all,

Except for Meng Jiang, who slowly walked up to the fire,
Causing the First Emperor to shout loudly, "My beauty,
Water and fire always have been most cruel elements.
Be careful not to damage your silk-like beautiful hair!"

Then all of a sudden Meng Jiang jumped into the fire;
As a whiff of smoke she ascended straightway to heaven.
The First Emperor shouted loudly, "My dear beauty,
How can you so cruelly betray all Our desires?"

He ordered his servants to search for her corpse,
So she could be put in a coffin and buried in a grave.
But when they searched the ashes, there was no corpse;
There was no corpse at all—gone without leaving a trace!

So Meng Jiang must have been an immortal maiden!
To the side was built a temple for the immortal maiden.
This temple that was built at the emperor's order
Has been preserved through eternity to this very day!

Let's not talk about the First Emperor back at his court,

BORN FROM A GOURD

But let's return to the immortal maiden Meng Jiang.
Her servants and maids returned and went home
To fully inform the squire of all that had happened.
    Let us now tell again of Wan Xiliang and Meng Jiang,
A couple made of an immortal lad and an immortal maiden.
The two immortals met each other and, holding hands,
Went home, riding a cloud, to repay their parents' grace.
    Riding a cloud, they arrived in the region of Songjiang,
Where they lowered their cloud and arrived at home.
As a pair, as a couple, they bowed before their four parents.
This day they were all reunited—a joy without bounds!
    The whole family shared in the joy of this reunion, and
They were told the whole story from beginning to end.
But all of a sudden they smelled an exceptional fragrance,
And an auspicious cloud descended into their house!
    This was the Bodhisattva Guanyin of the Southern Sea;
She came to take the six of them to see the Three Purities.

The bodhisattva addressed them as follows, "The two of you secretly descended to the mortal world. Even though you did this to save a myriad of men, you still should have asked the Jade Emperor for his permission. So when you now return to the heavenly palace, you unavoidably will be scolded by the Jade Emperor. But because the two of you have accomplished such an arduous feat, I have come on purpose to help you out and to take you with me to see the Jade Emperor. You have not yet repaid the grace of feeding and rearing of your parents on both sides, so I will also take them along to see the deity and await his decision." That very moment the servants and maids returned from the Long Wall. But just as they wanted to inform the squire of what had happened to his daughter at the Long Wall, they saw her standing at his side. And they also saw many people they didn't know, whose imposing mien was awe-inspiring! The servants and maids were so scared they didn't dare open their mouths! They noticed that the four elderly people were all seated in lotus position while music resounded through the sky. An exceptional fragrance filled the atmosphere with its wafting scent, as long clouds slowly rose up to heaven. They could only conclude that the four elderly people had escaped their mortal existence. There's no need to tell about the funerals at the Meng mansion.

The Mahasattva Guanyin took the six of them with her;
On a cloud they went straightway to the Tushita-heaven.[38]
When suddenly they heard the golden bell resound,
The Jade Emperor ascended the precious hall.

When the pearl screen was lifted and he wanted to speak,
He saw the Bodhisattva Guanyin prostrated before him,
"May I ask you, Mahasattva, what business you have?
What urgent matter made you come to heaven's palace?"

"I am here because of Sprout Lad and Seventh Sister,
Who in their ignorance secretly left the heavenly palace.
In their compassion they wanted to save a myriad of men,
So please forgive their crime and allow them to return."

When the Jade Emperor heard this, he was filled with joy,
"My dear Mahasattva, you really should not be doing this!
Otherwise all heavenly immortals will follow their example,
Secretly leave the palace and descend to the mortal world.

But today, out of consideration for you, Mahasattva,
I forgive them their crime and accept the situation.
They'll take up the position of their original function!"
The two immortals expressed their gratitude and left.

The Mahasattva Guanyin then addressed him again,
On the grace of feeding and rearing the two immortals,
"Their parents have attained the Way of immortality,
So they await your decision as to their assignments."

The Jade Emperor smiled and spoke as follows,
"Mahasattva, these people are disciples in your school;
Pure buddhas in possession of the Way and its Truth,
They are freed of vexations, illusions, and strife.

There's no need for Us to settle their assignment;
They may join the school of sovereign non-duality."

The mahasattva spoke, "May Your Majesty greatly display his compassion!
The merit of these four people is still shallow. They barely attain the realm of
the first *dhyana*-heaven,[39] and it is impossible for them to rise above the nine
firmaments. So I implore Your Majesty to bestow on them the exceptional
grace of assigning them to an office in the heavenly palace of Maya,[40] so they
may be promoted once they have doubled their merit and established their

virtue." The Jade Emperor said, "Your wish is granted! Now the heaven of Maya is actually the fruit of *pratyeka*-buddhas.[41] The two laywomen are assigned the task of inspecting the incense-candles and of welcoming guests, while the two laymen are assigned the duty of observing the cloud-terraces, including the assembly altars, and they will all be promoted according to merit. Would that be acceptable?" The mahasattva led her four charges in expressing their gratitude by kowtowing, "Your Majesty, may your sagely blessing be boundless as you display such compassion!" When the golden lads thrice sounded the gong and the curtain of pearls was lowered, all the immortal officials left the court, and the mahasattva took the four of them to the palace of Maya to take up their duties.

The *Precious Scroll of Meng Jiang* is told to the end;
May each and every one present now love the Way!
May young people devote themselves to their duties,
So their loyalty and chastity are renowned forever.

    May elderly people now be filled with compassion;
Self-sacrifice for the sake of others is not in vain!
You only have to consider the great vow of Xiliang.
The wisdom of the immortal maiden is without equal.

    The chastity of Meng Jiang is rare in this world;
She left behind a fragrant reputation for all eternity.
All you who have heard the *Scroll of the Immortal Maiden*
Will find this increases their lives as well as their luck.

5

BEING A FILIAL DAUGHTER-IN-LAW

THIS VERSION OF THE LEGEND, WHICH TURNS MENG JIANGNÜ into a perfectly filial daughter-in-law, belongs to the genre of "exposition" (*xuanjiang*). The term "exposition" originally referred to the prescribed bimonthly lectures, instituted under the Qing dynasty, on the *Sacred Edict*, which purported to summarize conventional Confucian morality. Once such lectures had been mandated, extensively annotated editions soon appeared, in which the maxims of the *Sacred Edict* were illustrated with gripping stories. In certain parts of China such as Hubei, the lectures evolved in a separate genre of storytelling that distinguished itself from other genres by its moral tone and aura of scholarship. Our example tells its story through prose and verse. Most of the verse sections are written in lines of ten-syllable verse (some lines contain additional three-syllable phrases), but there also are a few verse passages in seven-syllable lines. The text is introduced by a four-line poem. The translation is based on the edition of the text in Lu Gong's *Meng Jiangnü Travels for a Myriad of Miles to Find Her Husband*, which itself is based on an undated lithographic edition from Xi'an.[1] The text most likely dates from sometime in the second part of the nineteenth century.

The conclusion of this version of the legend conforms to a summary of the tale in the *Anatomy of Passion* (Qing shi) of around 1620:

> Meng Jiang of the Qin dynasty was the daughter of a rich man. She was the wife of Fan Qiliang, who had married into the family. After three days her husband left to take up his corvée at the Long Wall. When he did not return home even after a long time, she made winter clothes to take to him. When she arrived at the Long Wall, she learned that her husband had already passed away. She then called out to Heaven and stamped her feet, and the sound of her weeping shook the earth. The earth collapsed, but when she searched for her husband's bones, they were hard to recognize. She bit on her finger and dropped blood [on the bones]. Whenever the blood entered the bone and could not be wiped off, she knew this was a bone of her husband. Carrying the bones on her back, she set out for home, but when she arrived at Tong Pass, her strength was exhausted, and she realized that she would not be able to make it back home. So she placed the bones at the foot of a rock, sat down beside them, and died. The people at Tong Pass admired her chastity and erected an image for veneration.[2]

Tong Pass is located at the border of modern Shaanxi and Henan, where it dominates the narrow defile between the Yellow River and the mountains to its south. Throughout the ages, this heavily fortified location has played a strategic role in Chinese history, and from an early date, it achieved mythic status in popular lore.

Anonymous

MENG JIANGNÜ WEEPS AT THE LONG WALL

A poem reads,

> *Filial piety and fierce chastity, that's the maiden Meng Jiang—*
> *Delivering clothes to the border, she searched for her husband.*
> *The Long Wall collapsed over tens of yards for her weeping;*
> *For all eternity this maiden has left behind a fragrant reputation!*

Speak:

Once long ago the Qin dynasty had an emperor whose surname was Ying and who went by the name of First Emperor of the Qin. His ambition was such that he thought his sons and grandsons in later generations would rule the empire forever, and he also wished to live eternally, without aging. He ordered Xu Fu and the magician Lu Ao to search for the techniques of longevity, and he asked them about the rise and fall of dynasties in later days. When Lu Ao came to the Eastern Ocean, he obtained a manuscript that was written in tadpole script.[3] None of the civil and military officials of the court could make head or tail of it. Only five characters could be roughly made out, "The destroyer of the Qin will be *hu*." The First Emperor did not realize that this

162

referred to his own son Huhai. The northern lands belong to the *hu* barbarians, so he feared they would rob his descendants of their realm. Considering the national defense of prime importance, he issued his command: he ordered Meng Tian to be in charge and to conscript eight hundred thousand able-bodied men to build a Long Wall to be a protection against the *hu*. In the west it started from Linzhao in Longxi, and in the east it reached to Koguryo. The total length ran to more than nine thousand nine hundred *li*—a huge construction project![4] The people of the south improved the Five Ranges, the people of the west constructed the Epang Palace, and the people of the north built the Long Wall.[5] At first they conscripted only able-bodied men, but later they did not distinguish between old and young—any man was taken along!

But let's not indulge in idle talk. Let's just talk about a man with the name of Fan Qiliang. He had lost his father at an early age and had been raised by his mother. He was engaged to a daughter of the Jiang family. In ancient times, the names were Meng (Eldest), Zhong (Middle), or Ji (Youngest). She was called Meng Jiang and had reached the age of eighteen. Choosing her as the bride for her son, Fan's mother welcomed Meng Jiang into her house. Husband and wife respected each other like guests. But after three days, Qiliang was taken away by the imperial agents who were looking for men to build the Long Wall. Qiliang cried to his mother, "Your son has to go, but I will return, in the worst case after a year, but otherwise after a few months." He also said, "My dear wife, my old mother completely depends on you!" Meng Jiang answered him, "My husband, don't worry!" Mother-in-law and daughter-in-law were standing in the doorway, following him with their eyes until he had disappeared. They then went inside and wept.

From the moment Qiliang left, his mother always thought about him. Meng Jiang was virtuous and filial, and she served her mother-in-law with utmost diligence. When her mother-in-law shed tears out of longing for her son, Meng Jiang would always tell stories and jokes to cheer her up. But when Meng Jiang imagined how her husband would suffer hardship and hunger and cold in the border regions, and would be exposed to the sun by day and to the dew by night, to the extent that she had no idea what he would look like, she would, hiding herself from her mother-in-law, shed who knows how many tears.

Time flew by, and soon three years had passed. As his mother did not see Fan return, the longing for her son became ever more intense, and she spent each day in weeping and crying, and each night in sadness and gloom. Meng Jiang did her best to comfort her, but gradually the old woman stopped eating and drinking and took to bed. Meng Jiang's prayers to the gods remained without response, and the vows she made remained without effect, so all she could do was stand by the side of the bed and wait on her mother-in-law all those many days as she saw the condition of her mother-in-law grow worse and worse. Fan's mother told her, "My daughter-in-law, my illness is such that I will most likely soon leave this world. After I have died, you should not wear the hemp of mourning. It is unsure whether my son will ever return, and you are all by yourself and alone, so you should not let the season of spring pass by unused." When she had said this, she breathed her last and passed away. Meng Jiang wept bitterly, and the neighbors helped her dress the corpse. Wearing the hemp of mourning, a weeping Meng Jiang accompanied the coffin to the family grave-yard for burial. When she came home, she bought a sheet of paper and painted the likeness of her mother-in-law, to be used in the ancestral sacrifices.

Declaim:

> The maiden Meng Jiang
>> Painted her likeness,
>>> While wailing loudly for grief;
> She prepared the ink,
>> And took up the brush—
>>> Her heart pierced by arrows.
> She painted her mother-in-law
>> With silver-white hair
>>> Covering her head;
> She painted the old woman
>> While longing for her son,
>>> Not saying a word,
>>>> But cherishing him in her heart.
> She painted the old woman
>> With her brows in a furrow,
>>> Her eyes brimming with tears;
> She painted the old woman
>> Seated on a chair,
>>> Her staff leaning by her side;
> She painted the old woman
>> In front of a table
>>> With a pair of bright candles.

BEING A FILIAL DAUGHTER-IN-LAW

She set up a spirit altar
  And hung up this portrait
And called out, "Dear Mother-in-law,
  May your pure soul
    Come down and partake of these offerings!"

Speak:

The next day, after she had performed the morning libation, Meng Jiang thought to herself, "When my husband left, he was wearing thin and unlined clothing. At present the weather is very cold, and in the north it must be freezing. Earlier, when my mother-in-law still was alive, I didn't dare leave her alone. But now my mother-in-law has passed away, I will carry this portrait with me, so I can make offerings early and late, and I will make a bundle of my husband's padded garments and shoes and socks."

She waited till the first watch of the night of the next day; she thought of all the favors her parents had shown her and which she had not been able to repay and wept, overcome by emotion.

Declaim:

In the first watch of the night
  She wept, "My dear father-in-law,
    You died so young, while in the prime of spring!
Your daughter-in-law
  Will travel to the Long Wall
    To find her husband and bring him his clothes.
May you protect from above
  Your son, so he will be
    Free from danger and disease,
So he may return home
  And inherit
    The treasures of ten thousand years!"
In the second watch of the night
  She wept, "My dear father,
    The depth of your favors is beyond measure!
Your raised me, your daughter,
  Till I turned eighteen,
    Then married me off to young Fan.

On this day
    I depart for the borders,
        All by myself, searching for my husband,
And we will meet again,
    I am afraid,
        Only in our dreams!
In the third watch of the night
    She wept, "My dear mother,
        My heart feels as if wounded by knives!
You raised me, your daughter,
    And you did hope
        That I would be there at your funeral.
But I, your daughter,
    Disregard all your favors
        And leave you, my mother, to travel north.
My mother, you've suffered
    A thousand hardships
        To raise me—but all to no purpose!"
In the fourth watch of the night
    She wept, "My dear little brother,
        You and I were born from the same mother.
You also
    Have been arrested
        And taken north,
So I hope
    That you and my husband
        May share the same shed and same bed.
So I may find you
    And my husband,
        So you can return to take care of our parents."

Speak:
    After Meng Jiang had wept all night, she took her leave of the graves the next morning.

Declaim:
    She wept and cried,
        "My dear parents who died so young!

BEING A FILIAL DAUGHTER-IN-LAW

As soon as I see my parents' graves, I'm overcome by grief.
You, my father-in-law, departed at such an early date from this world,
And, sadly enough, this month my mother-in-law also passed away.

In conformity with your command, I ordered you properly buried;
You succeeded in achieving your widow's desire of bitter chastity.
Of course I should stay at home and always provide for your needs;
How could I dare abandon and neglect the graves of my parents?

But because your son had to leave and go to the Long Wall,
I will take these clothes to the border and search for my husband.
I, your daughter-in-law, have pondered all my possibilities;
If I want to maintain my fidelity, I have to forget about filial piety.

Because I have absolutely no other way, I now visit the graves,
And it is as if the cloudy souls of the two of you appear to me.
My father and mother, please accept this single stick of incense;
I will burn some paper money to ashes, please take it and use it.

May the souls of the two of you not turn in any other direction,
But may they follow me on my journey to those northern lands.
I carry my mother's portrait with me on my body, so please
Accept the libations that I will pour out, both early and late."

Speak:

When the neighbor women on all four sides saw Meng Jiang crying and weeping at the tombs, they all congregated to comfort her. But when they heard her weeping declaration that she wanted to go to the Long Wall to find her husband, some of them said, "Those thousand miles are an endless journey!" and others said, "You'll be a single person, all alone!" And they all tried to talk her out of going.

Meng Jiang said, "Many thanks for your good offices, dear aunts and sisters, but my mind is made up. I have sworn that I will travel all alone a thousand miles. I'll shirk no danger or threat till the day of my death!" The other women then all returned to their own homes.

In the village lived a certain Zhang Shixiu, an old and pious man. When he heard people say that Meng Jiang wanted to go to the Long Wall to deliver clothes to her husband, he heaved a sigh and said, "This is the most filial and chaste person between heaven and earth!" He told his two daughters-in-law, "Just look at her exemplary virtue! The two of you should send her off for quite a stretch and ask her to take a letter. If your husbands are still

167

alive, tell them to come back home as soon as possible. I will also send her off!" The two women obeyed his order and waited for her by the side of the road. When the neighbors heard that this old and pious man was seeing Meng Jiang off, it created such a stir that all the women wanted to see her off.

Meng Jiang back at home was getting ready for her departure.

Declaim:

In front of the gods
　　She burnt a stick of incense,
　　　　While tears coursed down her face.
She took her leave of the household gods
　　And of the ancestral spirits—
　　　　Her heart felt as if pierced by arrows.
She took down
　　Her mother's image
　　　　And hung it from her middle.
With her pack on her back,
　　She carried her luggage,
　　　　Holding her umbrella in her hand.
When she walked out of the gate,
　　All the assembled neighbors
　　　　Surrounded her on all sides.
When they saw the portrait,
　　All of these people
　　　　Said, "This is truly
　　　　　　The old lady herself,
　　　　　　　　Just as she was when alive!"
The maiden Meng Jiang
　　Closed the gate
　　　　And then turned around to discover
That old Mr. Zhang,
　　Leaning on his staff,
　　　　Was standing by the side of the road.
The maiden Meng Jiang
　　Quickly approached him
　　　　And greeted him with a bow.

BEING A FILIAL DAUGHTER-IN-LAW

Then she addressed him,
  "My dear uncle,
    You are too kind, and at this high age!
I have often heard
  My mother-in-law
    Tell me at length all about you.
Our family has often
  Enjoyed your favors—
    But we never repaid them in the least.
What kind of virtue have I,
  This insignificant woman,
    That you should come here without reason?
It is too great an honor
  That you see me off,
    At your age, your hair all gray!
Let me entrust the key
  To you, dear uncle,
    To look after the house,
And I hope you will also
  Kindly take care of
    The graves of my father- and mother-in-law."
Old Mr. Zhang
  Pulled Meng Jiang up
    As tears coursed down his face,
"You are taking winter clothes
  And looking for your husband,
    Making a journey of three thousand miles.
You are the very best
  Female Wenjun,
    Leaving an eternal reputation![6]
I will take care
  Of your parents' graves
    And the house and its business.
I have a few words
  That I want to tell you—
    Please remember them well.
You are only
  A girl in hairpins and skirt
    Who now shows her face to the public at large,

169

So how can you stand
  The hardships of the border
    And the dangers of the open road?
If you make a long trip,
  Do not be too hasty—
    Far better to take it slowly!
Whenever there is a road,
  Don't board a boat,
    As wind and waves may well spell danger.
If you ask for the road,
  Make sure to ask
    White-haired elderly people.
When talking to people
  Or finding an inn,
    Rely on your eyes;
Your greatest fear
  Is to run into villains
    Who harbor evil intentions.
When rising at dawn,
  Please inspect the skies—
    Cloudy or clear, bright or dark.
When looking for an inn,
  Don't wait until
    The sun is setting on western hills.
While on the road
  Do not weep and cry,
    As with blurry eyes
      You might well lose the road.
When you get to the border,
  Act according to opportunity
    But don't tarry there too long.
Whether you find him
  Or cannot find him,
    Return as soon as possible!
I've got here some ounces
  Of loose silver, which
    I am giving to you,
So you may buy some food

BEING A FILIAL DAUGHTER-IN-LAW

When you feel hungry
    While you are on the road."
When old Mr. Zhang
    Had seen her off,
        He went back with his daughters-in-law,
While the maiden Meng Jiang,
    Who had knelt down to thank him,
        Rose to her feet to set out on her lonely trek.

Speak:

All the way she was lonely and depressed. Day and night she was thinking of her mother-in-law, and every morning she longed for her husband—her desperation was beyond words! But fortunately she was in good health, so she made good progress, walking on for more than ten days in a row. As she was thinking of her mother-in-law, she was overcome by emotion and sat down by the side of the road, where she started to weep.

Declaim:

"Ever since I, your daughter-in-law, left home and village,
I never stopped thinking of you for a single moment or minute.
Mother, your kind compassion in life was an indescribable favor;
By day we shared our food, and by night we shared one bed.
    But since the day you all of a sudden passed from this world,
You left me without support and all alone, at a loss as to what to do.
Longing for my husband, I make my way to the Long Wall;
Looking for your son, / I am heading north.
    Even though I carry your portrait with me on my body,
I have no idea at all where your countenance may be."

Speak:

When Meng Jiang had finished weeping, she went on toward the north. With large steps she hastened on, and even though there were high mountains and steep ranges and difficult stretches through dangerous terrain, she walked on as before. When hungry she would eat, and when thirsty she would drink, and in this manner she walked on for more than twenty days. When the sky turned to evening, an old man was standing before a straw-thatched cottage. Meng Jiang asked him whether she could stay there for the night, and the old man led her inside the house. Meng Jiang asked him, "May I ask you for your name?" The old man replied, "I am called the Graybeard of the Border.[7] May I ask from whence you hail and from where you come, and what your purpose is?" Meng Jiang told him in great detail her name and place of domicile and that she was taking clothes to her husband. The Graybeard of the Border told her, "You should not have come these many thousands of miles to take clothes to your husband! You have experienced all the hardships of the road, and your problems and dangers cannot all be told, but how could you know the sufferings of life beyond the border? More than eight hundred thousand people are working on building the Wall, for over a continuous stretch of more than four hundred miles, so how can you locate one abducted common worker? They are exposed to the hardship of wind and frost, remain without food when hungry and without clothes when freezing. By day they are exposed to the sun and by night to the dew, and those who have died are without number! Truly, people go there but do not return. If your husband came here the year before last, most likely he is not to be found anymore!"

When Meng Jiang heard these words, she was awash in tears and said, "In case he has died, I want to find his corpse!"

The Graybeard replied, "When the people who work on the Wall die, their corpses are buried in the body of the Wall, so you would have no way to find him!"

But Meng Jiang said, "If I cannot find him, I will die at the Long Wall!"

The Graybeard then told her, "When loyal officers and righteous heroes die, their bones as a rule are not bright red but gold-colored, and in the case of filial sons and chaste wives, their bones are all white. If you find bones like these, bite on your fingers till you draw blood and drip a drop on the bones to test them. If they are not your husband's, the blood will not soak into them. This is the only way to establish their identity. From here it is still more than two hundred miles to the Long Wall through a largely uninhabited area, so take an ample supply of provisions with you so that you don't have to suffer hunger."

The next day Meng Jiang took her leave and set off, and all along the road she wept without end. All along the road there was no human habitation and no place to find food or water. But when she had ascended a high mountain, she saw the Long Wall. Overcome by hunger, she sat down by the side of the road and wept piteously. Out of the blue there appeared an old woman carrying a basket who approached her and asked her what she was doing. Meng

Jiang replied, "I am trying to find my husband, but I am starving right here!" The old woman then took a bun from her basket and gave it to Meng Jiang. After the latter had thanked her, the old woman went off. Meng Jiang forged on ahead, and when evening came, she spent the night weeping in the open field of the wasteland. The next day she searched for her husband all along the Long Wall, but without success, so she wept loudly.

Declaim:

> She cried out loudly,
>> "My dear husband,
>>> Where are you now?
>> When I look at the Long Wall,
>>> It looks as if made of bronze—
>>>> My heart feels as if pierced by arrows!

I traveled thousands of miles to find my man—but my hope was in vain;
The more I ponder the matter in my heart, the more I am filled with grief!

> The hardships you've suffered are too terrible to be put in words.
When your mother was eight months pregnant, your father died,
And only when she had managed to raise you to the age of eighteen
Did she succeed in bringing me as your wife to her home.

> Who did know that on the third day a major disaster would strike,
And that we, two mandarin-ducks, would be cruelly beaten apart?
It was just as if a brown hawk swooped down and grabbed a chick—
Your mother did not even get the time to say good-bye to you!

> Now I in my turn have come as your wife to bring you your things;
All by myself, completely alone I have traveled this far north.
You left behind your young wife and your elderly mother—
My mother-in-law already has passed away from this world.

> Only after I had properly buried our mother on a high hill
Did I come here to bring your clothes and find you, my husband.
Luckily old Mr. Zhang gave me some money, because without it
I would not have had the traveling money to reach this place.

> I carry with me on my body the true portrait of my mother-in-law;
Mother-in-law and daughter-in-law have been together on this trip.
All confused and bewildered, I've rushed forward toward the north,
Not knowing whether you, my husband, are still alive or already deceased!"

Speak:

   Meng Jiang had been looking for a day and had seen a number of piles of white bones, but none had absorbed a drop of her blood. As the sky turned to dusk and darkness, she sat down by the Wall and wept and cried. The next day she set out to search again.

Declaim:

   She cried out loudly, "My husband,
        It is unthinkable that you
            Would have a heart of steel or stone!
Traveling thousands of miles, I have come to find you.
For two days in a row I have been unable to do so;
When I call you, you don't reply, so I cry to Heaven!
   While you were here in the north, I was down south;
The clothes you wore when you left were unpadded.
I made you a set of winter clothes, a number of items,
Which I am bringing as a protection against the cold.
   I crossed mountains and rivers on this endless journey.
Is it possible that Heaven will display no pity at all?
I desire only to locate the bones of my husband;
As soon as I do, I am happy to leave this world!
   But if Heaven refuses to do me this single favor,
I'll butt my head against the Long Wall till I die!"

Speak:

   When Meng Jiang had finished weeping, she stood up and ran head-first into the Wall! A loud sound like a thunder crash was heard, the heavens collapsed and the earth was rent, and a number of yards of the Long Wall tumbled down, while an unconscious Meng Jiang lay on the ground. When after quite some time she came to and rose, she stepped forward, looked at the spot where the Long Wall had tumbled down, and found the bones!

   When she stepped inside the base of the Wall, she found many white bones, but none of them absorbed her blood. But from a distance she saw at the foot of a steep cliff a massive pile of white bones. When she walked up to the cliff, bit her finger, and dripped blood on the bones to test them, the blood was absorbed without leaving a trace. Whenever she tried it, the blood was completely absorbed, so she knew that this had to be her husband! She

BEING A FILIAL DAUGHTER-IN-LAW

threw herself on the skeleton and wept piteously. But after a while she thought, "I came here to find my husband, but now I have destroyed the Long Wall. If the court orders someone to come and inspect, I will be arrested and condemned, and then even the bones of my husband will not be able to return to his home village! I'd better flee as far away as possible!" She opened the bundle of clothes and carefully wrapped up the bones, which she had marked with the blood from her finger. With this pack on her back she took off.

Declaim:
> The maiden Meng Jiang,
>> Departing from the Long Wall,
>>> Wept and wailed most piteously,
> And she cried, "My dear husband,
>> May your spirit and soul
>>> Follow your wife on this southward journey!"
> Heading for her home village,
>> She trekked thousands of miles;
>>> Climbing mountains and crossing ridges,
> Protected by the gods,
>> Her body healthy and strong,
>>> She resembled a wind-blown cloud.
> Traveling day and night,
>> She just forged on ahead;
> She walked on, rain or shine,
>> Her feet never resting.
> A lonely shadow, a single person, overcome by sadness—
> Thinking of her mother-in-law,
>> Longing for her husband,
>>> She wept piteously without end.
> As she walked a mile,
>> She wept a stretch,
>>> And all people were wounded by sadness;
> After many days of walking,
>> She had no tears left,
> And when she arrived
>> In the Tong Pass area,
>>> Her eyes were crying blood.

She sat down below
    The Falling-Goose Cliff,
        Unable to take one more step.
Her husband's bones
    She placed by her side,
        And in moving tones she wept and told her tale.
Several thousands
    Of men and women
        Climbed the mountain to come and listen,
And there was not a single person
    Who did not for her sake
        Shed tears, deeply moved.
For three days and nights
    She narrated her woes—
        My brush is not up to the task.
Her tears of blood ran dry,
    Her heart broke, and so
        She breathed her last and passed away!
The people of Tong Pass,
    Overcome by pity,
        All joined in an act of charity
As they buried
    Husband and wife
        In one grave, in one tomb.
They asked for a recommendation
    And established a temple,
        Provided with their gilded statues,
Where millions of people,
    Travelers coming and going,
        Yearly and monthly burn incense.
You women and girls,
    When you hear these words,
        Be smart and intelligent in your hearts;
You all must emulate
    That maiden Meng Jiang's
        Filial piety and brave chastity!
You men and boys
    Who hear this account

BEING A FILIAL DAUGHTER-IN-LAW

And do not take it to heart
May wear a high hat
    And a long blue gown
        But fail to match hairpins and skirt!
If it had not been for
    This maiden Meng Jiang,
        Who sacrificed her life at the Long Wall,
How could we have
    At Goose-Gate Pass
        Open traffic between north and south?

PART II

BALLADS COLLECTED IN THE COUNTRYSIDE

6

SWITCHING THE DRAGON-ROBES

GANSU IS ONE OF THE AREAS OF CHINA WHERE PRECIOUS scrolls remained popular till recent times. Since the 1980s, Chinese scholars have reported on the continued performance of precious scrolls in the countryside, and they have collected and edited many of the texts that were current in the region. While many of these scholars are tempted to suggest a direct link between the modern traditions and storytelling traditions of ninth- and tenth-century Dunhuang, most of the precious scrolls that circulated locally in western Gansu derived from other parts of China. The plot outline of the *Precious Scroll of the Maiden Mengjiang Weeping at the Long Wall* (Mengjiangnü ku Changcheng baojuan), for instance, clearly shows the influence of the late-Ming *Precious Scroll as Spoken by the Buddha of the Chaste and Virtuous, Wise and Filial Meng Jiangnü at the Long Wall*, even though the current text may well have been composed locally—and at a relatively late date, to judge by its frequent use of ten-syllable lines in the verse passages.[1]

The text of the *Precious Scroll of the Maiden Mengjiang Weeping at the Long Wall* was collected and edited by the modern scholar Duan Ping, who describes the circumstances of the discovery of the text and the editing process as follows:

The third time I encountered a precious scroll on Meng Jiangnü was in March 1985. Together with some graduate students I again went to Hexi (western Gansu) to conduct fieldwork research on popular precious scrolls. This time our focus was the two districts of Zhangyi and Minle in the Zhangyi region.

In March we obtained a precious scroll on Meng Jiangnü from the hands of an eighty-year-old man. He said he called it the *Precious Scroll on Weeping at the Long Wall*, and we now call it the *Precious Scroll of the Maiden Mengjiang Weeping at the Long Wall*.

This was a damaged copy. The old man told us that he had inadvertently allowed his innocent little granddaughter to tear out a number of pages, and that in the sections before and after there were not a few omissions, but he still could remember it in outline, because he had read it god knows how many times during his lifetime and simply knew it by heart. We then promptly asked him to recite the text. Everybody copied [what he said], but his local pronunciation was difficult to understand. Words like *zhong* and *gong*, *yang* and *yan*, *zhuang* and *guang*, and *chuan* and *guan*, quite common characters with a well-established pronunciation, were all mixed together in that place and not distinguished. We often made mistakes, occasionally leading to much laughter. Fortunately, among our companions there also were some colleagues from the same region whom we could consult, and in the end we furthermore collated the text a number of times using a tape recording, in order to achieve a faithful and reliable text that avoids mistakes.

The old man was, alas, already in failing health at the time, and also deaf and of poor eyesight, which made it impossible to understand more about the related circumstances, and we were already very elated that we had been able to fundamentally complete this precious scroll on Meng Jiangnü. We promised that we would come back later and wished him well, but unexpectedly he soon thereafter left this world. This means we had been able by happy coincidence to save a popular precious scroll.

The *Precious Scroll of the Maiden Mengjiang Weeping at the Long Wall* we now present is the manuscript provided by this eighty-year-old man from Minle in Gansu. Its strong points are,

1. Religious superstition is very limited; its contents basically consist of actions by humans. The contradictions that are reflected are contradictions of this world, and the methods to solve them are decided by human intelligence and effort. One may say there still is the shadow of karma and retribution, but that is a reflection of the good and simple peasant psychol-

ogy of "the good will have a good retribution, and the evil will have an evil retribution."

2. The incidents are moving and the style is beautiful. Throughout the text there are no questionable parts that defy interpretation, and the many dialect words and local expressions are appreciated by the local audience. . . .

3. It is rich in Hexi (western Gansu) characteristics. It has been performed and distributed among the local population for a long time and established roots in the local psychology.[2]

This translation is based on the text as established by Duan Ping and printed by him in his *Fieldwork and Research concerning the Precious Scrolls of Western Gansu* (Hexi baojuan de diaocha yanjiu).[3] The text is composed of sections in verse alternating with sections in prose. While some verse sections employ the seven-syllable line, many others are written in ten-syllable verse. The text also contains two sets of songs of "weeping through the five watches of the night" and a set of ten four-line songs linked to the first ten months of the year.

Anonymous

THE PRECIOUS SCROLL OF THE MAIDEN

MENGJIANG WEEPING AT THE LONG WALL

Come here and listen, all my fellow villagers and relatives,
Now the Precious Scroll of the Long Wall has been opened.
The goose separated from its flock sadly crying with each call
Resembles Mengjiang weeping and wailing at the Long Wall.

The story of the maiden Mengjiang weeping at the Long Wall is a heartrending story to startle Heaven and Earth and move gods and ghosts. Now listen attentively as I will tell it to you from the very beginning. Once long ago, when the First Emperor of the Qin had unified all of China, winds and rain came in timely fashion all through the world; the nation was prosperous, and the people were at peace now the wars and disturbances of many years had come to an end. But one night the First Emperor of the Qin had a bad dream. In his dream the many flocks of sheep of the northern grasslands all crowded his golden palace and cried in a human voice, "You have unified the whole world and all the people are enjoying themselves. Because of the banqueting and feasting all day, you slaughter countless pigs and sheep, and we want you to pay for their lives!" The First Emperor of the Qin was so scared that he was covered in cold sweat, and he woke up with a start. When he summoned his ministers to explain his dream, most of them wanted to please him, so they all told him something to cheer him up, something he would love to hear. But there was one general who said, "This must mean that the northern barbarians are about to rebel!" And when the First Emperor promptly asked him what was to be done about it, he replied, "Build a long wall to block their way so they cannot enter [China]." The First Emperor agreed that this was the best solution and ordered the Heaven-Measuring Foot-Ruler taken from the rear palace and handed it over to that general. The latter assumed command and left the court, and he started the construction of the Long Wall, starting from Mountain-Sea Pass and proceeding toward the west. From his capital Xianyang the First Emperor issued an order that, throughout the world, from every family of five able-bodied males two persons had to serve, and from every family of three able-bodied males one person had to serve; that in case a family refused to comply, all able-bodied males in that family would be arrested and taken away; and that in case a family dared to resist, even its women would all be arrested and taken away. Suddenly all people throughout the world were overcome by fear and trepidation, and complaints and laments filled the roads.

Our story also tells that in the area of Hongshui out west there lived a gentleman of over sixty years by the name of Fan Yanyu. He had two sons. With himself included, he figured they made for three able-bodied males, so one of them would be drafted to work on the construction of the Long Wall. His elder son was a blind boy, and the younger son of seventeen was still in school reading his books. So he thought to himself, "Whom should I send?" The squire and his wife considered all possibilities, but they didn't see any solution. As they were beset by this unsolvable sorrow, their younger son came home from school. As soon as he had learned the reason of their sorrow, he immediately responded, "Best if I go! On the one hand I will be able to manifest my filial piety and set my parents' minds at rest, and on the other hand I will be able to show my loyalty, protecting the rivers and mountains of the current dynasty!" When the squire and his wife heard these words, their hearts felt as if cut by scissors, but they saw no other solution, so they could only say, "Our son, when will we be able to see you again once you have left?"

His parents cried,
"Fan Qilang!"
And they loudly wept:

185

The mother looked at her son,
    The son cried out to his mother,
        Completely filled with pain.
"Once you arrive
    At Mountain-Sea Pass,
        You'll suffer day and night;
Once you've abandoned
    The books of the Sages,
        It's hard to make a career.
If you're not careful,
    And offend
        The authorities in charge,
You will be condemned
    And sentenced to death—
        You will never return.
You leave behind here
    Your two parents
        With no one to care for us,
Longing for you each day,
    Yearning for you each night,
        Sleeplessly tossing and turning till dawn."
He told his father and mother,
    "Set your minds at rest
        And do not worry too much.
After three autumns
    Or after five years
        I am bound to come back.
And at that time I will
    Devote myself to study
        To pursue an official career.
The world will be happy,
    The people filled with joy,
        And the family will be reunited."

Fan Qilang urged his father and mother not to be too sad and not to cry,
"You two also will have to take care of my elder brother. If something happens to you, our family is even worse off!" That very moment he took his
leave from his parents and joined the twenty or more drafted neighbors

SWITCHING THE DRAGON-ROBES

from the village, and all together they departed for Mountain-Sea Pass to build the Long Wall.

After they had marched for two months, they passed the Tong Pass,[4] and only after they had marched for another two months did they arrive at Mountain-Sea Pass. When one saw the crowds of laborers assembled from the whole world, they looked just like ants, one huge black crowd, without head or tail, farther than the eye could see! The commander-in-chief of the First Emperor of the Qin was busy conducting a roll call, but not one of the leaders that had come from each place could tell the number of his own men. This was because on the road not a few people had died owing to the high mountains and steep roads and the lack of food. Only the leader who had come from the west could promptly report the exact number of his men who had arrived. The commander immediately asked him, "Why do you know?" The leader replied, "We have with us a certain Fan Qilang, who can read and write. He is conversant with military affairs and knows how to conduct a roll call." The commander-in-chief immediately summoned Fan Qilang and had him conduct a roll call. Within a day he had finished the count, nine million nine hundred ninety thousand and ninety nine men! By this feat Fan Qilang established his fame, and the commander kept him at his side for odd jobs.

This Fan Qilang
    Had studied the Odes and the Documents
        And deeply understood the great principle;
Conversant with military affairs,
    He could conduct a roll call
        And distinguished himself from the crowd.
For the sake of the nation
    He wanted to build the Long Wall
        And did not spare any effort of body or mind,
And all his fellow villagers
    Crowded around him—
        United in purpose, they all joined forces.
His only aim was
    To build a high wall
        To block the advance of attacking bandits;
He never had thought
    That the common people
        Would suffer beyond any description.

This Fan Qilang
    Cried out, "My fellow villagers,
        Listen to my instructions!
This government corvée
    Is truly backbreaking,
        More than I ever had thought.
It is not that I
    Willfully on purpose
        Want to harm others and myself—
Such behavior
    Is without any human decency
        And goes against Heaven's principle!
Let the young guys
    Do some extra work
        As they have the strength,
And let those who are older
    Take some extra rest
        So as to preserve their health.
The youngsters
    Can do small jobs,
        Running in all directions.
We all together should
    Take care of one another
        And not distinguish between you and me.
As soon as we have finished
    Building this Long Wall,
        We will quickly go back home,
To see our parents,
    To meet our wives—
        The whole family reunited again!"
When the common people
    Heard him speak,
        Each word made sense,
But the truth of it was
    That there was no end
        To their days of suffering.
And soon one saw
    One after another man
        Collapse and die on the spot,

SWITCHING THE DRAGON-ROBES

While those who survived
    Lacked any strength—
        So how could they do any work?
Dust clouds emerged
    And trees lost their leaves
        As the northern winds started to blow;
Heaven and earth turned cold,
    Snowflakes fluttered about,
        And a lonely goose flew southward.
Those who had families
    Received from their families
        Clothes to wear and food to eat,
But those without families
    Died from starvation at
        The foot of the Long Wall.
Their corpses were taken up
    And dumped into
        The body of the Long Wall,
And it was even said
    That they could subdue evil
        And stabilize the foundations!
For every mile
    Another man,
        White bones all over the place!
Below the Long Wall
    Their ghosts wept and wailed,
        Crying out to Heaven and Earth.
Resisting this corvée,
    The common people rebelled
        In conformity with Heaven's intent,
As throughout the world
    The First Emperor was hated—
        "Raising sticks, they rose up!"
The people were united,
    The world was in turmoil,
        The dynasty was in imminent danger;
By building the Long Wall,
    The First Emperor of the Qin
        Harmed both the people and himself!

As heaven and earth were freezing over and sufficient clothing was lacking, the millions and millions of conscripted laborers were living in misery. In truth,

When the First Emperor built the Long Wall,
The myriad people were unable to survive.
Their complaints and laments filled the roads;
No peace was found throughout the world.

When Fan Qilang saw how each and every one of these conscript laborers was beset by hunger and cold, he found this completely unbearable and went to see the commander with the request that the men be provided with more food and clothing so they might survive the severe winter. Who would have thought that at the commander's office he would run into the First Emperor of the Qin, who, on a tour of inspection, had arrived at Mountain-Sea Pass? When the First Emperor saw that Fan Qilang distinguished himself from the crowd by his talent and bearing, and that the way he expressed himself was out of the ordinary, the emperor immediately took a liking to him and appointed him deputy commander for the construction of the Long Wall. When Fan Qilang heard this, he was not elated at all. Actually, this increased his sorrow, because this put him in an even tighter spot: he could not bear in his heart to oppress the people, but if he did not oppress the people, he would not succeed in building the Long Wall, and he would be punished by the First Emperor. In truth,

Caught on the horns of a dilemma without any solution,
And with no idea how to deal with this dangerous problem—
Even if I am able to survive by chance for a single day,
The next one will bring even greater suffering for me!

But before we go on talking about all of Fan Qilang's problems and sufferings in building the Long Wall, let's first talk about the family of the maiden Mengjiang.

Close to the Long Wall lived a certain Squire Xu Weiliang. He had plenty of land and plenty of money, but he had no son. He had only a beautiful daughter with the name of Xu Mengjiang. She had just turned eighteen and was not yet engaged. She had studied the books and knew the rites and was perfect in both chastity and filiality. The squire's wife, lady Hu, was a woman of wisdom and virtue. Both Squire Xu and his wife were more than sixty years of age, and they were totally dependent on their daughter's care. One day Squire Xu said to his wife, "I want to find our daughter Mengjiang a husband who will join our household. First of all, we will then have taken care of the most important matter of her life, so we won't have to fret and worry anymore. Secondly, we will have someone to rely on, so we can all be relieved." His wife said, "You're right. Too bad there is no suitable candidate!"

Let's not continue to talk of the deliberations of these two elderly people, but let's return to the subject of Fan Qilang. After he had taken on his job, even though he was overcome by an unsolvable sorrow, he still made every effort to find a way to comfort the people. But after less than a month of building the Long Wall, he was so tired out that he looked emaciated and had become a bag of bones. That general of the First Emperor of the Qin had wanted only to make use of Qilang's talent and never had thought of letting the laborer become an official, as he was afraid that Qilang might surpass him and that he might then lose his own position. Now that the emperor himself had appointed Fan Qilang, there was nothing the general could do about it, but he felt very unhappy about it and was brooding on a dirty trick. So one day this general of the Qin, most friendly, said to Fan Qilang, "You are far from home and your parents are advanced in years. So I was thinking about allowing you to go home and visit them. Are you interested?" Fan Qilang immediately responded, "Many thanks, commander, for your kind nurturance. I will need only four months. I will make haste while traveling and leave again after only three days at home." With a deceptive smile the general said, "I will give you a fast horse, so you will need only three months on the road. That way you can stay more than a full month at home." Fan Qilang was elated when he heard these words; he hastily knelt down, and, expressing his gratitude by kowtowing, he said, "Many thanks, general, for your care and consideration. I'll leave quickly and return even more quickly!"

The next day Fan Qilang got on his horse and set out. Who would have thought that soon after he had gone out of the gate, a fierce storm would suddenly start to blow, raising dust and pebbles. This black wind blocked his way, and soon a heaven-piercing whirlwind sucked him up and carried him off!

The skies were invisible,
    The earth was darkened—
        Where was his home?

Our young Fan Qilang
    Had left the camp—
        But where had he gone?
When he fell to the ground
    And lifted his head,
        He seemed to be in a flower garden,
But he felt
    Dizzy and dazed,
        As if in the land of dreams.

The maiden Mengjiang was just enjoying the flowers in the flower garden, when she suddenly discovered a man moving about in the shade of the tree before her feet. Hastily she lifted her head and asked her servant girl, "Who is this man?" At this moment Fan Qilang came around, and he promptly said to the servant girl, "Please tell your young mistress that I am the student Fan Qilang. I'm here because yesterday a whirlwind sucked me up and deposited me on your parasol-tree, and for a while I lost consciousness. Please don't be alarmed when I now come down." The servant girl hastily explained the situation to her young mistress, who thought to herself, "My parents were just now worrying that they cannot find me a groom who will join our family. This must mean that the heavenly gods have delivered such a groom! Let me step forward and have a look."

Qilang addressed the young girl in the following way,
"Please allow me to provide you with a full explanation.
If you ask for my family, we live a myriad of miles from here;
In the region of Hongshui I have a father and an elder brother.
    My mother originally was a daughter of the Jiang family;
She has a virtuous character and a good disposition.
My elder brother, when four years old, lost his sight,
So I became responsible for the family's continuation.
    Unexpectedly one day an edict was issued, and
The First Emperor drafted me to build the Long Wall.
I've worked for a full three years on the Long Wall
Without being able to send a letter back to my family.
    Recently I got this opportunity to go back home,
But a freak storm deposited me in this flower garden.

SWITCHING THE DRAGON-ROBES

I pray you, young lady, to help me out, please allow me
To leave this flower garden and resume my journey!"
    When the young lady heard this, she was elated
And said, "Dear Mr. Fan, you should not be alarmed!
    I will go and tell my father and mother about you and
Borrow the fastest horse to see you off on your journey,
But when you go back and meet with your parents,
Don't forget to mention the way I came to your aid!"

The maiden Mengjiang stepped forward and helped Fan Qilang to his feet
and let him sit in a flower pavilion to rest for a while. She herself went off to
inform her parents. When her parents heard about this, they were truly elated,
and they promptly ordered a servant girl to invite Fan Qilang into the reception room. They treated the young man with courtesy, and the old squire then
asked him, "Young student, are you already married by any chance?"

Fan Qilang hastily replied, "I've just turned twenty, and I have not yet
taken a wife."

Because the old squire was not yet assured, he asked again, "And your parents have not made engagement arrangements on your behalf?"

Qilang replied, "Not at all! I was only seventeen when I left home, and later
I was engaged in the building of the Long Wall and couldn't send a letter, so
how could they make arrangements for a marriage?"

When the old squire's mind had been set at ease, he said with a smile, "I
would like to invite you as a groom to join the family. How about it?"

Fan Qilang replied, "I would have to go back home and inform my parents
first before I could agree to such a proposal, because otherwise I would be
acting in an unfilial manner."

The old squire secretly praised him as a student who really had studied the
books and understood the rites—a hard-to-find excellent groom! So he said,
"Your parents are so far away from here. They are advanced in years and in
declining health, and every day may be their last, so how do you know whether
they are still alive? You'd better agree to my proposal!"

Fan Qilang considered that he was right, so he [agreed] but asked for a full
ceremony with three matchmakers and six witnesses.

The old squire said with a smile, "As I am in charge, we can dispense with
all of that." The bride and groom promptly bowed to the ancestors to be married in a happy union for a hundred years!

The maiden Mengjiang
    Hastily raised incense
        And knelt down on both her knees
As she called out,
    "My dear Fan Qilang,
        The two of us now are married!
Heaven was the matchmaker,
    Earth was the witness,
        My parents were in charge:
You wanted to take a wife,
    I wanted to be married,
        Joy fills my heart.
Mountains may crumble
    And rocks may rot,
        But my love will not change;
Heaven up above,
    Earth here below,
        And stars and moon are my witness."
When Fan Qilang
    Heard these words,
        He also promptly knelt down,
And he called out,
    "My darling wife,
        You are a person of devotion!
The two of us are
    Friends in adversity,
        United by love and affection.
Heaven brought us together,
    And obeying our parents
        We bowed before buddhas and gods.
When I have finished
    Building the Long Wall,
        I will return home to be with you,
To plow and sow together,
    To share our joys together,
        One in purpose, one in mind!
And if my parents
    Are still alive,
        I will move them to this place,

So the two families
  Will be united into one,
    Enjoying wealth and status for ever!

Once the two of them were married, their love and affection was without compare, but after three days Fan Qilang made ready to depart for the west to visit his parents. Who could have known that the general of the Qin had reported [Fan Qilang's absence] to the emperor, and that throughout the world an edict had been issued for the arrest of Fan Qilang? It stated that he had cruelly harmed the conscript laborers and had deserted the troops on the eve of battle—those who delivered him up to the authorities would receive a thousand *liang*, and those who reported his whereabouts would be rewarded five hundred *liang*, but those who dared to hide him would see their whole family confiscated and beheaded![5] When a servant girl showed him the announcement, which had been brought home by a dependent of the family, Fan Qilang was dumbstruck. The maiden Mengjiang hastily asked him, "What is this all about?"

"This is that general trying to trap me!" As he said this, Fan Qilang started to weep.

The young lady hastily said, "Don't be afraid! Let me find my parents and talk things over."

She had barely finished these words, when the old squire entered their room. "What can we do about this?"

As soon as the maiden Mengjiang and Fan Qilang heard this, they realized that the old squire was already informed, so the two of them stepped forward and knelt down, and the maiden Mengjiang said, "Father, you must know some way to save us!"

But Squire Xu replied, "This is too big! The edict mentions him by name, and those who dare to hide him will see their whole family confiscated and beheaded. What way could I have?"

Fan Qilang then stood up and declared, "My father-in-law, don't worry! I will step forward and report myself to the authorities." As he said this, he walked out the door. Looking around, he urged his wife, "My dear wife, take good care of yourself and serve your parents with filial respect."

Once Fan Qilang had reported himself to the authorities, he was quickly transported to Mountain-Sea Pass. The general buried him alive in the Long Wall and reported to the emperor that the case was closed. Now that the general himself was once again solely in charge and didn't have to share his power, he treated the common people even more cruelly. Those who died were beyond counting, and night after night wolves were weeping and ghosts were howling. No human eye could bear to see this hell on earth at the foot of the Long Wall!

When the maiden Mengjiang saw that Fan Qilang had been taken away, she promptly fainted and collapsed on the ground, unaware of the world around her. Only after her parents had called out to her for more than an hour did she slowly come around and open her eyes, all the while calling, "Young Master Fan, my Young Master Fan!" All those around her were moved to tears as they heard this.

The first words she said were
    "Young Master Fan,
        This is truly too sad and painful!
When I saw you
    Report yourself to the authorities,
        I fainted and lost consciousness.
The two of us had been
    Married as man and wife
        For barely three days altogether—
You suffer an injustice,
    I suffer a hardship
        Enough to shake Heaven and Earth!
This fatal disaster
    Strikes all too suddenly—
        The whole family is saddened and pained.
Once you are gone,
    In what month and year
        Will you be revenged for this injustice?
Oh, how I hate
    That general
        For his willful abuse of power!
The common people
    Throughout the world
        Suffer bitter hardship and trouble.
Husband and wife are separated,
    Mother and son are dispersed,
        Crying and moaning, weeping and wailing.
But the day will come when

Heaven opens its eyes
And tramples the palaces of the Qin!
Young Master Fan,
Please wait for me,
So we can travel together,
Husband and wife while alive,
Companions forever in death—
The sun inseparable from its shadow!"

The more the maiden Mengjiang wept, the more heartrending it was, and she implored her parents, "I want to go and find Fan Qilang. In life I am his wedded wife, in death I'll be his wedded ghost, and we will stay together for all eternity!" Her parents time and again tried to change her mind, but she did not answer them at all but just kept weeping and crying, and the whole family was at a loss as to what to do. After this had gone on for three days, Squire Xu had no other way out but to allow her to leave and look for her husband. This was because he did not want her to commit suicide—if he let her go, she perhaps would be able to find her husband and come home together with him.

The maiden Mengjiang wanted to leave the next day to go and look for her husband. That night she had a dream, and in her dream Fan Qilang told her, "I am still in prison, so come quickly. If you are late, you may not be in time to find me.

As soon as I think of my wife, my tears will not dry;
If you want to see me again, come to the border region!
My parents, advanced in years, I cannot see again, so I
Entrusted a letter to a messenger to ask how they're doing.
I bit on my middle finger and wrote my letter in blood
But do not know whether it ever will reach my home.
My darling wife, please listen to what I have to say,
Set out as fast as possible to visit me here in this prison,
So once we, husband and wife, will have been reunited,
We may go together to the Pass of the Gate of Ghosts!"[6]

The next day the maiden Mengjiang set out on her journey. Before her departure she lit three long sticks of incense in the flower garden, praying to the heavenly gods for their protection, so husband and wife might be reunited.

Loudly weeping and wailing, she prayed to Heaven and Earth,
"I am the maiden Mengjiang of the Xu family, and my husband,
While unjustly accused, reported himself to the authorities, and
I do not know for sure whether he may have died or is still alive.

Today I am leaving from home and setting out on the road;
Please protect me on my journey, so things will go smoothly.
When I have arrived at the border and met with my husband,
We will together appear before King Yama to seek redress![7]

High Heaven up above and Earth here below, may you both
Open up your eyes and carefully scrutinize our condition here—
The common people in their multitudes are crying and weeping,
When will they be able to be free from this wearying labor?"

After she had bowed before Heaven and Earth, she took her leave of her parents and set out on her journey to find her husband. Throughout the trip her servant girl meticulously took care of everything, and also because of protection by the heavenly gods she smoothly finished the first half of the road. But after a few more days her servant girl fell ill from exhaustion, and even though the maiden Mengjiang took good care of her, she did not get better. One night the servant girl said, "Young lady, you go on by yourself! Once I have recovered, I will catch up with you. If, in the worst case, I die here, I won't cause you any more problems."

The maiden Mengjiang hastily replied, "The two of us grew up together and shared pleasure and pain, so how could I bear to leave you behind and go on alone?"

When the servant girl heard this, it made no sense to insist, but she thought to herself, "I have to find a solution for the young lady!" She thereupon crawled up and crushed her head against the wall. When the young lady saw that she had died, she loudly wept.

She cried out, "My servant girl,
    Please listen to me
        As I tell you my innermost feelings.
For so many years
    The two of us
        Were inseparable by day and by night.
We were just like

Real sisters,
  Sleeping in the same bed,
And when I left to find my husband,
  You accompanied me,
    Sharing all hardship and suffering.
Throughout the journey
  I depended on you
    For matters of food and clothing,
And master and servant,
  We had just arrived
    At the inn in this place.
Who would have thought
  That once we got here
    Heaven would remain blind—
You contracted an illness,
  And, fearing to be a burden,
    You sacrificed your own life.
I pray that you
  In the world of shade
    Will be spared all torture.
If my husband has died,
  I too will die, and
    Master and servant will be reunited!"

After the maiden Mengjiang had buried her servant girl, she continued her journey, and after three days she arrived at Mountain-Sea Pass.

She knelt down on both her knees there on the ground
And prayed again to the heavenly gods for protection.
  She did not mention all the bitter hardship on the road;
She only wanted to go inside the prison to see Fan Qilang!
If only she could meet her husband again face-to-face,
This loving couple would never again be separated!

When the maiden Mengjiang arrived at the gate of the prison, the soldier guarding the gate did not dare tell her the truth but said, "For seeing the prisoners you need the general's permission." So she could only go and see that archenemy. As soon as the general saw this beautiful woman, he immediately was totally captivated by her, and hastily he helped her to her feet with both his hands, "There is no need to kneel down! Please rise to your feet! Where are you from, my lady, and what business brings you to the border regions?"

The maiden Mengjiang replied, "I'm looking for my husband Fan Qilang!" Oomph! This gave the general such a scare that he retreated three steps. Once he had recovered his composure, he feigned to fly into a rage, "Your husband committed a crime and was buried inside the Long Wall, and you dare come and look for him? Are you aware of your crime?"

As soon as the maiden Mengjiang heard that her husband had died, she was filled with rage, and she loudly questioned the general, "What crime did my husband commit? It is you who trapped him! I will clarify his case and be revenged!" As she spoke, she threw herself at the general, who was so scared that he hastily had her tied up and put in jail.

As soon as the general closed his eyes that night, the maiden Mengjiang appeared before him, and the more he saw of her, the more beautiful she appeared to him, and the more beautiful she became, the more he loved her. And throughout the night in his dream he was "weeping the five watches":[8]

In the first watch of the night the evening cool set in;
The general suffered from an acute case of longing!
His longing eyes seemed to drop from their sockets.
His nose had turned blue and his face was all swollen,
Oh my lord Buddha!
His nose had turned blue and his face was all swollen,
Oh my lord Buddha!

In the second watch of the night the night seemed endless;
Because of his longing the general was filled with sorrow,
And he was seated stark naked in the great hall, oh yeah!
He longed to see the maiden Mengjiang face-to-face,
Oh my lord Buddha!
He longed to see the maiden Mengjiang face-to-face,
Oh my lord Buddha!

In the third watch of the night the moon stood high;
Because of his longing his eyes were bloodshot and red,
And the general seemed to be bereft of spirit and soul.

SWITCHING THE DRAGON-ROBES

One had to fear for his life, he might not survive this night,
Oh my lord Buddha!
One had to fear for his life, he might not survive this night,
Oh my lord Buddha!

In the fourth watch of the night the moon sank in the west;
Because of his longing our general was in greatest distress,
So much that he was hovering on the brink of death, oh yeah!
It was clear that King Yama was about to claim his life,
Oh my lord Buddha!
It was clear that King Yama was about to claim his life,
Oh my lord Buddha!

In the fifth watch of the night the sky slowly brightened;
Because of his longing he did not wake up from his sleep.
As long as he was alive he would be unable to meet her!
In death the general only wanted to be reborn with her,
Oh my lord Buddha!
In death the general only wanted to be reborn with her,
Oh my lord Buddha!

When he had wept through the five watches, he awoke with a start from his dream. The sky was already bright, so he ordered his people to lead the maiden Mengjiang as quickly as possible before him, so he could feast his eyes on her. "Because of her I could not sleep at all last night—I could only weep through the five watches!"

The maiden Mengjiang was only too well aware of the general's intention, so she adapted her plans accordingly and said, "I want to embroider a dragon-robe and offer it to the emperor, in order that he will bury and ennoble my husband, so we will not have been husband and wife in vain."

The general agreed enthusiastically and had his underlings ready an embroidery room for her. Everything she needed was provided, and he waited on her with greatest care. "Just let her finish the business of her husband's burial, and then I will force her to marry me. We'll see whether this weak woman can escape from the palm of my hand!"

The maiden Mengjiang suppressed her anger and stilled her mind, and stitch by stitch she embroidered the dragon-robe.

One little lamp was brightly shining before her eyes
As she took into her hand the gold and silver threads.
Her limitless hatred and rage were pressing on her mind;
By embroidering the dragon robe she would take revenge!

Stitch after stitch / thread after thread, all these thousands
Of stitches and threads all would turn into as many arrows
That would shoot right through the heart of that general
And send him off to hell to be cooked alive in boiling oil!

The maiden Mengjiang / her tears never dried, as she pondered,
"I left behind my father and mother, they're truly pitiable!
During daytime there is no one to bring them tea and rice,
And at nightfall there is no one to ask them how they are.

My poor parents, you are both well advanced in years,
And your daughter is thinking of you, here at the border,
But because I first want to take revenge for my husband,
I cannot now come back home to be reunited with you.

I hope and pray that Blue Heaven will soon open its eyes,
So I may soon take revenge and then soon return home.
Pressed down by a desire for revenge beyond compare,
I must concentrate my thoughts on my embroidery work."

She took the yellow silk and inspected it carefully;
This one dragon-robe measured three *zhang* three feet.[9]
On all three sections dragons brandished their tails,
And the collar was cut into a perfectly round circle.

She tightly joined the seams, willows swaying in the wind;
In front and behind she embroidered a star-studded sky.
To the east she embroidered the great Eastern Ocean;
To the west she embroidered Buddha's Western Paradise.

To the south she embroidered the Final-South Mountain,
And to the north she embroidered Mountain-Sea Pass.
Above she did the Jade Emperor in his dragon-clouds hall;
Below she did the infernal world and Ghost-Gate Pass.

She also embroidered the Queen-Mother's Peach-Party,
Where immortal maidens were performing their dances.
She also embroidered all the many heavenly immortals,
And the eighteen arhats were arranged on both sides.

She embroidered the heavens; she embroidered the earth.

SWITCHING THE DRAGON-ROBES

Vividly portrayed, the eight immortals seemed to come alive.
She embroidered the civil officials and military officers,
Incapable of preserving rivers and mountains for eternity.

She embroidered the Yellow River as one long thread,
Carp jumping across the Dragon Gate, overturning the seas![10]
She also embroidered her husband, His Excellency Fan,
While engaged in building the Long Wall at the border.

"That rotten scoundrel of a general, too evil in nature,
Caused the death of my darling husband, truly to be pitied!
Revenge follows revenge, an injustice follows injustice;
I will not be satisfied until I have fully taken revenge!"

As she thought of Fan Qilang / her tears coursed down.
Wiping away her tears, she embroidered the four borders.
On the border in front she embroidered a single dragon—
When taking revenge, it'll rip out his heart and his liver!

On the section in back she embroidered a single tiger—
When seeking redress, it will be the vanguard captain!
On the left border she embroidered an eagle on a branch
That with its beak would gouge out the general's eyes!

On the right border she embroidered a huge rooster—
If that cock announced dawn, she had taken revenge!
The hatred in her heart / the rage in her belly—
She expressed these through her embroideries of birds,

Working at her embroidery from late at night till dawn,
And then again throughout the day till late at night.
After working at her embroidery for a full ten days,
The embroidered dragon-robe was finally completed.

When she had finished embroidering this dragon-robe, the sky had not yet turned bright, a north wind was blowing, snowflakes had covered the whole wide world, and the maiden Mengjiang came to think of her "sufferings throughout the ten months."

"In the First Month of the year / people celebrate New Year,
But only I, Mengjiang, feel truly at a loss.
Everybody else has a great time eating baked buns, but I
Long for Fan Qilang who suffered such a pitiable fate.

In the Second Month of the year / with Second-Month weather,
Clouds of dust cover the sun, and my clothes are unpadded.
All other people are happy at heart on their heated brick-beds,
But my Fan Qilang has departed from the world of the living.

In the Third Month of the year / people celebrate Clear and Bright,
When every family and every household visits the graves.
When others visit the graves, they go in pairs and couples,
But only I, Mengjiang, am left all alone, without a partner.

In the Fourth Month of the year / on the eighth day of the month,
People go and burn incense in the temple of the Mothers.[11]
Other people go and burn incense for the sake of their children,
But I, Mengjiang, burn my incense for the sake of Fan Qilang.

In the Fifth Month of the year / on the holiday of Double Fifth,
Every family and every household is busily planting willows.
Other families all have a man, who can go and plant the willows,
But I alone have no man at home to go and plant the willows.

In the Sixth Month of the year / when the heat is unbearable,
People cook rice porridge on the banks of the Yellow River.
But I don't have a man who serves as backbone by my side,
So to whom can I fully express my feelings of sorrow?

In the Seventh Month of the year / when autumn winds are cool,
Every family and every household is busy bringing in the harvest.
All other people have a man around who brings in the harvest,
But I, Mengjiang, have no man to help me bring in the harvest.

In the Eighth Month of the year / when the moon is fully round,
Watermelons and mooncakes celebrate 'a fully-rounded reunion.'
In other families the watermelons resemble the moon's shape,
But when I, Mengjiang, watch the moon, it still lacks one half.

In the Ninth Month of the year / when chrysanthemums bloom,
I am waiting for my husband, not knowing when he'll return.

SWITCHING THE DRAGON-ROBES

The chrysanthemums bloom only so late, so late in the year—
When I take them to the grave, they are ruined by the wind.

In the Tenth Month of the year / on the first of that month,
People deliver winter clothes and cold sesame buns.(?)[12]
I walk for one mile, and then yet another mile,
But where oh where do I find my Fan Qilang?

Fan Qilang has been buried inside the Long Wall—
Weeping only once, I'll bring down its myriad miles!
How I hate that general for his inhuman cruelty, as he
Buried my Fan Qilang in the body of the Long Wall!"

The maiden Mengjiang was truly pitiable. When she had wept her sufferings
throughout the ten months, she also wept the five watches.

"In the first watch of the night the moon rises in the sky—
With both my hands I open the two doors in the gate.
The large red blanket is folded in a pile by the wall—
On the mandarin-ducks cushion one person is lacking.
Oh my heaven!
On the mandarin-ducks cushion one person is lacking!

In the second watch of the night the moon rises higher—
As soon as I think of Fan Qilang, I feel as if cut by a knife.
You have left me now to go to the realm of the shades,
Causing me to endure bitter suffering, night after night.
Oh my heaven!
Causing me to endure bitter suffering night after night!

In the third watch of the night the moon is in the sky—
Looking for my man, I have come to Mountain-Sea Pass.
Below Mountain-Sea Pass my weeping voice carries far:
My Fan Qilang, where have you gone, where oh where?
Oh my heaven!
My Fan Qilang, where have you gone, where oh where?

In the fourth watch of the night the moon tilts to the west—
Fan Qilang has been buried in the body of the Long Wall.
Loudly I call out to Heaven, and softly I call out to Earth:
Return me my Fan Qilang, so we can be husband and wife!
Oh my heaven!
Return me my Fan Qilang, so we can be husband and wife!

In the fifth watch of the night the sky slowly brightens—
Finding my husband has turned into a figment of a dream.
But I, Mengjiang, will take revenge and seek redress,
And I will happily risk my life to engage in the fight!
Oh my heaven,
And I will happily risk my life to engage in the fight!"

When she had wept through the five watches of the night, the sky had turned bright. The maiden Mengjiang went to seek the general, asking him to present the dragon-robe as quickly as possible to the First Emperor of the Qin so that she could at the earliest opportunity provide her husband with a fitting funeral. The general agreed enthusiastically, and carrying the dragon-robe he entered the capital. When he had arrived at Xianyang, he presented the dragon-robe, and he expected he would receive a large reward, after which he would go back and marry the maiden Mengjiang. Who could have thought that when the emperor opened the package and had a look, he would find a white robe for a burial! The First Emperor flew into a rage and said, "You, this traitorous villain! If you today offer me this burial shroud, it must mean you wish me dead and want to steal my rivers and mountains!" He called to his guards to have him arrested and beheaded. The general shouted time and again, "A myriad years!" but even so his life was not spared.

After he had beheaded the general, the First Emperor of the Qin came in person to Mountain-Sea Pass to inspect the building of the Long Wall. Once he had arrived at the construction site, the maiden Mengjiang requested an audience. She presented the true dragon-robe and explained that the one the general had taken was a false one. Next she also told the whole story of how the general had killed Fan Qilang. The First Emperor of the Qin feigned some tears, telling her that Fan Qilang had died unjustly and that the general should have been executed much earlier! When he had accepted the dragon-robe the maiden Mengjiang had presented, it indeed shimmered with true gold—it was a truly rare, top-grade, precious object! On top of that he saw that the maiden Mengjiang was of a surpassing beauty, so his evil desire was raised, and he hastily asked her, "If you have any further request, I will happily grant it. And if you still have any business that has to be taken care of, I will happily do so on your behalf. And when everything is finished, you go back with me to the palace to become empress. How about it?"

The maiden Mengjiang promptly said, "That evil villain has been eliminated, so my husband has been revenged. But there are still three things you have to do for me, and then I will come along with you."

The First Emperor of the Qin hastily asked her, "Which three things?"

The maiden Mengjiang said, "First of all, you have to find the bones of Fan Qilang and provide them with a lavish burial. Secondly, I want the emperor and his high ministers in person to weep for the deceased and to send off his spirit. And thirdly, I also want you to appoint Fan Qilang to high office!"

The First Emperor of the Qin said, "I will do all these things for you, but I have no way to find those bones."

The maiden Mengjiang replied, "That will be my responsibility!"

The First Emperor of the Qin then said, "Fine!" and the maiden Mengjiang kowtowed to express her gratitude.

In order to find the bones of Fan Qilang, the maiden Mengjiang wept by the Long Wall. Her tears gushed forth like a spring, and all the people passing by on the road who heard her weeping could not stop themselves from being deeply moved. No one knows how long she wept, but suddenly she heard the mountains shake and the earth move, and with a rumbling sound that oh so high Long Wall collapsed. All at once it was in ruins for a hundred miles, and countless skeletons of victims appeared. The maiden Mengjiang rubbed her tear-filled eyes and went forward to inspect them, but each skeleton was the same, and she could not distinguish which one was her own Fan Qilang. She looked again and again, and after much thinking, she finally thought of the following way, "I will use my blood to identify my man." She bit her middle finger till it bled and dripped the blood on the bones so as to establish their identity one by one. "If they are not my husband's, the blood will run off, but if they are my husband's, it will be absorbed by the bone." One bone after another—she wasted no end of blood—but in all cases it ran off, until she suddenly dripped her blood on a bone, and the blood did not run off, but each and every drop soaked into the bone. "These must be Fan Qilang's!" The maiden Mengjiang immediately embraced the skeleton, wept, and fainted.

But when a gust of wind awoke her from her unconscious state, she hastily placed her husband's bones in the golden casket that the First Emperor of the Qin had given her, and with it she went to see the First Emperor of the Qin. Not only was the First Emperor of the Qin not offended at all that she had crumbled the Long Wall by her weeping, but he also had his underlings make preparations for a lavish burial.

The maiden Mengjiang / was awash in tears,
And she bit through her middle finger to one third.
    Blood kept streaming out in one uninterrupted flow.
"In finding Fan Qilang, it truly proved miraculous!
You may want to insist that white bones cannot speak, but
For me it equals meeting my Fan Qilang face to face!"
    She wept for a while, / and she cried for some time
And said, "Husband, listen to the words of your wife.
    Ever since you left to report yourself to the authorities,
I have felt inside as if I were cooked in boiling oil.
Later, once I had seen your face in my dream,
I decided to find you and traveled to the borders.
    From the start of the journey / I encountered hardship,
And my servant girl fell ill at an inn on the road.
Her undiluted loyalty will not change for eternity;
She found peace by going to the Western Paradise.
    Upon my arrival at the Pass, I found that villain;
I tricked him by a clever scheme to go to the shades.
    The First Emperor of the Qin / has seen me
And wants to take me to the palace as his queen,
But I will come up with another clever scheme—
We, husband and wife, will remain forever united."

The maiden Mengjiang wept as if she would never stop. At this sight the First Emperor of the Qin was overcome by pity, and he promptly ordered his underling to make preparations as quickly as possible for an early funeral and an early marriage. When the day of Fan Qilang's funeral arrived, the First Emperor of the Qin and all his officials wore the white of mourning and accompanied the deceased in a long row. The emperor himself even walked in front of the hearse with the coffin. But when they arrived at the grave, the casket absolutely refused to move. The maiden Mengjiang promptly said, "Fan Qilang is unwilling to be buried in the earth. Because your evil scoundrel killed him using earth, he refuses to enter the earth once again. Now he must be buried in water, so take him to the sea!" The First Emperor of the Qin hastily ordered his people to carry the casket of Fan Qilang to the seaside and to put it in the water. But the strange thing was that this coffin, which was filled with gold and silver, pearls and jewels, and which was extraordinarily heavy, refused to sink! Just like a boat it drifted now in this direction, now in that direction!

The First Emperor of the Qin asked the maiden Mengjiang, "Why doesn't he sink?"

The maiden Mengjiang replied, "You first have to appoint him to office."

The First Emperor of the Qin said, "Would it be sufficient if I appointed him district magistrate for Hongshui in his next life?"

A disappointed Mengjiang said, "That office would be too small!"

In order to please the maiden Mengjiang, the First Emperor of the Qin then said without any further thought, "Then I appoint him the Dragon King of the Eastern Ocean!" The maiden Mengjiang hastily knelt down to express her thanks for the imperial grace.

This is the way in which Fan Qilang became the later Dragon King of the Eastern Ocean.

Fan Qilang's coffin refused to sink into the sea;
Even as Dragon King he still was not satisfied.
He was waiting for Mengjiang, so they might
Together as immortals enter the gate of heaven!

Our story goes that, after the First Emperor of the Qin had appointed Fan Qilang dragon king, the coffin, just like a human being, thrice nodded its head, but after that it continued to drift about, refusing to sink.

The First Emperor of the Qin asked again, "By now we have done everything according to your conditions, so why does it still not sink?"

The maiden Mengjiang replied, "He wants me to go aboard to bow and sacrifice." The First Emperor of the Qin then hastily ordered people to take her there in a rowboat, so she might bow and sacrifice to Fan Qilang.

When the maiden Mengjiang in this boat had come close to the coffin, she made three deep bows, and her tears coursed down like a rain.

She called out, "Fan Qilang,
   Now listen to me,
      Please stand still for a while,
Because I want
   To make fun of
      The First Emperor of the Qin.
In the end
   He will lose
      Both me and his treasure,
And on the seaside
   Heave a sad sigh,
      Filled with remorse for a myriad of years!"

The coffin stood absolutely still just like a human being and did not move at all. The maiden Mengjiang, all dressed in the white of mourning and with tears streaming down her face, stepped out of the boat and onto the coffin, and that boat quickly moved away from the shore as if blown by the wind. The First Emperor of the Qin hastily cried, "I have met all three of your conditions, so come back to land for a return to the palace and the marriage!"

The maiden Mengjiang stood on the coffin with both her eyes wide open but not saying a word. The First Emperor of the Qin was as panicked as an ant on a hot wok. Pacing back and forth on the beach, he had no clue by what means he could induce that physical heavenly immortal to come back to the shore.

At this moment the maiden Mengjiang laughed loudly, and by her laughter she robbed the First Emperor of the Qin of his soul. She asked him, "Whom do you think I look like?"

The First Emperor of the Qin hastily replied, "You resemble the Bodhisattva Guanyin who saves from hardship and danger!"

"Let me once again express my gratitude for the imperial grace!" As she said this, the maiden Mengjiang started to sink together with the coffin of Fan Qilang into the sea. A gust of wind blew down from heaven, as the maiden Mengjiang in a towering rage cursed the First Emperor of the Qin on the beach, "You shameless and deluded ruler, you cruelly hurt the common people by building the Long Wall, and you caused the unjust death of my husband of three days, Fan Qilang. I came to take revenge on behalf of my husband, who is harboring his grief in the world below. How could I ever marry you and leave a vile reputation!" As she was speaking and cursing, she sank to the bottom of the sea. Then a huge wave rose up, and husband and wife—a couple, a pair—rose to heaven as immortals!

The First Emperor of the Qin / was truly stupid;
He had happily met all the conditions set by Mengjiang.
She wanted to take revenge on behalf of her husband,
But he believed that she sincerely wanted to be his wife.
  The deluded rulers of this world are all besotted by lust;
Once they've won the empire, they only cultivate flowers,[13]
Not realizing that in the world of men there are smart girls
Who can trick even an emperor and turn him into a fool.
  Today as the emperor stood on the bank of the Eastern Sea,
He was both startled and terrified, and he concluded,
"Had I known from the start that this would be the outcome,
I would have done better by killing her straightaway!"

Our story goes that the First Emperor of the Qin was overcome by sadness and remorse. He did not say a single word, and when he had returned to Xianyang, he fell ill. The people who had accompanied him all knew he was suffering from lovesickness, but the great ministers who had stayed behind thought the illness was caused by exhaustion. For three days on end he did neither eat nor drink, and all he did was softly whisper, "Mengjiang, Mengjiang, you are causing Us great suffering!"

The great ministers panicked and didn't know at all what to do, so they brought in a roaming Daoist master. It was said that he possessed three magic weapons—the first was a whip to move rocks, the second was a ladle for scooping out the sea, and the third was a pill for refining the ocean.

As soon as the First Emperor of the Qin heard about this man, he was elated, and his health improved considerably. He immediately ordered people to use his whip for moving rocks to fill the sea with them. But even after seven days in a row the sea was still the same old sea, and when they used the ladle to scoop it out, the water did not appear to decrease. In the end only the pill for refining the ocean was left to cook the ocean dry. This was really a terrible weapon! It overturned heaven and shook earth, and all divine immortals of the Eastern Ocean could not live there anymore—they were scorched to such an extent that they had no place to hide. The Dragon King could only go up to heaven and see the Jade Emperor, and then the Jade Emperor appeared in a dream to the First Emperor of the Qin, telling him that he could not go on cooking the ocean. "If you go on cooking the ocean, even the dragon palace will be destroyed, and your empire will also be cooked to smithereens!" But the First Emperor of the Qin thought only of the maiden Mengjiang, and if the world of men had to suffer, the divine immortals would suffer too, so he did not heed the words of the Jade Emperor, and the cooking went on day and night.

As the Jade Emperor was incapable of talking sense to this totally irrational tyrant, he could only dispatch an immortal maiden to the mortal world, to take on the guise of the maiden Mengjiang and become the wife of the First Emperor of the Qin. When the latter saw this false maiden Mengjiang, he took her for the true one and was immensely elated. He ordered the Daoist master to reverse the effects of his pill for refining the ocean. Immediately the winds subsided and the waves calmed down, and the whole wide world was at peace.

The overjoyed First Emperor of the Qin treated all his ministers to a banquet. With gongs and drums resounding to heaven, they celebrated the consummation of the nuptials. Because of his excessive elation, the emperor forgot about the Daoist master and his pill for refining the ocean, so the latter left the palace in a pique and was nowhere to be found anymore.

After three days the Jade Emperor had the immortal maiden return to the heavenly palace. She left behind a First Emperor of the Qin suffering from lovesickness, and he quickly died.[14] In truth,

The next time around he lacked the pill to refine the ocean;
The common people had taken revenge and found redress.

The First Emperor of the Qin
  Built the Long Wall
    And left a vile reputation;
The maiden Mengjiang
  Wept at the Long Wall
    And left a fine reputation.
Under heaven
  Lord and subject
    May not be the same,

SWITCHING THE DRAGON-ROBES

But in listing the good
    And listing the evil,
        We have to distinguish clearly.
Fellow villagers and relatives,
    You have listened to
        The Precious Scroll of the Long Wall;
The maiden Mengjiang
    Looked for her husband
        With sincerity and clear-sightedness.
On behalf of her husband
    She sought revenge
        And cooked up a clever scheme;
She took revenge,
    Obtained redress,
        To be praised for eternity!

Revenge follows revenge, and injustice follows injustice,
But revenge and injustice in the end have a final reckoning!
Acting as a human being, we must follow the common Way;
Hurting Heaven and harming reason cannot be done.
    Upon hearing this scroll, may your heart-ground be opened;
Come again tomorrow if you want to hear another scroll.
The many affairs of rising and falling from the beginning of time
Are each and all recorded and listed in the precious scrolls.

7

MOBILIZING THE GODS

SINCE THE EARLY 1980S, FOLKLORE SCHOLARS OF THE PEOPLE'S Republic of China have been engaged in a number of massive projects documenting the traditions of folk narrative, folk song, and folk music throughout their huge country. Based on extensive collections of firsthand materials compiled at the county level, massive tomes are published to present a summary of the findings for each province. One of these projects documents popular song, and so far some ten volumes have been published in the series *A Complete Collection of China's Songs and Ballads* (Zhongguo geyao jicheng). The songs collected in these tomes are arranged thematically and are mostly short lyrical songs. But each volume also includes a section devoted to narrative songs, and here we usually find one or more long texts devoted to the tale of Meng Jiangnü.

Meng Jiangnü Weeps at the Long Wall (Meng Jiangnü ku Changcheng) comes from Pingdingshan in central Henan. The translation is based on the text provided in the Henan volume of the collection.[1] According to a note appended to this edition, Wang Chuxue and Huang Wenbo recorded the ballad in 1984, in the rural section of Pingdingshan, when it was performed by Mrs. Zhang-Wang. The ballad is composed throughout in lines of seven-syllable verse.

This retelling represents the northern versions of the legend, which omit the bathing scene and present Meng Jiangnü as a prim and proper filial daughter-in-law. Nevertheless, she leaves her parents-in-law in order to join her husband at the Wall. This retelling derives from a much shorter Henan ballad (also titled *Meng Jiangnü Weeps at the Long Wall*), which is preserved in at least two printings of the nineteenth century.[2] In view of discussions about evaluation of the First Emperor in China, it is interesting to note that the detailed account of the misgovernment of the First Emperor in the version translated here hardly has a counterpart in the earlier ballad.

MENG JIANGNÜ WEEPS AT THE LONG WALL

Let's talk about a virtuous person, tell the story of a virtuous person!
Don't you know from where this virtuous person hailed?
    South of the Yangzi River you may find Jiangning county,
And in Jiangning prefecture she had her home and village.
In Jiangning prefecture there lived a certain magnate Xu;
He was married to a lady Meng, who ran his house and home.
    He had many of hundreds of acres of wet fields and dry fields;
The storied buildings and tiled dwellings glistened in the sun.
His mules and horses formed herds, his cattle were many,
But he lacked a son to wear mourning in front of the grave.
    Husband and wife at all times practiced good works;
They built bridges, paved roads, dispensed medicines,
Comforted the elderly and the poor, gave alms to clerics,
Constructed temples, and revered the divine immortals.
    After the couple had practiced goodness for long days,
Heaven gifted them a daughter who was smoothly born.
After three days they gave her a name, a proper name,
And they also invited a godmother for the little girl.
    The father was surnamed Xu, the mother was a Meng,

And the godfather and godmother were surnamed Jiang,
So they named her by listing all three surnames;
The name by which they called her was Xu Mengjiang.

The first year and the second: carried in her mother's arms;
The third year and the fourth: never far from her mother!
The fifth year and the sixth: her feet were tightly bound;
The seventh year and the eighth: she was sent to school.

She continued the study of books till the age of twelve;
She memorized the Five Classics and the Four Books.

She fully understood loyalty and filial piety and the four rites;[3]
She knew the basics of rites and duty, of honesty and shame.
She constantly pondered Threefold Obedience and Fourfold Virtue;[4]
She memorized the texts of poems and lyrics, songs and rhapsodies.

Once she turned thirteen, she entered the embroidery room;
She learned needlework by embroidering mandarin-ducks.
First she learned to sketch dragons and do embroidery;
She surpassed all others in large and small cutting and sewing.

When this young lady had reached the age of sixteen years,
She was married to Fan Xiliang, who lived south of the city.
Husband and wife were of the same age, a handsome couple;
The two of them were also a fitting match in sophistication.

She served her father- and mother-in-law with filial piety,
And she urged her husband to devote himself to his studies.
But after she had come to his home for only a few months,
Her life was changed by that sinful First Emperor of the Qin.

He had gobbled up the six other states, achieved unification,
And the common people of the whole world met with disaster.
He chased mountains and trampled seas: the people suffered;
Burning the books and burying scholars, he harmed good men.

Descendants of noble houses now tended plow and harrow;
Sons of academic families now changed into peasant garb.
People who reached the age of sixty were all expected to die,
And those who didn't die really had no way to make a living.

All graves throughout the world were leveled and removed;
Once the graves had been leveled, grain was grown there.
The sins of the First Emperor cannot all be told in detail—
He also constructed his Wall of a Myriad of Miles at the border.

Conscript laborers were drafted to execute the project;
They all had to be young men in the spring of their youth.
All young men between the ages of fifteen and twenty
Had to go to the border region in order to build the Wall!

Xiliang was drafted by name to go and build the Wall:
This couple of beautiful mandarin-ducks was ripped apart!
Husband and wife, so young of years, cruelly separated:
A couple of mandarin-ducks beaten apart with a cudgel!

He found it hard to abandon his elderly father and mother.
How could this not cause one's heart to break?
Xiliang first took his leave of his parents with a bow;
Then he turned around and also bowed to Xu Mengjiang.

"Now I leave for the border region to work as a laborer;
My parents completely depend on you for their care.
If you serve my parents at their bedside with filial piety,
I will never forget this virtue of yours, even in death."

The young lady addressed him in the following way,
"My dear husband, listen to my most sincere thoughts.
When you leave for the border to work as a laborer,
I will be responsible for serving your father and mother.

I further have some words of good advice for you;
Each and every one you should record in your heart.
One traveling away from home is less than one third;
Polite behavior comes first of all, never rely on force.

When you meet someone your senior, call him 'uncle';
Call those who are younger than you 'elder brother.'
On no account drink cold tea and uncooked water;
You'd better not eat any raw melons, pears, or dates.

Stay good friends with your fellow workers at work;
Make sure you do not get into a fight and get hurt.
Whatever good or bad may happen in the outside world,
You will never get the same kind of care as at home!"

The young man thereupon walked out of the house;
Mengjiang saw him off, overcome by her emotions.
One awash in tears saw off someone also awash in tears;
A brokenhearted person accompanied a brokenhearted person.

The young man gnashed his teeth, leaving on his journey,

MOBILIZING THE GODS

敕伯。哥。方喝冷茶

While Mengjiang returned home with tears in her eyes.
Overwhelmed by sorrow, she went to her embroidery room;
Filled with longing, she felt oh so lonely and miserable!

    The First Month and the Second were still manageable;
The Third Month and the Fourth: the wheat turned yellow.
The Fifth Month and the Sixth bring insufferable heat;
The Seventh Month and the Eighth: a cool autumn breeze.

    From the Ninth Month onward, the weather becomes chilly,
And in the Tenth Month one sees the freezing frost.
Once the freezing frost appears, the weather gets chilly,
And every house and family prepares their padded clothes.

    The young lady also started making winter clothes
While longing for her husband, her Fan Xiliang.
"You are in the border regions, working as a laborer.
How can you withstand this terrible cold weather?

    Come to think of it, this cold is really insufferable.
How can it fail to cause me to be heartbroken?"
The young lady wept till her tears fell like rain,
And sinking into a heavy slumber, she had a dream.

    In her dream her husband had come back home;
By the side of her bed he yawned, awash in tears.
With each and every word he told of his sufferings;
His body was shaking all over, like winnowing chaff!

    "My darling," he said, "I am truly freezing to death,
So quickly get me my cotton-padded winter clothes!"
The young lady stepped forward and grasped his hand,
But when she woke up, it actually was only a dream!

    When she woke up, it actually had only been a dream;
Tears of pain coursed down, the drops soaking the bed.
While weeping and crying, she opened her eyes
Just as the red sun appeared in the eastern sky.

    When the young lady saw the sky had brightened,
She stole away and got up and went to the kitchen.
Tottering and stumbling, she prepared the breakfast
And then waited on her father and mother in the hall.

    When the two elderly people had finished eating,
The young lady told them her deepest feelings,

"Last night your daughter had a dream, in which
Your son had come back to his old hometown.

I saw him walking and entering into my room,
And he stood by the side of my bed, awash in tears.
With each and every word he told of his sufferings;
His body was shaking all over, like winnowing chaff!

He told me he was freezing to death in the border region
And told me to get him his winter clothes immediately!
I found this impossible to bear and dissolved into tears,
But when I woke up, it was actually only a dream.

I have been pondering this dream all night long:
This dream bodes disaster and spells little luck!"
Her father- and mother-in-law replied as follows,
"Dear daughter-in-law, please listen to our thoughts!

Dreams, the proverb says, are the heart's fantasies;
If you worry too much, you're bound to be anxious.
Daughter-in-law, we urge you, don't worry so much;
When the work is done there, he will come home!"

Mengjiang replied to them in the following manner,
Weeping, she shouted: "Dear father- and mother-in-law,
You may not believe the words he spoke in his dream,
But how can you not give any thought to his situation?

Now in the Tenth Month the weather is getting cold,
So how can he not be shivering in his unlined clothes?
Other people all have elder brothers or younger brothers,
Who travel to the border regions to deliver clothes.

We here have no one who can take him his clothes,
So he's set to freeze to death in some strange land.
I have therefore decided today to take him his clothes;
I, your daughter, will deliver the clothes to the border."

The two elderly parents-in-law replied as follows,
"Darling daughter-in-law, please listen to our thoughts.

The road to the border is many thousands of miles,
And do you know where he is working on building the Wall?
If you cannot find him in those overgrown marshes,
You'd better stay here at home to live with your parents!"

MOBILIZING THE GODS

The young lady did not follow the advice of her in-laws;
Her mind was made up to find her husband at the border.
The startled neighbors came by to talk her out of it,
To talk that virtuous woman Mengjiang out of this idea.

"If you want to go to the border to deliver his clothes,
It's thousands and thousands of miles, a long journey!
You'd better wait for him here while staying at home—
When the work is done there, he will come home."

Mengjiang replied to them in the following words,
"Dear Auntie Zhang, and you too, dear Auntie Li,

Now in the Tenth Month the weather is getting cold,
So how can he not be shivering in his unlined clothes?
I've made up my mind today to take him his clothes;
I will deliver his clothes in person there at the border.

If I meet with my husband there at the Wall face-to-face,
We will return to our hometown together, man and wife.
And if I do not find my husband there at the border wall,
I will die there at the border and never return back home!"

She came to her embroidery room and opened the chest;
She took out that set of cotton-padded winter clothes.
"Let me take two sets of coarse linen clothes for him;
Let me take two pairs of old and new shoes and socks."

She wrapped them all up in a nice little bundle;
She picked it up and carried it over her shoulders.
First she took her leave of her two parents in the hall;
Next she said good-bye to the neighbors on both sides.

"I am leaving for the border to deliver these clothes;
My parents-in-law depend on you for their care.
When I come back from the border region,
I'll prostrate myself as an expression of my gratitude."

After she had said this, the young lady left the house;
She left through the main gate, all awash in tears.

After one mile of weeping she passed Zhang Village;
After two miles of weeping she passed Shi Hamlet.
After three miles of weeping she got to Peach Blossom Station;
After four miles of weeping she passed Li Hamlet too.

The travelers from north and south were all gentlemen;
Spring scenery flourished on both sides of the road.
But once she got to hamlets where the going was rough,
She could not help being beset by doubts.

"All I knew was I longed for my husband with all my heart,
But I have no clue at all where that border wall may be."
Weeping and crying, however, she continued to walk on;
Alas, wandering and roaming in all four directions!

That day she rested for the night in a Guanyin temple,
And the startled bodhisattva noticed her loyal virtue.
Old Mother Guanyin was seated on her lotus-pedestal;
Her ears got hot, her eyes jumped, she was not at ease!

When she'd made some computations with her fingers,
She realized that this virtuous woman needed help.
"If I don't come to her rescue, who will help her out?
If I don't take care of her, who will take care of her?"

She bowed down to the ground to get somewhat closer;
Then lifted that virtuous Xu Mengjiang from the floor.
On a single cloud she traveled three thousand miles
And arrived right at the middle of the border wall.

She reined in the cloud, brought the haze to a halt,
And deposited virtuous Xu Mengjiang on the ground.
Old Mother Guanyin returned to her original position,
Abandoning there the young lady Xu Mengjiang.

When the young lady opened her sorrowful eyes,
She discovered in front of her the endless Wall:
So high it had to be at least thirty-five feet high,
So long that nobody knew how long it might be!

The laborers working there were without number;
Common people from the whole world in one mass!
The young lady stepped forward and asked them:
"Mr. Workman, please be so kind as to listen to me!

There is a conscript laborer here from Jiangnan
Who goes by the name and surname of Fan Xiliang.
This year he had barely reached the age of seventeen—
Where is he now working on building this wall?

MOBILIZING THE GODS

If you would want to know what I may be to him,
I am his wedded wife—my name is Xu Mengjiang.
I have come thousands of miles to bring him his clothes,
But I do not know where to look for my husband."

Hearing this, the conscript laborer started to cry;
Looking toward his hometown, he wept for his parents,
"I have elder brothers and younger brothers at home—
How come I do not see them here to deliver clothes?
I too have a wedded wife and children at home—
How come they are not as virtuous as you?"

The conscript laborer answered her as follows:
"You, lady, who are delivering clothes, please listen!
This wall at the border goes on for myriads of miles,
And a single laborer works on one hundred of those miles.

Who knows here who may be from Jiangning county?
Who knows here who may be your Fan Xiliang?
It would be much better if you went back home to wait;
When the work is done here, he will come home!"

Mengjiang knelt down before everyone she met
And asked everyone she met about her Fan Xiliang.
When she did not find him here, she asked over there;
When she did not find him there, she went farther on.

One step after another she went forward and asked,
And in the end she had been asking for quite some days,
But there was not one person who could tell her a thing,
Until an old man arrived on the scene, and until
Mengjiang stepped forward and asked for information.

He answered her question in the following way:
"Dear virtuous lady, you who are looking for your husband,
We both originally are from Jiangning county,
We both actually are from the same township.

Your husband Fan Xiliang once upon a time
Shared a room at the academy with my son.
But people who study cannot stand this hardship;
Once he had died, he was bricked into the Wall."

When the lady heard that her husband had died,

She collapsed with a thud on the ground.
Her three souls wandered off to the realm of shades;
Her seven spirits ascended Looking Back Home Terrace.[5]

But King Yama refused to hold a ghost who had died unfairly;[6]
He returned her breath to her so she could come back to life.
While her eyes continued to be flooded by tears,
She wept for her husband while facing the Wall.

She wept, "My dear husband, how cruel your death!
Alas for your fine writing skills, which you acquired
During ten years of bitter toil in front of the window,
Hoping to become a pillar and beam to the state!

Who could have known the First Emperor of the Qin
Would grab you to become a laborer and build his Wall?
I only thought you were laboring, building the border wall.
Who knew you had died and were bricked into the Wall?"

With each and every word she wept for her husband Fan;
With each and every phrase she cursed the First Emperor.
She wept till the heavens darkened and the earth darkened,
Till the sun and moon and all the stars had lost their light.

As she wept, the artisans could not lift a finger;
Those engaged in selling could not cry out their wares.
As she wept, the farmers abandoned plow and harrow,
And the officials did not dare leave their offices.

She wept for seven days and seven nights, and
By her weeping startled the Jade Emperor, Zhang.
The Jade Emperor ascended the throne in high heaven
And summoned the old Dragon Kings of the four seas,
The Thunder Lord, and the Thunder Mother and said,

"All of you have to go speedily to that border wall;
Bring down that border wall and show Fan Xiliang!
Transfer the corpse to that Mengjiang, so she may
Take it back with her and return to her village."

Once the divine immortals had received their orders,
They left the hall of heaven as fast as they could.
With the thundering roar of a peal of thunder
A huge downpour of rain arrived at the Wall!

Gusts of wind, large and small, displayed their violence;

MOBILIZING THE GODS

The thunder continued to rumble and roar without end.
Flashes of lightning blinded a man with their light,
As a huge downpour came down in great haste.

After that downpour had lasted for three full days,
Three miles of wall there at the border had collapsed.
When the storm abated and the clouds had dispersed,
The gods returned to heaven to report on their mission.

The young lady, whose tears kept coming down,
Suddenly saw the white bones appear with a rumble.
The white bones buried in the Wall were without number.
How to know which ones were those of Fan Xiliang?

As the young lady was standing there, quite confused,
A Daoist priest suddenly appeared by her side.
"The drops of blood from a wife will enter the bone;
The drops of blood from a mother will fall to the side.

If you do not believe what I am telling you now,
Just drip a drop on the bones and see what happens."
As soon as the Daoist priest had told her these words,
He disappeared again in the wink of an eye.

The young lady knew he had come to enlighten her,
So she knelt down on both knees before the sky.
After she had prostrated herself, she got to her feet—
"There can be no harm at all in trying this out."

As soon as her jade teeth had bitten her middle finger,
Blood trickled down on all sides in rapid ripples.
One after another she dripped her blood on more than ten,
But in each case it fell to the side in rapid ripples.

When the young lady saw this, she became fearful,
Fearful that the blood she shed might fill a vat!
From early morning she kept on dripping till noon,
And then finally she found that Fan Xiliang.

The young lady stepped forward and embraced him;
She embraced the corpse, crying, "My Xiliang!"

She wept: "My dear husband, you died too early;
Who will take care of me now—I'm still so young!
Wait for me on the roads of the realm of shades;
I'll have your corpse moved back to your home."

She spread the cloth of her bundle out on the ground
And placed the corpse exactly in the middle.
She wrapped him up into a nice little bundle,
Which she lifted up and carried over her shoulder.

As the young lady was about to start walking,
There appeared that sinful First Emperor of the Qin.
Lances, knives, and swords were gleaming in the sun:
Surrounded by his officials, he inspected the Wall.

When he in his imperial conveyance lifted his head,
He saw the young lady Xu Mengjiang and thought:
"I may have three palaces and six courts, but none
Of those women is as beautiful as this woman is!"

He ordered his people to call the girl over; he wanted
To summon her to the palace, appoint her to be empress!
The young lady replied to him in the following way:
"You sinful king," was the way she addressed him,

"You first were the cause of the death of my husband,
Now you want to raise me to the rank of empress.
You will have to meet three major conditions,
And then you may raise me to the rank of empress!"

When the stupid king heard this, he laughed happily,
"Tell me those three conditions in all detail!"
The young lady said: "The first condition is
A golden casket, a silver coffin, and an imperial funeral
Will be used to dress and encoffin my husband.

The second condition is:
Officials and officers will all wear heavy mourning,
And you, stupid king, will follow the hearse as a son.

The third condition is:
As my husband was unable to rule the level land,
He must be buried at the beach of the Eastern Sea.
If you can meet these three major conditions,
Then you may raise me to the rank of empress."

When the stupid king heard this, he laughed happily,
"No problem at all in meeting your three conditions!"
He ordered people to bring a golden coffin and casket,
In which Fan Xiliang was encoffined in greatest haste.

MOBILIZING THE GODS

Officials and officers all wore heavy mourning;
The stupid king followed behind as the filial son.
With great pomp and circumstance they walked on,
Resting at night, departing at dawn—no need to tell.

Eventually they reached the bank of the Eastern Sea
And put down Fan Xiliang's golden coffin and casket.
Who was the one who knelt down in front of the grave?
The one who knelt down was the young lady Mengjiang.

She prayed and she prayed, and she prayed once again,
As she prayed to her husband, her dear Fan Xiliang.

"You may have died without any rank or title,
But your wife has arranged for quite a show.
Officials and officers all wear heavy mourning,
And that stupid king plays the role of a filial son.

I will not have you buried on any level land;
You'll be buried on the bank of the Eastern Sea.
Even though you may have died a bitter death,
Your wife has given you quite some status.

Wait for me there on Looking Back Home Terrace;
I, your wife, will climb the terrace together with you."
Once she had covered her face with her ample gauze skirt,
She used all the strength in her lotus-feet and jumped into the river!

The civil officials and military officers laughed heartily;
They laughed at the stupid king who had lost much face.
"Had I known that you were such a chaste woman,
I would never have played the role of a filial son!"

That stupid and sinful king became a virtuous ruler
Who ordered all men never again to build such a wall.

Now hurry home and show respect to your parents!

8

STEPPING INTO THE POND

I N LATER IMPERIAL TIMES, MENG JIANGNÜ WAS POPULARLY
venerated in the northwestern part of Hunan. Her story was widely
performed, both as a ritual opera onstage and as a ballad in other set-
tings. This chapter presents one ballad from the area, *Jiangnü Steps Down into
the Pond* (Jiangnü xia chi), which focuses on the meeting of Meng Jiangnü
and Fan Qiliang at a pond and so does not provide a full account of the legend.
As is also clear from the conclusion, this ballad was intended for performance
at a wedding. This version of the legend was current in an area that belongs
to the old prefecture of Lizhou, a region that nowadays has an ethnically
mixed population. The majority of the population has been officially classified since the early 1950s as the Tujia (The Locals) minority. Tujia culture
shares many features of mainstream Han culture, and the ballad was popular
with Tujia, Han, and Miao as wedding entertainment.

The translation is based on the text provided in *An Anthology of Materials
on Meng Jiangnü* (Meng Jiangnü ziliao xuanji).[1] The editors appended the
following note:

According to the collector (Jin Kejian), there originally existed manuscripts transmitted by the folk artists for *Jiangnü Steps Down into the Pond*, this folk ballad that was popular in the region of Dayong and Yuanling in western Hunan, but later these manuscripts were lost. This text has been edited by the collector on the basis of three periods of fieldwork and collecting (May to December 1977; July to September 1980; and October 1984). It is very rare to find among our contributions a long ballad, popular in a minority area but written entirely in the vernacular language.[2]

The Shanghai editors next mention the claim that Meng Jiangnü was born in Lizhou. A certain Gong Sizhong, who was ninety years old at the time of recording, and a certain Xiang Zechang, who had turned seventy-eight, are listed as singers.[3] The ballad is composed throughout in seven-syllable lines, but some lines contain one or two additional syllables. The white lines in the translation follow the typography of the printed edition.

Anonymous

JIANGNÜ STEPS INTO THE POND

The waters of the Li flow on and on below Chu's heaven;[4]
Mount Heaven's Gate, oh high so high, provides the singing stage!
The one song about Lizhou's Jiangnü has been performed
For hundreds and thousands of years, still going strong!

Who was the one who gave the Yellow River its winding way?
Who was the one who planted the sal tree up in the moon?
Who was the one who opened up the barbarian wastelands?
Who was the one who wrote the song of "the orchids of the Li"?

King Yu gave the Yellow River its winding way;[5]
The Old Gardener planted the sal tree in the moon;[6]
Huandou opened up these barbarian wastelands;[7]
Qu Yuan wrote the song of "the orchids of the Li."[8]

A Li river orchid, sweetly fragrant, blooming in Li county:
Jiangnü was born here in Jiang Family Stronghold,

230

A lotus flower that emerges from the water—
She had been reared in the inner chambers till age eighteen.

Jiangnü unbound and shook her hair like black silk,
And in her hand she took her comb made of ivory.
Combing her hair on the left—a coiling-dragon bun;
Combing her hair on the right—she put in some flowers.
    In her coiling-dragon bun she wore some silver pins,
And in her ears she wore hangers of gold and of jade.
A garment of cotton covered her jade-white body;
A pinkish gray skirt was wrapped around her middle.
    Her tiny feet were bound with long bands of silk;
Her small shoes were embroidered with lotus flowers.
As the front gate was locked, she took the back door;
Opening the back door a little, she left her own room.

Dragon-boats and mandarin-ducks float in pairs on the Li.
She feels flustered and hurried; she is at a loss as to what to do—
"How well I remember the Double Fifth of that year;
The first fifth of the Fifth Month is Double Fifth Festival.⁹
    My errand boy and serving maid whispered into my ear,
And every one of their words struck the strings of my heart,
'Your life is just the same as that of other men and women,
But those men are all married, those women are wed!
    All other people are married and enjoy Heaven's bond,
But you're sitting all alone by yourself in your cold room.
How often is a woman young and eighteen years of age?
Once spring is gone and autumn comes, leaves wither!'"

After she had carefully considered the matter all by herself,
Jiangnü decided to go to a temple and light a stick of incense.
She hid her action from her father; she hid it from her mother;
She hid it from the errand boy and from her serving maid.
    When she had sneaked through the gate and into the temple,
The many bronze incense-burners were all arrayed in a row—
"I do not burn my incense to ask for wealth and power,

Nor do I pray the gods to provide me peace and health.
I only want to know about the decisive affair of my life—
Will I marry a perfect lover who will stay with me till old age?"

Jiangnü got up on her feet and bowed to the east:
"Divine gods of the east, please listen to me!
    Please show a response if you want me to marry!
Even a granddad of eighty I will not think too old.
People are free to make fun of me, I'm not afraid—
Taigong was eighty when he wrote his essays!"[10]

Having bowed to the east, she bowed to the south:
"Divine gods of the south, please listen to me!
    In case you have knowledge about my marriage,
Please open your mouths and tell me about it.
Even a three-year-old baby I'll not think too young;
I'll happily take him as husband and be his wife."

Having bowed to the south, she bowed to the west:
"Divine gods of the west, please listen to me!
    Even a blockhead or fool I will not think too ugly—
If it's determined by fate, that man will be the groom.
Mistakes made by ghosts or by gods—I'll not complain;
I'll not continuously compare my husband to other men."

Having bowed to the south, she bowed to the north:
"Divine gods of the north, please listen to me!
    I am not looking for some prince or nobleman;
I will only love the finest guy in the entire world!
I will love him with all my heart, not fearing poverty—
This fresh flower may be planted in buffalo dung!"

· Even after she had bowed to all gods on the four sides,
All four parties refused to open their golden mouths.
Who could understand even an inkling of her desire?
Her floating girdle trailing, she left the temple building.

STEPPING INTO THE POND

From the east of the village she walked to the west;
From the south of the village she walked to the lotus pond.
By the side of the pond was a well of pure water—
Golden sand and weeping willows and butterflies!
　　Jiangnü then thought that she might take a bath,
To untie the hundred knots of her sorrowing guts.
　　Up the road she saw no one coming for five miles;
Down the road it was all wilderness for five miles.
All around the wide sky let down a curtain of fog,
And inside that curtain Jiangnü took off her clothes.
　　She took off not only her shirt made of silk
But also her hundred-plaited pinkish gray skirt.
She also took off the white cloth for binding her feet,
And she even took off the pair of embroidered shoes.
　　Not encumbered by a single thread: light as a swallow!
Her lotus-pouch, filled with shame, exuded pure fragrance.
She lightly stroked the willow strands covering half her face—
She was the very image of Seventh Sister entering the pond![11]
　　In cold winter one seeks comfort around a coal burner;
In the heat of summer one can only cool off in the water.
When a man takes a bath, he first washes his face, but
When a woman takes a bath, she first cleans her chest.
　　She took her handkerchief and shook it out once or twice;
When her left arm was cleaned, she washed her right arm.
She took her handkerchief and wrung it out a few times.
A carp turning its belly up—she washed her back.
　　After washing, her upper body was as white as snow;
After washing, her lower body was as white as silver.
When she had washed, body and limbs spotlessly clean,
She brushed aside the duckweeds to look at herself.
　　The eyes below her brows were black as a candlewick;
Her eyebrows were as curved as the new moon sickle.
Her teeth were like white rice kernels sieved in a golden tub;
Her lips were like the pure lotus flower emerging from the water.
　　Her ten fingers were slender and tapering like bamboo shoots;
She was even prettier than Guanyin of the Southern Sea![12]
　　Suddenly a faint breeze arose, light as a thread—

The lotus leaves rustled, and their shadows moved.
As the blowing wind scattered the duckweeds in all directions,
One person watching herself observed two reflected faces!
    "This one reflection here—that is mine own,
But that reflection there—whose can it be?
Is it a heavenly god who has descended to earth?
Is it an earthly ghost who ascends to the sky?
    Is it a living person who is hiding himself?
Is it a ghost from the pond who is haunting me?
Is it perhaps a cattle rustler or a horse thief?
Is it a criminal who commits heinous deeds?
    Is it an ancestor who shows himself to me?
When I'm back home, I'll light a stick of incense.
Is it the Master of Life from the ninth heaven?[13]
When I'm back home, I'll light a candle in the kitchen.
    If you are a human being, then quickly speak up,
But if you are a ghost, then give off some light!"

All of a sudden someone burst out in laughter;
From the willow branches a soft voice trembled,
    "Immortal maiden in the pond, don't harbor doubt,
And please listen carefully to me, point by point.
First, I am not a heavenly god, who has descended to earth;
Second, I am not an earthly ghost who ascends to the sky.
    Third, I am not a ghost who wrongfully died in this pond;
Fourth, I am not a ghost in the water who's haunting you.
Fifth, I definitely am not a cattle rustler or a horse thief;
Sixth, I am not a criminal who commits heinous deeds.
    Seventh, I am not an ancestor who appears to you,
So there's no need to light a stick of incense back home.
Eighth, I'm not the Master of Life from the ninth heaven,
So there is no need to light a candle in the kitchen at home.
    If I were a ghost, I'd be unable to give some light,
But as I am a human being, I can tell you my background."

When she heard this human voice coming out of the tree,
Jiangnü was so scared that she lost all her souls.

STEPPING INTO THE POND

"Please be so kind as to turn your face to the east,
So I can come out of the water and meet with you.
Please be so kind as to turn your face to the south,
So I can come out of the water and put on my clothes.
	Please be so kind as to turn your face to the west,
So I can come out of the water and get dressed.
Please be so kind as to turn your face to the north—
Aiyah! With a man around, I cannot get dressed!
	Please hide yourself behind three layers of leaves,
So I can come out of the water and put on my skirt.
Dear elder brother, please show compassion and pity,
As human beings we all are the children of parents!"

"First of all, I will not turn my face to the east—
What do I care whether I meet with you or not?
Secondly, I will not turn my face to the south—
What do I care whether you come out of the water?
	Thirdly, I will not turn my face to the west—
What do I care whether you put on your clothes?
And fourthly, I will not turn my face to the north—
What do I care if you cannot put on your clothes?
	I hide myself behind three layers of willow leaves
And do not care whether you can put on your skirt.
I jump from an eastern branch to a southern branch,
From a western branch back to a northern branch."

Only when she saw he had turned his back toward her
Could Jiangnü feel relieved enough to breathe again.
She plucked some lotus leaves to cover her body;
Walking through the water, she came out of the pond.
	She put on her blouse, and she put on her skirt,
Wrapped her feet, and put on her embroidered shoes.
Politely she stepped forward and made a light bow,
Opened her lips and asked the young man the following,
	"From which county do you hail? Which prefecture?
Of which noble family are you the son and heir?

235

Are you perhaps surnamed Zhou or surnamed Chen?
Are you perhaps surnamed Quan or surnamed Jin?
　　How many elder and younger sisters do you have?
What is your birth ranking amongst your siblings?
For what reason did you end up here as a fugitive?
Why were you hiding yourself in that tree?
Please tell me your surname and also your name—
People when passing leave a name, geese their call!"

"My dear young lady, I will make all things clear!
Your voice is even sweeter than the red bayberry.
When you ask me for my name, I really feel ashamed;
I am shivering as if my palms were covered with salt.
　　We live in Kuilin prefecture in Guangxi;
We're the Fan family below Hundred Flowers Ridge.
In a straw-thatched cottage we were spending our days;
My mother bore three sons, so I have two brothers.
　　My eldest brother has the name of Fan Qiyu;
My second brother has the name of Fan Qiyun.
From age seven I've studied the books with a teacher,
And Fan Qiliang is the name that I've been given.
　　Before the *bingyin* year the rivers rose in a flood,
And all the nine lands and ten regions were struck.
The northern nation of Qin produced a Son of Heaven,
Who through his many campaigns united the world.
　　That king of Qin, bereft of reason, rules the world;
At Xianyang he wants to build a myriad-mile wall.[14]
He wants to build a wall that's a thousand rods high—
A drunken dream of enjoying peace in life and death!
　　A golden plaque was transmitted throughout the world:
From every country and prefecture men were drafted!
Of a family of three sons, one person was drafted;
Of a family of five sons, three names were drafted!
　　As we were three brothers in our family, one of us
Had to fulfill the draft and go and build the wall.
When my parents heard this, they were shattered,
And tears poured from their eyes like a copious rain.

STEPPING INTO THE POND

The whole family huddled together, weeping and crying,
'How are we going to deal with this problem?

Actually we should order your eldest brother to go,
But who would plow and hoe the fields, pay the taxes?
Actually we should order your second brother to go,
But who would take care of your nephews and nieces?

Your duties in serving your parents are still limited,
But the family's livelihood depends on their labor.
So we would have to order you, our third son, to go,
But we find it impossible to abandon you, our baby!'

When I heard these words from my parents,
I knelt down on my knees and answered as follows,

'If my eldest brother cannot go, my second brother goes;
If my second brother cannot go, I will do my duty.
My dear parents, please allow your baby son to go;
I am the youngest, without duties, I'll build the Wall!

If it takes long, I'll be gone for three or five years;
If shorter, I'll come back home after half a year or so.
If you don't let me go, you'll disobey the emperor;
If you don't let me go, the family will be confiscated!'

My father wept till his throat was all hoarse;
My mother wept till she was all dazed and befuddled.

My elder brothers poured me a cup of farewell-wine;
In each and every cup the wine was mixed with tears.
They saw me off at the pavilion ten miles out of town;
None of us three could stop his tears from flowing.

In many ways they urged me to take good care of myself,
And, brokenhearted, I pronounced the following vow,

'Even if I may not be able to come home for ten years,
I will never forget my family, wherever I may wander.
Even if my body may be buried in that Long Wall,
My soul will travel back to Hundred Flowers Ridge!'

Then I, the youngest, wiped away my tears, left the village,
And after an autumn journey arrived at the capital city.
In this way I discarded the brush to be a border conscript;
A student of books, I became a laborer building the Wall.

One carrying pole balances two large baskets of earth—

火

和

水

That flat pole looked more like a fire-and-water cudgel![15]
Each and every carrying pole was far too heavy,
And both my shoulders turned into one bloody mess.
    In the morning we went up the eastern hills to carry earth;
At night we went down the southern gully to haul stones.
    In one day we had to build up three feet of earth;
In three days we had to build up nine feet of wall.
But each day we got only half a cup of rice;
For nine days they gave us only one liter of rice.
    Our water was the foul and fetid water of the steppe;
Our firewood was the dung of horses and of mules.
The trees all over the hills were stripped of their bark;
All around the grass had been eaten down to the roots.
    And then there were the officers like wolves and tigers;
Again and again they would hit you with their whips.
Millions of conscript laborers died of exhaustion;
The field was covered with holes for burying people.
    I, Fan Xiliang, was originally a student of books;
I was so worn, I was reduced to this bag of bones!
Cursing the Emperor of the Qin as bereft of all reason,
I decided to flee, hoping to escape from this pit of fire!
    In the first watch of the night I walked along the Wall;
In the second watch of the night I ran along the Wall.
In the third watch of the night I came to the parapets;
Clutching the parapets, I was scared out of my mind!
    Because the officers who pursued me were so close behind,
I risked my life, courted death, and jumped down the Wall!
I feared that I would die and that my three souls would dissolve,
But eventually I came back to life when my seven spirits revived.
    When I came to, I hurried on, pursuing my journey;
I didn't dare halt my step, whether by night or by day.
For three months I've been crossing hills, fording rivers,
And all by chance I arrived here in this village of yours.
    My stomach was one empty hole, the hunger unbearable,
So when I found this lotus pond, I met my lucky star!
The water from the well near the pond slaked my thirst;
I gobbled down the lotus roots with the leaves attached.

STEPPING INTO THE POND

When I looked up, I suddenly saw this willow tree,
And it seemed to me as if I saw my own dear mother.
Embracing the willow tree, I wept my heart out;
In the shade of its leaves I sank into a deep slumber,
    Not knowing at all that you were taking a bath and
In the water would see the reflection of me, up in the tree!
Young lady, I hope that you will show me some pity
And not disclose my presence here to other people.
    I also hope, young lady, that you will tell me your name,
So I may pay you back for this favor in a future life!"

"Young man, your story has been very long indeed,
But your words, drenched in blood, wrench my guts.
When I speak to you now, my eyes are filled with tears,
So, young man there in the tree, please listen carefully.
    If one beats a drum on a high hill, its sound carries far;
If one plants a flower in the sea, its roots will be long.
This place here belongs to Lizhou prefecture, and it is
Jiang Family Village, to the east of the Li county capital.
    My father is the famous 'Millionaire Jiang';
My mother is the very virtuous lady Fan.
I am my parents' only daughter, Meng Jiangnü;
Eighteen springs old, I'm locked up in inner chambers.
    Because I wanted to consult the gods about my desire,
I secretly left the embroidery room and burned incense.
Because of the fiery summer heat of the Sixth Month,
I took off my clothes to take a bath here in this pond.
    Who could have known that you would be up in that tree?
For shame I don't know what to do, me, such a pretty young girl!
You have seen my body, fully disclosed, from top to toe!
How can I ever live down such a terrible scandal!
    When I secretly think about this in my heart,
My heart's in turmoil, I'm at a loss as to what to do.
A screw-pump irrigating dry fields—it should stay locked;
I've something to say but don't dare open my mouth."

"Young lady, please feel free to say whatever you want;
I am not some cannibal tyrant who eats his victims.
Only when a screw-pump is opened does its ingenuity show—
You'll remain upset as long as you don't speak your mind!"

"You may not want to do this, but this is what I want:
I will tell it to you straight, and I will stick to my words.
Karma brought us together when I stepped into the pond;
It is all because of that one stick of incense that I lit!
    If you don't have a wife, I will marry you as your wife;
If you already have a wife, I'll become your concubine.
I pledge myself to you for the rest of my life, and so
I ask you to climb down from the tree and become a couple!"

"Young lady, your words are not very well considered!
A marriage bond of floating duckweeds cannot last long.
You are the daughter of a lofty family, a great house;
I am a boy from a very simple straw-thatched cottage.
    I have no hat on my head and no shoes on my feet;
My clothes, patched a hundred times, give off a sheen.
My gown has no collar, and my pants have no bottom;
My socks have no soles, and my shoes have no uppers.
    A student of books down on his luck, turned into a beggar—
How could I ever be a match for such a pretty young lady?
So I urge you, young lady, plant your flower elsewhere;
Select a scion of a lofty family, of some great house!"

"If you need clothes, we have plenty of them at home;
All the baskets and chests are filled with clothes of all kinds.
If you have no hat to wear, I'll embroider one for you;
If you have no shoes to wear, I will make you a pair.
    Darling brother, you make sure to wait here in the tree,
And I will go off to my house to get you some clothes.
Don't sneak away as soon as I have left, because
Then all my good intentions will have been in vain!"

STEPPING INTO THE POND

Jiangnü hurried back home as fast as she could;
Running all the way, she went to her embroidery room.
She took the keys that dangled and jangled on the ring,
And she opened the chests, and she opened the boxes.

She took out one single hat embroidered with flowers;
She took out one pair of socks made of glistening silk.
She also took out new embroidered shoes from Suzhou;
She also took out a silken gown that shimmered in the sun.

Her little heart wanted to go even faster than her feet;
As if flying on her feet, she arrived back at the pond.
She called out, "Brother!" she called out, "Darling,
Please stretch out your hand and get these clothes!"

When Qiliang received the clothes that Jiangnü had brought,
He panicked as if doused by a bucket of water!
Holding on to the willow, he descended step by step and
Made up his mind to argue the matter with Jiangnü:
    "What kind of whore are you, what kind of prostitute,
That you step into a pond in clear daylight, for all to see?
Why would a virgin, a proper young lady, take such a bath?
You have done this on purpose to seduce me, Fan Qiliang!
    In the event your father comes to know of this affair,
I am afraid you may be in danger of losing your life!
In the event your mother comes to know of this affair,
She will skin you alive and then pull out your tendons!
    Even if your parents stopped you from making mischief,
I would send back the eight characters, destroy the red card!¹⁶
In the end this is as useless as fetching water in a bamboo basket—
For all eternity, a thousand years, your name will be cursed!"

"You may curse me for being a whore and a prostitute,
But you are a criminal on the run from the king of Qin!
If you refuse to marry me and become my husband,
I will go back to my house and inform my parents.
    I will tell them that you are a criminal on the run
And tell them you tried to rape their little Meng Jiang!

心
田
。

思
心

魚

和

為

They'll inform the magistrate, who'll have you arrested;
Then he will put you on transport, back to Xianyang!
　　You'll be led before the king of Qin in his golden palace,
Who'll allow you to taste a hundred kinds of tortures.
From a student once again a conscript laborer at the Wall,
Whose corpse will be buried far away from his home.
　　Add 'heart' to the character 'field':[17] think it over—
The outcome, good or bad, is all up to you, Mr. Fan!"

"Mention the king of Qin, and I am trembling with fear,
Just as if I had run into a living Yama, king of hell!
I am just like a fish that has escaped from the hook;
I am just like an eagle that has fled from its cage.
　　But as I am a fugitive conscript laborer of the king of Qin,
How could I ever be a match for you, young lady?
If ever the king of Qin came to know of this,
I'd implicate two families in my problem with the law.
　　I love you for your thousand kinds of friendliness, but
I couldn't bear to be the fire that would burn your body!"

"You may be a fugitive laborer of the king of Qin,
But the king of Qin has not carved your name in stone.
When the two of us, you and I, have become a couple,
The name fits the facts, and the words are correct."

"When taking a groom, he should be an official's son;
When finding a husband, he should be a man of power.
Please, young lady, don't marry a man who carries earth,
A match with a man who carries earth cannot last for long."

"I do not want to marry the son of an official family,
Nor do I want to marry a man of power and wealth.
I love only the king of Qin's man who carries earth;
I'll marry the king of Qin's guy who hauls earth!
　　You, elder brother, down on your luck, are so nice,
This match with a man who carries earth will last long!"

STEPPING INTO THE POND

"You are like heaven, and I am like the earth;
Compare heaven to earth: they are no match at all!
I am like a black crow, and you are like a phoenix;
How can a black crow be a match for a phoenix?"

"You are like heaven, and I am like the earth:
All creatures are born from the union of heaven and earth!
You are like the dragon, and I am like the phoenix:
From the union of dragon and phoenix comes eternal spring!"

"Please, young lady, please, please allow me to mention
The pitiable hearts of parents, the same all over the world.
My parents are waiting for their son, a son who doesn't return;
I've been separated from my brothers now for a few years!
    Even a wandering son and a drifting ghost hope to get home;
Let me go back, and then I'll return to be married to you!"
    "Once you and I have tied the knot as husband and wife,
I'll saddle a horse so you may go and fetch your parents.
Your parents-in-law will receive them in their house,
And the two families will be united together as one.
    From early till late I will serve them most obediently;
I will make sure they feel comfortable and at ease."
    "Without clouds in the sky there will fall no rain,
And without a matchmaker there will be no marriage.
Who are you going to use as the matchmaker for us?
What are you going to use as the wedding wine for us?
    Tell me the three matchmakers and the six witnesses;
Only then can we tie the knot as husband and wife."
    "The camphor tree to the east will be the male matchmaker:
The tree is big, its roots run deep, it grows to a thousand rods!
The willow tree to the west will be the female matchmaker,
Because the willow tree hid my lover amongst its leaves.
    The lotus leaves will serve as the wine cups we exchange:
The threads in their roots so hard to break, a love so strong.[18]
The water from the well by the pond is the wedding wine;
As long as we are loving and good, even water is fragrant!

243

These four are all things that live forever and forever—
As long as heaven and earth we will be mandarin-ducks!"

"With one stroke you have settled the sound of the drum;
Such a pure love as yours, darling, is rare to find indeed.
I'll go to Main Street to have our eight characters compared
And also rent a bridal sedan to come and fetch the bride."

"There's no need for you, darling, to compare the characters;
There's no need for you, darling, to bring a bridal-sedan.
There's no need for you, darling, to hire trumpet players;
All I want you to do, my darling, is to have a loving heart.
    Don't be like the sieve that has a thousand eyes;
Just be like a candle of wax, which has only a single heart!"

When Fan Xiliang heard this, he hastily made a bow,
And our little Meng Jiang blushed even behind her ears!
She took the clothes and gave them to Fan Xiliang to wear,
And she took the hat and put it on his head for him.
    He put on the socks, and he also put on the shoes,
And his whole body now was dressed sparklingly new.
The beggar had been turned into a handsome young fellow;
The pond served as a mirror when he looked at the groom!
    They plucked two lotus flowers that were full of buds,
And each affixed one flower to the other's breast.
As a pair, holding hands, they bowed to Heaven and Earth,
And they also bowed to the willow tree as their matchmaker.
    They plucked a lotus leaf to hold the water from the well;
They exchanged this wedding wine: it sweetened their hearts.
They plucked a lotus leaf to serve as their blanket of silk;
They plucked a willow branch to serve as their ivory bed.
    This enticed pairs of butterflies to flutter all about them;
This seduced numberless couples of larks to sing their songs.
The willow tree felt so ashamed it deeply lowered its head;
Its myriads of strands serving the couple as their bridal chamber.

STEPPING INTO THE POND

The lotus root was so ashamed it sank deeply into the pond,
Thread after thread connected together: an everlasting love!
It is commonly said that a man carrying earth married Meng Jiangnü;
We all sing the story of Meng Jiangnü, who married her Fan Qiliang.
We celebrate a couple of stars that flies across, growing old together;[19]
Our only wish being that this hundred-year marriage may last forever!

9

SLEEPING WITH THE BONES

IN THE DISTRICT OF JIANGYONG, IN SOUTHERNMOST HUNAN, the local women developed their own script. This women's script, or *nü shu*, most likely developed from standard Chinese characters (locally designated as "men's script") through continuous simplification until one sign was left for each distinct syllable in the local dialect. The local women used this script in the nineteenth and twentieth centuries not only to write their own compositions but also to transcribe ballads and songs written in standard characters. Their choice of tales for transcription is very interesting as it represents a selection from traditional narrative by women for women. Not surprisingly perhaps, almost every ballad transcribed into women's script features a strong female protagonist. At the same time, many of the selected stories stress a wife's loyalty to an absent husband.

The first outside reference to Jiangyong's women's script dates to shortly before the Anti-Japanese War (1937–45). When the Liberation Army entered this area in 1949, they initially took women's script for a secret code of the enemy. Later attempts to train women to sing the praises of the new regime using women's script were not very successful, and during the Cultural Revolution a considerable quantity of materials in women's script were destroyed.

Many of the currently available materials in women's script were written down in the 1980s when local cultural workers and outside scholars encouraged the few remaining elderly women who still knew the script to record these tales from memory. Yi Nianhua (1907–1991) was one of the very productive women in this endeavor. Printed collections of texts written in women's script contain two texts on Meng Jiangnü. One of these texts, written down from memory by Yi Nianhua, is clearly fragmentary. But in 1986, Yi Nianhua, with the assistance of the local cultural worker Zhou Shuoyi, also prepared a complete transcription of a long ballad that was locally available as a songbook. This latter version is presented here.[1] The text is composed in seven-syllable verse from beginning to end.

The translations are based on the texts in Zhao Liming's *A Collective Edition of Writings in China's Women's Script* (Zhongguo nüshu jicheng).[2] In this edition, each line of verse is accompanied by a transcription in the International Phonetic Alphabet and in standard Chinese characters. My translations are based on the Chinese-character transcriptions.

Anonymous

THE MAIDEN MENG JIANG

The maiden Meng Jiang wept at the Long Wall—
For all eternity, a thousand years, her fame will endure.
    If you want to know why Meng Jiang acted this way,
Just listen as I will tell you everything very clearly.
The maiden Jiang was born in the region of Youzhou;[3]
Her father was known by the name of Meng Nengren.
    The maiden Meng Jiang was his one and only child,
So she was not allowed to leave the house at will.
But because of the First Night of the First Month, she
Put on her jewelry and dressed up to view the lanterns.
    She combed her hair, did it up in a coiled-dragon bun,
And she dressed herself in a dress of fresh new colors.
In her hair she placed eight-jewel golden hairpins;
She looked just like Guanyin of the Southern Sea.
    When she observed her face in the bright bronze mirror,
She truly was the most beautiful person in the world!
When she came out of the room and stepped forward,
She resembled an immortal maiden descending to earth.

Ever since she had seen the First Night festival crowd,
Her passion was roused and her love-longing stirred.
When she returned to her room, she thought to herself,
Thought to herself, "This year I've turned eighteen!

Since earliest times an adult man will take a wife;
When a girl is grown up, she should marry a husband.
I'm afraid my parents are not paying any attention
And have no intention as yet to arrange my marriage!"

Let's not talk about Meng Jiang and her longings,
But let's turn our attention now to the king of Qin.
The king of Qin, fearful of an invasion by others,
Wanted to build a myriad-mile wall in the east.

This meant the people's star of disaster appeared:
It was the First Emperor, that ruler bereft of the Way!
He summoned the hundred officials to hear his orders;
He also summoned all the high officers in his court.

That very day the First Emperor issued an edict:
Each region, prefecture, and county was to make known
That one man out of three was drafted, two out of five;
Based on money and grain the people were to be fed.

In Nanyang in Dengzhou lived a certain Fan Changchun,
Whose family owned more than five hundred *mu* of good fields.[4]
His only child was a son by the name of Fan Qilang,
A student who lived at home and studied the books.

He was drafted as a laborer to work on the Long Wall,
And his family hired one replacement after another.
So when the district once again delivered a notice,
No money was left to hire yet another replacement.

There was no other way out than to go by himself;
He prepared his luggage and set out on the journey.
After he had been in the Eastern Capital for more than a year,[5]
Not a penny was left of the ready cash he had brought.

And so he had no alternative but to work hauling rice;
For each load he transported, he made five coppers.
How many heroes died in that way of exhaustion!
And how many fine young men died of starvation!

Fan Qilang then thought to himself in his heart:

249

"If I continue this way, I'm bound to lose my life.
My best chance is to sneak away, flee for my life,
And return back home to continue the family line."

He would have liked to travel over the broad open road,
But feared he might be caught there by soldiers.
It would be better to take the small country roads;
On those small country roads it was easier to hide.

If he traveled by daylight, people might spot him,
So he could walk on the road only during nighttime.
After he had traveled on for a number of nights,
He happened to arrive in Meng Family Village.

In front of the Meng mansion was a lotus pond;
The lotus leaves in the pond provided protection.
At this time it happened to be the sixth of the Sixth;[6]
The grains in the fields promised a fine harvest.

Every family and household was filled with joy
And burned incense and paper to thank the gods.
Nengren, who wanted to thank Heaven and Earth,
Ordered Meng Jiang to burn incense at the temple.

He ordered his daughter first to go to the pond
And purify her body before thanking the gods.
When she had received this order from her father,
Meng Jiang happily walked out onto the street.

When she arrived at the pond, she looked around:
Not a person was to be seen in whichever direction.
Only after she had carefully looked all around her,
Only then did she start to take off her clothes.

She started by taking off her silk upper garment;
Next she took off her embroidered gauze skirt.
The tender skin of her body a lotus-root white—
She was ready to step in the pond to bathe her body.

Just as Meng Jiang stepped forward stark naked,
She all of a sudden discovered a student. No need
To tell of her panic as she hastily fled. Even that
Fan Qi was completely frightened out of his wits!

Meng Jiang promptly started to put on her clothes,

SLEEPING WITH THE BONES

But as she put on her clothes, she watched the boy.
And while putting on her clothes, she told him,
She immediately told him to meet her parents!

Fan Qi, afraid that a police officer might arrive,
Had no option at all but to go along with her.
When the two of them arrived at the Meng mansion,
Nengren immediately asked, "Who is this boy?

Why did you try to rape my daughter at the pond?
We will definitely hand you over to the magistrate!"
Fan Qi was so scared, his heart jumped in his throat,
And he called out, "Dear sir, please let me explain!

My family lives in the Nanyang district of Qinzhou;[7]
My father is surnamed Fan and is quite well known.
It's the fault of the First Emperor, who, bereft of the Way,
Wants to build a myriad-mile wall at Chang'an.[8]

My family had a few hundred *mu* of fields,
But we sold them all to hire replacements for me.
When the county had yet another notice delivered,
There was, alas, no alternative but to go myself.

When I had gone and worked for more than a year,
Not a penny was left of the money I'd brought.
From then I had to rely on government rations:
Each man each day got only half a pint of rice.

How many heroes there died of exhaustion!
Watching it from nearby, my heart was broken!
That is the reason I took flight that very night,
And I only dared to walk on the roads at night.

When I came to the pond, I hid myself there;
Running into your daughter gave me quite a scare!
Dear sir, if you today are willing to pardon me,
I'll burn my flesh as incense to repay your grace!"

When Mr. Meng heard him speak like this, he
Realized this was someone who was to be pitied.
So he asked him this time, "How old are you now?
What are the year, month, and day of your birth?

Do you or don't you already have a wife at home?

And what is your business? Please let me know!"
Fan Qi answered Mr. Meng in the following words,
"Dear sir, please allow me to provide an explanation.

This year I am now eighteen years old, and I was
Born at noon on the first day of the Tenth Month.
At home I occupied myself by studying the books,
And since my youth I've never been engaged."

Mr. Meng and his wife addressed him as follows,
"Young student, please accept our proposal.
You right now are eighteen years of age
And of exactly the same age as our daughter.

Since ancient times a girl at that age should marry,
And when a man turns eighteen, he should take a wife.
I will marry my daughter to you to be your wife
And ask Third Uncle to serve as the matchmaker."

His wife replied, "You have spoken quite well.
The events of today really please my heart."
They invited Third Uncle to be the matchmaker
And treated relatives and neighbors to a banquet.

When these guests had finished the wedding wine,
Meng Jiang and her husband entered the bridal chamber.
Husband and wife entered the red gauze bed curtains:
A pair of mandarin-ducks, joined together by Heaven!

In the first watch: just like the phoenix seeking a mate,
Cooing together with a common tone of voice!
In the second watch: just like the Western Wing story,
They resembled Student Zhang wedding Yingying!⁹

In the third watch: just like the fish playing in the stream,
They acted like the carp jumping across Dragon Gate!
In the fourth watch: just like a pair of turning millstones,
Mouth against mouth and heart against heart!

In the fifth watch the Golden Rooster announced dawn,
And only after a little sleep the sky had turned bright!
One day turned to three, and three days turned to nine:
Husband and wife spent their time in happy harmony!

Mr. Meng and his wife too were filled with joy;

The whole household was enjoying this plenitude.
Who could know that misfortune soon was to strike
And that a terrible disaster was about to befall?

　　The laborers building the Wall all had fled;
Each region, prefecture, and county put up posters.
Those who were arrested counted in the millions;
Each one who was arrested substituted for two.

　　The Meng mansion was visited by a ward-leader,
Who declared that Fan Qi was an escaped laborer.
He also went to the county to report his name, and
Two runners were dispatched to arrest their man.

　　The two police officers arrived in great haste;
Once they arrested Fan Qi, they set out to depart.
Meng Jiang stepped forward and cordially said,
"Dear officers, please do not be in such a hurry!

　　I have golden hairpins that weigh three ounces;
I also have here twenty ounces of finest silver.
Since ancient times enlightened officials do good;
Whenever they can spare a man, they'll spare him."

　　The two officers replied as follows to her words,
"We police officers have to be very circumspect;
We would not dare demand your gold and silver!
Please ready his luggage quickly so we may go!"

　　Meng Jiang at that moment fainted and collapsed,
And her two elderly parents were awash in tears.
Fan Qi hastily helped his wife to her feet again,
And, once revived, Meng Jiang sent her husband off.

　　She saw her husband off for one mile, coming to the gate,
All the while stamping her feet and beating her breast.
"I'd hoped that husband and wife would stay together forever.
Who could have known this flower would bloom in vain?"

　　She saw her husband off for two miles, passing by the gate,
And a pair of mandarin-ducks took wing and flew off.
"When mandarin-ducks take wing, they fly a thousand miles;
They only long to be a couple, refusing to be separated!"

　　She saw her husband off for three miles, to the pavilion;

She led Fan Qi by the hand, had him accept a jacket-front.
"I give these two pieces making up a jacket-front to you—
It is so easy to see you off, it'll be so hard to see you again!"

She saw her husband off for four miles, to a field,
And as she looked at the field, her tears coursed down.
"I will sow the seeds of the five grains in this field,
But if the field lacks water, they will not grow!"

She saw her husband off for five miles, to a bridge;
Both of them, hand in hand, watched the water flow.
"Never be like the water below the bridge, as it only
Flows off toward the Eastern Ocean and never returns!"

She saw her husband off for six miles, to a pond;
The wind on the lotus leaves spread their fragrance.
"Because of roots and leaves the flowers bear fruit;
Without roots and leaves they'd not form a couple."

She saw her husband off to the seven-mile rapids,
Reminding her of the Weaving Maid and the Oxherd.
"Never be like the Oxherd and the Weaving Maid—
Husband and wife for eternity but forever divorced!"

She saw her husband off for eight miles, to a garden;
She saw the bright flowers, and her tears coursed down.
"Flowers bloom and flowers fade, every year anew,
But human beings are unable to regain their youth!"

She saw her husband off for nine miles, across a hill,
And wildflowers were blooming all over that hill.
"My husband, never pluck wildflowers on a hill,
Because if you do, you'd be breaking my heart!"[10]

She saw her husband off for ten miles, to a dike,
Where she gave her gold and silver to her husband.
She also implored his escorts in a friendly manner
To take good care of Fan Qi, "my darling husband!"

Let's not talk about Meng Jiang seeing her husband off;
Let's speak of Fan Qi, arriving in the Eastern Capital.
As soon as his commanding officer saw Fan Qi return,
He gnashed his teeth and repeatedly cursed him.

As a greeting he gave him thirty strokes of the rod;
Afterward he had him taken to the jail and locked up.

SLEEPING WITH THE BONES

Alas, Fan Qi had had no food or drink for three days,
And he died there in the jail of hunger and starvation.

As nobody came and claimed his body for burial,
His bones were dumped inside the myriad-mile Wall.

Let's not go on about Fan Qi's return to the shades,
But let's return again to the subject of Meng Jiang.
Ever since her separation from her darling husband,
She waited at home every day for his return home.

In the First Month of longing it was the New Year!
"Lanterns of glass are hung up in front of the hall.
Other families now are all drinking New Year wine,
But it's only my Fan Qi who is far away from here."

In the Second Month all the flowers were blooming!
"I'm just like Zhao Wuniang longing for Cai Yong.[11]
The swallows on the rafters know to come and go;
It is only my husband I do not see coming back home."

In the Third Month it was the time of Clear and Bright.
"Every family and household goes out to sweep the graves.
All other people sweep the graves with their husbands,
But only I, Meng Jiang, have to walk alone."

The Fourth Month is the season for picking mulberry leaves,
And Meng Jiang went out alone to pick mulberry leaves.
"My hand grabs the branches, but I don't pick the leaves,
As my heart is taken up by longing for my Fan Qilang."

In the Fifth Month people celebrate Double Five, and
On the racing boats the beaten drums roar and rumble.
"Other people now all drink their Double Five wine,
But I still don't see my Fan Qilang coming back home."

In the Sixth Month it was again the feast of Double Six;
Last year on this same day she had found her husband.
"When I think back to the day of our first meeting,
I cannot stop myself from weeping as he still is not back!"

In the Seventh Month people celebrate Middle Prime,
"Every family and household welcomes its ancestors back.[12]
Your wife here has been waiting for you past the fifteenth;
Out of longing for my Fan Qi, my tears keep on flowing."

In the Eighth Month people celebrate Mid-Autumn.

"The moon is fully rounded, yet I'm filled with sorrow;
My Fan Qilang is far away, and I never got any letter.
My longing for my absent husband increases my grief."
    In the Ninth Month people celebrate Double Nine.
"I'm just like Li Sanniang longing for Liu Zhiyuan.[13]
In other homes husband and wife together drink wine,
But my husband is staying in a region far away."
    In the Tenth Month it was the beginning of winter.
"Without karmic cause man and wife don't come together.
Can it be that in a former life I did not practice virtue,
And that now I am in the west and he is in the east?"
    In the month of winter the snowflakes swirled about;
Her longing for her husband was wrecking her heart.
"Despite the cold weather my husband is still not back;
I'd like to go and find him, but the journey is so far!"
    In the Last Month she longed till New Year's Eve,
"All year long I have been waiting and watching.
All other families now drink New Year's Eve wine,
But Fan Qilang and I still are not yet together again."
    She waited for him for a year, and then another year:
In this life husband and wife were never complete.
All day long she longed for her husband, each day!
In her room by herself her tears coursed down.
    After she had considered the case from all directions,
She decided to go to the capital to find her husband.
So Meng Jiang addressed her parents as follows,
"I will go and travel in person to Chang'an!
    And because the weather is so terribly cold,
I will take my husband an extra set of clothes."
    Her parents in the hall answered her as follows,
"My child, please listen to what we have to say.
You are only a girl, so how would you be able
To travel all by yourself to such a faraway place?"
    Meng Jiang addressed her parents once more,
"Your daughter really has made up her mind!
A good woman can enter a crowd of a thousand men;
She doesn't fear the other party, more than a myriad!

But because of my love for my married husband,
I am not afraid of high mountains or long roads.
When I find my husband, we'll come back together,
And I'll leave a lasting reputation for all eternity.

If something or another untoward might happen,
I can stand a myriad cuts or a thousand wounds.
Here in front of my parents I make the vow that I
Will not return home unless I find my man!"

She took her leave of her parents, and she left,
Crossing rivers and mountains to seek her husband.
Holding a lute in her hands, she walked in front;
Her servant girl followed, carrying the luggage.

She crossed thousands and thousands of mountains;
She crossed thousands and thousands of rivers.
She suffered endless hardship on her journey;
Seeking her husband, she arrived at the Long Wall.

Seeking here and there, she did not find him,
And unexpectedly she arrived at a temple,
Where she asked the priest to tell her fortune;
Her question was where to find her husband.

The priest replied to her in the following words,
"This hexagram I obtained is not very lucky.
It is hard to tell you the hexagram's message:
Most likely he's dead and will not revive!"

When Meng Jiang heard these words,
She burst into tears and could not stop crying.
She went to the office of his commanding officer,
And she asked him for her husband, Fan Qilang.

He replied to her, "Indeed, we had a Fan Qilang;
Last year he was killed on the execution ground.
Because nobody claimed his bones for burial,
We then buried him in the myriad-mile Wall."

When Meng Jiang heard this, she wept loudly,
Weeping and wailing in a most saddening way.
She wept for three days and then for three nights,
Moved Heaven and Earth, and crumbled the wall!

Meng Jiang recovered her husband's bones;

She carried them home and put them in her room.
Each night she slept alongside her husband's bones,
And never in her life did she marry any other man.

    This is the end of the story of Meng Jiang, who left
A beautiful reputation that will last through eternity.

10

FORBIDDEN DESIRES

THE FOLLOWING TEXT, TITLED SIMPLY *MENG JIANGNÜ*, provides a highly idiosyncratic version of the legend. It was recorded in 1984 on Dongtou, a small island off the Zhejiang coast near Wenzhou, in Dayao village, Sanpan township. The translation is based on the text in *A Complete Collection of China's Songs and Ballads: Zhejiang* (Zhongguo geyao jicheng: Zhejiang juan). The final note appended to this edition of the text informs us that the ballad was performed by Huang Zhicai and Zhu Honghua and recorded by Cai Gengyao. The genre of the ballad is given as *shange*, or "mountain songs," a term that is widely used to refer to folksongs and popular ballads.[1] *Meng Jiangnü* is composed in lines of seven-syllable verse.

This relatively short text is included because it provides a quite novel explanation for the First Emperor's desire to build the Wall. During a visit to the heavenly palace of the goddess Nü Wa (who gave birth to mankind after marrying her brother Fu Xi), the First Emperor makes a pass at the Weaving Maid, and her sisters punish him with an incestuous desire for his mother, who sets him the impossible condition of building a wall that will rise up to the sky and block out the sun.

Anonymous

MENG JIANGNÜ

Look at this wooden wall, with its marvelous painting,
A painting of times long ago, of the Emperor of the Qin:
Riding a deer, he ascended the Heavenly Terrace;
On the road he passed by the palace of Nü Wa,
And there he met with all of the seven heavenly sisters.
  The Seventh Sister came and served him a cup of tea;
The Qin emperor was filled with evil desire at first sight.
The immortal maiden, he saw, was of exceptional beauty,
And he stroked her arm for the length of three inches.
  Once a mortal had stroked her, she smelled like a human,
And the Jade Emperor up in heaven was fully informed.
As soon as he saw this, the Jade Emperor flew into a rage;
He drew his sword and chopped off Seventh Sister's head.
  Her discarded corpse fell down to the world of men;
One half of it was yin, and the other half of it was yang.
The part that was yin became Meng Jiangnü of Qingzhou;
The part that was yang became Fan Xiliang of Hangzhou.[2]
  Her six immortal sisters were outraged in their hearts

And blamed the Qin emperor for his evil behavior.
They plucked a magic flower and also a magic blossom
And had the Qin emperor take these to the mortal world.

When the empress wore this flower, the flower wilted;
When the empress-dowager wore the blossom, she shone.
Alas, the emperor of the Qin was evil in all his ways;
The empress-dowager, he saw, was of exceptional beauty,
And he wanted to make the empress-dowager his empress![3]

The empress-dowager said:
"If you want to raise me to the rank of empress, you must
Build a wall in the Eastern Capital that will block out the sun!"
That stupid ruler, obeying the words of the empress-dowager,
Dispatched the commander-in-chief, someone called Zhang.

At low tide they then built the first three feet of the Wall,
But at high tide it was completely washed away by the waves.
The commander-in-chief reported to the throne that he needed
A myriad of men to make a firm foundation for the Wall.

That stupid emperor agreed to the commander's request,
And the good citizens, the common people, suffered sorely.
From three they drafted one, from four they drafted two,
And in this way they drafted Fan Xiliang from Hangzhou.

When Young Master Xiliang heard this information,
He could do nothing else but leave his home and village.
He fled to Qingzhou, to the house of Meng Jiangnü, and,
Once they had met, they tied the knot as mandarin-ducks.

After seven days in the bridal chamber, six nights together,
The imperial commissioner arrested him: off to the steppe!
Other wives see their husbands off in front of the gate,
But Meng Jiangnü accompanied him for more than ten miles!

She informed her father and mother in the hall that she
Wanted to deliver his clothes to her husband and lord,
That she wanted to take him his padded clothes to wear,
Wanted to take him his winter clothes: off to the steppe!

When her six immortal sisters learned about this,
They gave her a danger-candle and some danger-incense.

When she wanted to cross the river at Silvergrass Ford,
Zhang San and Li Si were both filled with evil desire.[4]

They brought the boat to a stop in the middle of the river;
They wanted to force her to tie the knot as mandarin-ducks.
As soon as Jiangnü saw this, her scared souls scattered;
She lighted the danger-candle, burnt some danger-incense.
Her six immortal sisters immediately arrived, all together,
And huge waves rose up right in the middle of the river.
Zhang San and Li Si were half dead with fright
And could not but ferry her across the Yangzi River.
When Jiangnü arrived at the Eastern Capital,[5] she was
Obsessed with finding her husband there on the steppe.
She walked all along the Wall but found not a trace;
Weeping and wailing, her sad tears would wound you.
Alas, that emperor of the Qin was evil in all his ways.
Jiangnü was, he observed, of an exceptional beauty,
So he wanted to raise Jiangnü to the rank of empress.
    Jiangnü said:
"If you really want to raise me to the rank of empress,
You must construct a floating bridge across the river.
You have to invite five priests and Buddhist monks
To secure the release of Young Master Fan Xiliang;[6]
You yourself have to wear mourning as a filial son,
And then I will be happy to become your empress."
That stupid lord promptly obeyed Jiangnü's request,
And a floating bridge was constructed across the river.
He himself wore mourning and mourned as a filial son
To ensure the release of Young Master Fan Xiliang.
Jiangnü walked onto the floating bridge, while she
Stamped her feet and beat her breast, weeping piteously.
If she walked one step, she stamped her feet once;
If she stepped two steps, she stamped her feet twice,
Then she sank into the Seven-Continent Yangzi River[7]
And rushed off to the land of a myriad of Springs.[8]
The eastern corridor's wooden wall—its painting is long!

NOTES

MENG JIANGNÜ: THE DEVELOPMENT OF A LEGEND

1   Waldron, in *The Great Wall of China*, provides a detailed discussion of the wall-building activities of the Ming dynasty, the earlier walls, and the changing interpretations of the Wall over the centuries. A more popular account is provided in Lovell, *The Great Wall*. Both books contain only brief references to the story of Meng Jiangnü. Also see Claire Roberts and Geremie R. Barmé, eds., *The Great Wall of China* (Sydney: Powerhouse Publishing, 2006) for a fine catalogue of an exhibition on the theme of China's border walls and the border culture through the ages, accompanied by a number of historical essays. In featuring the Great Wall on their maps of China, the Jesuits were actually following the example of those Chinese maps from the Song dynasty (960–1278) and later, which mark the border between Chinese lands and their northern neighbors by a conspicuous wall.

2   For the various meanings of "weeping" (*ku*) in pre-imperial China, see Harbsmeier, "Weeping and Wailing in Ancient China." "Weeping" or "wailing" was a strictly prescribed part of the mourning ritual. Whereas in late centuries, upper-class women were not expected to engage in loud and public displays of grief as part of mourning and funeral rituals, peasant women continued to do so in many parts of China until quite recently; see, for instance, Johnson, "Grieving

for the Dead" and "Singing of Separation" (both based on fieldwork conducted in the New Territories of Hong Kong). *Kusangge*, edited by Ren Jiahe et al., is a collection of funeral laments from Nanhui (near Shanghai).

3 While this is the accepted text of this sentence, various early sources strongly suggest that it originally read: "Approaching the corpse of her husband, she wept at the foot of the wall."

4 Wang Zhaoyuan, *Lienü zhuan buzhu*, 68–69.

5 Ch'iu-kuei Wang, "Formation of the Early Versions," 117–18.

6 DeWoskin and Crump, Jr., *In Search of the Supernatural*, 137–38.

7 Dunhuang is a small town in westernmost Gansu. In medieval times, it was a major station on the Silk Road. Shortly after the year 1000, the library of one of the Buddhist monasteries was stored in a side cave of a cave temple outside the city, and the side cave was then walled up. This library of up to fifty thousand manuscripts was rediscovered in 1900.

8 Arthur Waley, *Ballads and Stories from Tun-huang*, 56–64.

9 Ma Changyi, "Li Fuqing Meng Jiangnü yanjiu," in Gu, Zhong, et al., *Meng Jiangnü gushi lunwenji*, 180–203.

10 As quoted in Waldron, *Great Wall of China*, 17 (transcription of Chinese terms adapted). A *li* measures roughly six hundred meters; as the basic measure of distance, it is often translated as "mile."

11 *The Zuo Tradition* has been preserved in the shape of a commentary of the *Annals of Spring and Autumn* (Chunqiu), one of the Five Classics.

12 In my translations, I prefer a more literal rendition of "Changcheng" as "Long Wall," rather than "Great Wall."

13 This translation is based on the Chinese text as reproduced in Huang Ruiqi, *Meng Jiangnü gushi yanjiu*, 51.

14 As for the date of this particular commentary, one can say only that it must have been compiled after 732.

15 This translation is based on the Chinese text as provided in Huang Ruiqi, *Meng Jiangnü gushi yanjiu*, 74. Li Shan is a famous seventh-century commentator of the *Selections of Refined Literature*.

16 This translation is based on the Chinese text as provided by Huang Ruiqi, *Meng Jiangnü gushi yanjiu*, 69.

17 This translation is based on the Chinese text as provided in ibid., 74.

18 The phrase "the mountains of Long" refers to the border area of modern Shaanxi and Gansu.

19 In drafts of a sacrificial text, the exact dates are often left blank, to be filled in later when the dates have been set and the formal text, which often will be burned as part of the ritual, is prepared.

20 This translation is based on the extensively annotated Chinese text provided in

Xiang Chu, *Dunhuang bianwen xuanzhu*, 94–105. For an earlier translation, see Waley, *Ballads and Stories from Tun-huang*, 145–49. Also see Ch'iu-kuei Wang, "Tun-huang Versions," 67–81.

21 Many vernacular stories recovered from Dunhuang conclude with the recital of a funerary text of some kind, strongly suggesting that this text on Meng Jiangnü would have ended with the text of her prayer.

22 Some more recent versions of the legend from outside Shaanxi confuse Tongguan county (now Tongchuan municipality, to the north of Xi'an) with Tong Pass (Tong Guan, to the east of Xi'an). Tong Pass is the name of the fortifications that dominated the main road from Henan into Shaanxi.

23 Zheng Qiao, "Yue zhi," in his *Tongzhi*, quoted in Huang Ruiqi, *Meng Jiangnü gushi yanjiu*, 107.

24 Sun and Huang, *Fengyue jinnang jianjiao*, 633.

25 The motif of the lovers who break a bronze mirror in two and each keep one part so that they can confirm their identities after a forced separation is first encountered in the tale of the Lechang princess and her husband. The story dates from the Tang dynasty and was often adapted for the stage.

26 No early vernacular novel on the life of Meng Jiangnü has been preserved, and it is not known that one ever existed. Her story is retold only in a collection of vernacular stories of the final decades of the Ming dynasty, the anonymous *Vernacular Tales on Personalities of Seventy-two Reigns* (Qishi'er chao renwu yanyi), as an "introductory tale" (*ruhua*) to "How the Wives of Hua Zhou and Qi Liang Changed the Customs of Their State by Being Good at Weeping for Their Husbands" (Hua Zhou Qi Liang zhi qi shan ku qi fu er bian guosu) . See *Qishi'er chao renwu yanyi*, 422–23.

27 The title given here is the one used for the excerpted edition of the text in Lu, *Meng Jiangnü wanli xunfu ji*. This work most likely is a somewhat later redaction of a precious scroll known as *Xiaoshi Meng Jiang Zhonglie zhenjie xianliang baojuan*. For a detailed discussion of the text in this latter edition, see Ch'iu-kuei Wang, "The *Hsiao-shih Meng Chiang Chung-lieh Chen-chieh Hsien-liang Pao-chüan*." Wang's discussion was based on the manuscript in the possession of Sawada Mizuho. A reprint of an edition of 1714 (Kangxi 53) may be found in Zhang, *Baojuan chuji*, vol. 11.

28 Lu, *Meng Jiangnü wanli xunfu ji*, 313. Lu Gong has often been criticized for his sloppy editing, but his compilation remains useful as it brings together many texts that are not easily found elsewhere.

29 Needless to say, versions of the legend originating outside the Jiangnan area provide quite different accounts of Meng Jiangnü's journey to the Great Wall.

30 Hung, *Going to the People*, 46–49, 93–99. For a recent evaluation of Gu Jiegang's contribution to the study of traditional popular literature, see Gu Chao, "Gu

Jiegang de suwenxue yanjiu," in Chen, *Xiandai xueshushi shangde suwenxue*, 449–56. For a modern edition of Gu Jiegang's publications concerning Meng Jiangnü and the works of many other scholars of the time, see Gu Jiegang, *Meng Jiangnü gushi yanjiu ji*. Gu's own writings are also reproduced in *Gu Jiegang minsuxue lunwenji*.

31 Lu, *Meng Jiangnü wanli xunfu ji*, 1.

32 *"Meng Jiang nü" shi yizhu zunru fanfa de da ducao*, 1. This pamphlet credits all versions of the tale to "literati" (*wenren*).

33 Lee, "Tears That Crumbled the Great Wall." *Meng Jiang nü*, a Chinese-style comic book by Guo Shuzu and Li Wendou, "based on a draft provided by the Bureau for the Administration of Cultural Relics of Shanhaiguan," solves the problem of the negative portrayal of the First Emperor by replacing him as the villain of the piece with the eunuch Zhao Gao, whose machinations, according to traditional historiography, were instrumental in hastening the downfall of the Qin dynasty.

34 For brief discussions of this text, which was widely available and has also been reproduced by Lu Gong in his *Meng Jiangnü wanli xunfu ji*, 113–216, see Ch'iu-kuei Wang, "From Pao-chüan to Ballad," 62–63, and Yang, *Meng Jiangnü yanjiu*, 254–56. Wang notes the link of this text to the Jiangnan ballads (a representative of which is translated in chapter 3 of this volume). Yang Zhenliang points out that the same Wenyi Bookstore that published this version also published a twelve-chapter retelling, *Meng Jiangnü, a Sentimental Novel* (Aiqing xiaoshuo Meng Jiangnü). In the sixteen-chapter prosimetric version, Meng Jiangnü accidentally falls into the garden pond as she is trying to capture a butterfly. When she travels to the Wall accompanied by one male and one female servant, the two servants are killed by the evil servant Meng Xing, who earlier had been dispatched to the Wall but had squandered the money entrusted to him. When Meng Xing tries to force Meng Jiangnü to have sex with him, she tricks him, and he falls to his death in a ravine. After various other new incidents on the road, the Bodhisattva (or Mahasattva) Guanyin assists Meng Jiangnü to reach the Wall in seven days and nights. Following her confrontation with the First Emperor, in this version, Meng Jiangnü jumps into the Yalu River.

35 Occasionally, strong local oral traditions survived in the countryside outside the big cities. The rural areas of southern Jiangsu and the municipality of Shanghai turned out to be the home of a rich tradition of orally transmitted, long, narrative "mountain songs" (*shange*) in the Wu dialect. The mountain song on the legend of Meng Jiangnü as performed by Yao Yonggen and recorded by Ma Hanmin and Bo Jinxing runs to almost two thousand lines of verse. The role of the evil servant Meng Xing is further expanded in this version of the legend. See Zheng, *Wuyu xushi shange yanchang chuantong yanjiu*, 58–59. For the edited text of Yao Yonggen's version, see Jiang, *Jiangnan shi da minjian xushishi Wugeji*, 503–98.

This essay is based on Haiyan Lee, "Tears That Crumbled the Great Wall: The Archaeology of Feeling in the May Fourth Folklore Movement," *Journal of Asian Studies* 64, no. 1 (February 2005): 35–65, and is published courtesy of the Association for Asian Studies.

1   In the narrow sense, the May Fourth movement refers to a series of public protests, first in Beijing on May 4, 1919, and then in major cities throughout China, against the handing over to Japan of former German concessions in northern China as stipulated in the Treaty of Versailles. Led by students, who were joined by workers and merchants, the movement was the broadest demonstration of nationalism in modern China. It was preceded by the New Culture movement launched in the mid-1910s by Western- and Japanese-educated intellectuals who attacked Confucian values and institutions as being responsible for China's weaknesses and powerlessness on the international stage and who advocated radical language, literary, and sociopolitical reforms aimed at regenerating Chinese culture and revitalizing the Chinese nation. In historiographical writing, "the May Fourth movement" is commonly used to designate the effervescent decade between the mid-1910s and mid-1920s.

2   Certeau, *The Practice of Everyday Life*, 131.

3   Gu Jiegang, *Meng Jiangnü gushi yanjiu ji* (hereafter *MJN*), 2.

4   Ibid., 4–5.

5   Ibid., 8.

6   Ibid.

7   Ibid., 9.

8   Ibid., 10.

9   Ibid.

10   Ibid., 12–23.

11   See Lee, *Revolution of the Heart*.

12   *MJN*, 71.

13   Ibid., 169.

14   Ibid.

15   Certeau, *Practice of Everyday Life*, 137.

16   *MJN*, 199. This ballad circulated independently in many versions; one version, included in a larger narrative, is translated in chapter 3.

17   Waldron, *The Great Wall of China*, 196.

18   Ibid., 194–226.

19   Liu Fu, "Dunhuang xieben zhong zhi Meng Jiangnü xiaochang" [Songs about Meng Jiang nü in the Dunhuang manuscripts], in Gu Jiegang, *Meng Jiangnü gushi yanjiu ji*; translation adapted from Hung, *Going to the People*, 98.

20 Waltner, *Getting an Heir*, 36–46.

21 *MJN*, 291.

22 Jay, *Throughout Your Generations Forever*, 31.

23 This also explains why medicinal broth made from a daughter-in-law's flesh or organ is believed to be efficacious in healing an ailing parent-in-law. The trope of consanguinity seems sufficiently elastic to overcome "the physical barrier to the assimilation of an outsider into the family, metaphorically expressed by the barrier between blood and bone" (Waltner, *Getting an Heir*, 45).

24 *MJN*, 191–92.

25 See Elvin, "Female Virtue," 111–52.

26 Duara, *Culture, Power, and the State*.

27 See Butler, *Antigone's Claim*.

28 Zhang Zichen, "Meng Jiangnü yu Qin Shi huang" [Meng Jiangnü and the First Emperor], in *Meng Jiangnü gushi lunwenji*, ed. Gu, Zhong, et al.

29 Appadurai, "Topographies of the Self," 106–9.

30 *MJN*, 7.

31 Feld, "Wept Thoughts," 257.

32 Ibid.

33 Ibid.

34 Hung, *Going to the People*, 65.

35 For more on this argument, see Lee, *Revolution of the Heart*.

36 *MJN*, 71–72.

37 During the Qing dynasty, women who had been widowed at a young age and never remarried, living a life of chastity devoted to serving their parents-in-law and rearing their children (if any), might be reported to the Throne by local authorities for special recommendation. When the request was granted, the family of such a woman might be allowed to erect a memorial archway in her honor, often spanning the street in front of her house. By the early twentieth century, cities all over China were dotted with such public monuments to chaste widows.

38 Liu, *Geyao yu funü*, 133–34.

39 See Giddens, *The Transformation of Intimacy*; Luhmann, *Love as Passion*; and Singer, *The Nature of Love*.

40 Certeau, *Practice of Everyday Life*, 132.

41 Ibid., 160.

42 Geertz, *Local Knowledge*, 149.

1 TREKKING TO THE WALL

1 Lu, *Meng Jiangnü wanli xunfu ji*, 43–49. I also consulted the annotated edition in Guan and Zhou, *Zidishu congchao*, 541–53.

2 Lü Buwei (d. 235 B.C.E.) was a rich merchant. While in Handan, he befriended Zichu, a prince of Qin who had been sent as a hostage to Zhao, and gave him one of his concubines. This concubine quickly gave birth to a boy (Ying Zheng), and it has often been stated that Lü Buwei was the father. Upon Zichu's return to Qin, he became crown prince and later king of Qin, appointing Lü as his chancellor. Lü also served as chancellor following the king's death, during the minority of Ying Zheng. The latter would later unify the world and assume the title of First Emperor. As emperor he reportedly buried dissenting scholars and burned their books, so as to stamp out any criticism of his grandiose policies.

3 In one of his widely popular poems, the poet Bai Juyi (772–846) noted that while the written texts on steles are often sycophantic in the extreme, the oral tradition of the common people provides a more reliable testimony as to the virtue (or vice) of a ruler.

4 Master Meng, or Mencius (372–289 B.C.E.), was one of the most respected Confucian philosophers in Ming and Qing China.

5 Traditional criticism of the First Emperor condemned him for relying on law and fear, not on virtue, in ruling the realm. A virtuous emperor was expected to transform his subjects by his example and his teachings.

6 "Right breath" is here the translation of zhengqi.

7 In early China, upper-class women plucked out their eyebrows and painted brows that were more curved on their foreheads. In the first century C.E., a certain Zhang Chang became famous as a loving husband by painting his wife's brows.

8 From the Song dynasty (960–1278) onward, more and more Chinese women bound their feet from an early age, bending the toes under the sole of the foot. These disfigured small feet required special curved shoes and socks. The bound feet were often referred to as "golden lotuses." Needless to say, bound feet greatly impaired a woman's ability to move around; walking long distances was extremely painful. To describe Meng Jiangnü as a woman with bound feet is of course an anachronism.

9 In traditional Chinese physiology, the gall is the seat of courage.

10 A couple who married in youth was said to have hair that was tied together.

11 The Toad Palace is the palace of the moon, because the moon is said to be inhabited by a toad. Chang'e is the goddess of the moon.

12 That is, something unfathomable. Here it refers to the possibility of his death.

13 That is, my long journey.

14 Lovers swear their love by stating that it will last as long as Heaven and Earth.

15 Meng Guang (first century) showed her respect for her husband, the poor recluse Liang Hong, by lifting his tray as high as her eyebrows whenever she served him food.

16 In poetry, the one left behind will constantly climb a tower to look out for the return of the beloved.

17 In a lyric addressed to her husband, the famous twelfth-century poet Li Qing-zhao described herself as "even skinnier than the yellow flowers." "Yellow flower" is the common designation of the chrysanthemum.

18 This line is based on a famous couplet from the poem "Setting Out Early on Mount Shang" (Shangshan zaoxing), by Wen Tingyun (812?-866): "The call of the rooster below the moon over the thatched inn; / A traveler's traces on the frost on the wooden bridge."

19 The "peach flowers" refer to her cheeks, and the "willow leaves" designate her eyebrows.

20 That is, she might be either kidnapped or murdered.

21 The cruel king of Song buried Han Ping and his wife on opposite sides of a road so that they would remain separated forever, but trees sprouted from their graves, the branches of these trees intertwined, and a couple of mandarin-ducks came to rest in them. The local people took these ducks for reincarnations of the loving couple. Ever since then, "intertwined branches" and "mandarin-ducks" symbol-ize true and abiding love.

22 A "floating stick" is at the mercy of winds and waves and has no chance of return-ing home.

23 "Mountain-Sea Pass" is a literal translation of Shanhaiguan.

24 Meng Tian was one of the First Emperor's major generals. According to historical sources, the First Emperor charged him with building a connected line of forti-fications along the northern border.

25 The paper money is sacrificial money, meant to be burned for the benefit of peo-ple who have passed away.

2 GUIDING THE SOUL

1 For a more detailed discussion of this way of writing the Minnanese dialect, see Klöter, *Written Taiwanese*, 71–87.

2 Minnanyu suqu changben "Gezai ce" quanwen ziliao ku [The texts database of folk songs in Southern Min dialect], at Academia Sinica's general Web site, Hanji dianzi wenxian [Electronic documents in Chinese], ASCC, http://www.sinica.edu.tw/~tdb=kau-a-chheh (accessed July 11, 2006). Access is by permission of Professor Wang (Ong). The full title of our text is *Xinke Jiangnü ge* (Newly cut: A song of Jiangnü), which is listed as no. 23 in the category "woodblock editions."

3 The same text also survives in an undated printing from Sibao, in Western Fujian, by the Wenhailou. The Wenhailou was founded in the middle of the

eighteenth century and continued to be in operation throughout the nineteenth century. See Cynthia Brokaw, *Commerce in Culture: The Sibao Book Trade in the Qing and Republican Periods* (Cambridge, Mass.: Harvard University Asia Center, 2007), 501. The Hakka publishers and booksellers of Sibao distributed their publications throughout Fujian, Jiangxi, Guangdong, and Guangxi, especially in those areas with a large Hakka population.

4   Wang Shunlong, "Qi zhong quanben *Meng Jiang nü ge*."

5   Traditional Chinese beliefs credited a single person with three souls and seven spirits.

6   In the course of time, the story of the pilgrimage to India of the seventh-century monk Xuanzang or Sanzang (Tripitaka) developed into the legend of his pilgrimage to Vulture Peak. The legend is best known through the sixteenth-century novel *Journey to the West* (Xiyou ji), usually ascribed to Wu Cheng'en. In this version, the monk is assisted by the acolytes Monkey (Su Wukong) and Pigsy (Zhu Bajie) and has to pass through eighty-one ordeals.

7   Mulian (Maudgalyayana) was a disciple of the Buddha. He was best known for his miraculous powers and, in China, for the legend in which he rescues his mother from the tortures of the Avici-hell. This legend provides the charter for the Ghost Festival on the fifteenth of the Seventh Month, when offerings to the deceased are believed to be especially efficacious.

8   Meng Zong is one of the famous twenty-four exemplars of filial piety. When his elderly mother was ill and developed a craving for bamboo shoots in the middle of winter, the sincerity of his weeping in a bamboo grove moved Heaven and Earth, and bamboo shoots miraculously appeared.

9   Wang Xiang is one of the famous twenty-four exemplars of filial piety. When his evil stepmother demanded fresh fish in the middle of winter, Wang Xiang lay down on the ice. His body warmth miraculously melted the ice, and two carp jumped out of the water.

10 Guo Ju is one of the famous twenty-four exemplars of filial piety. He had become so poor that he could not feed both his elderly mother and his infant son, and he and his wife decided to bury their son. When he dug a hole in the ground, he found a pot filled with gold bearing the inscription "For the filial son Guo Ju."

11 Dong Yong is one of the famous twenty-four exemplars of filial piety. Upon the death of his parents, he sold himself into bondage so he could raise money for a decent burial. After the mourning period, he set out for the house of the man who had bought him in order to work off his debt and was joined by the Weaving Maid, who produced enough silk in ten days to pay off his debt. Thereupon she returned to heaven.

12   Ding Lan is one of the famous twenty-four exemplars of filial piety. He lost both his parents at an early age and made wooden images of them, which he venerated sincerely. His wife treated these images without any respect, and when she pricked them with a needle, they bled. Ding Lan then divorced his wife.

13   The fifteenth night of the First Month is called First Night because it is the first night of the full moon in the new year.

14   The Bodhisattva Guanyin has been widely venerated in female form in China since the tenth century. The female Guanyin is often mentioned as the perfect type of feminine beauty. One of her main pilgrimage sites is the little island of Putuo, off the coast near Ningbo.

15   Clear and Bright, celebrated 105 days after the shortest day of the year, was the day for cleaning graves. Families would visit the family graves and picnic out in the open.

16   In Chinese, the word for "fruit" used here, zi, has the same pronunciation as the word for "son."

17   Meng Guang, the wife of the noble but poor recluse Liang Hong (first century C.E.), showed her respect for her husband by raising the tray bearing his food as high as her eyebrows whenever she served him his meal.

18   The Three Jewels are the Buddha, the Dharma (his teachings), and the Sangha (the monastic community), but the term is often used as a designation for the Buddha.

19   Chang'e is the beautiful goddess who lives on the moon.

20   "The Third Son of the Li family" most likely is a reference to Li Si (d. 208 B.C.E.), the chancellor of Qin. In the power struggles that followed the death of the First Emperor in 210 B.C.E., he and Meng Tian lost out to the main eunuch, Zhao Gao.

21   The later rewritings identify the bird not as a phoenix, which displays all colors, but as a parrot, which fits the description better.

22   The Oxherd and the Weaving Maid are stars on opposite sides of the Heavenly River (Milky Way). The two lovers are allowed to see each other only once every year, on the seventh night of the Seventh Month, when magpies form a bridge across the Heavenly River.

23   The Springs are the Yellow Springs, in ancient Chinese belief the abode of the deceased below the earth.

24   Jiangnü here is throwing the oracle blocks, two pieces of wood in the shape of a half moon. Depending on the way the two blocks fall on the ground, the answer is positive (a Sage) or negative.

25   The Star of the Great White (the planet Venus) often appears in popular tales and legends. At his own initiative, or at the behest of the Jade Emperor, he descends to earth (often in the guise of an old man), manifests himself to virtuous persons who are facing insurmountable obstacles, and helps them out.

26 "Release" here refers to release from the sufferings of the Underworld so that Fan Qilang may be reborn in the Western Paradise.

27 The meaning of this line is unclear to me. Perhaps the author wants to say that the First Emperor never fought a war against the northern barbarians and the building of the Wall was a waste of effort.

28 I am puzzled by these two lines. Liang Shanbo is one of the main characters in the legend of Liang Shanbo and Zhu Yingtai, which was very popular in Southern China. Liang Shanbo dies from grief when he learns that he cannot marry Zhu Yingtai because her parents have promised her to someone else.

29 By washing clothes soiled with menstrual blood or blood shed in childbirth, women pollute the gods. For this sin, they are condemned to the Blood Pond Hell upon their deaths and can be saved only through special rituals.

3 RETRIEVING A FAN

1 Ch'iu-kuei Wang, "From Pao-chüan to Ballad," 54.

2 Lu, *Meng Jiangnü wanli xunfu ji*, 99–112. Ch'iu-kuei Wang compared this edition with an edition put out by the Zhuangyin Shufang in Shanghai in 1920 and concluded that Lu Gong's version lacked fifty lines, while ten lines showed important differences ("From Pao-chüan to Ballad," 62–63, n. 57). So far I have been unable to locate a copy of either lithographic edition.

3 Wang, "From Pao-chüan to Ballad," 63–64, n. 61.

4 "Yellow Springs" is one of the many designations of the Underworld.

5 The cuckoo is said to cry tears of blood.

6 In Ming and Qing China, the same city, now known as Songjiang, served as the capital of both Songjiang prefecture and Huating county.

7 The *Classic for Girls* (Nü'er jing) is a short tract in verse on the moral and practical duties of women. The earliest known editions date from the Ming dynasty.

8 The *Four Books for Women* (Nü sishu) is a collective designation for four moral tracts: *Precepts for My Daughters* (Nü jie), often translated as *Precepts for Women*, by Ban Zhao (ca. 100 C.E.); *Classic of Filial Piety for Women* (Nü xiaojing), by a certain Lady Zheng (early eighth century); *Analects for Women* (Nü lunyu), usually credited to Song Ruozhao (ca. 800); and *Instructions for the Inner Quarters* (Neixun), by Empress Xu (1371–1407). *Biographies of Exemplary Women* (Lienü zhuan) was compiled by Liu Xiang (79–8 B.C.E.).

9 The family name Wan also has the meaning "ten thousand, a myriad." The theme of Wan Qiliang's substitution for a myriad of men who were to be buried as sacrificial victims, one for each mile of wall, is developed at much greater length in some other versions of the legend.

10 The Chinese names of the parasol-tree and the palm tree are homophones of words that mean "together" and "companions."

11 Some of these fishes may have been chosen for the connotations of their names. The syllable *qing* (black) in *qingyu* (black carp) has the same pronunciation as *qing* (emotion, passion, desire). The *bimuyu* (sole, flounder, flatfish) is of course a saltwater fish and out of place in this pond, but it is said to be able to swim only in pairs.

12 The City of Those Who Unjustly Died is a special section of the Underworld.

13 Meng Xing is the name of a family servant of the Meng family.

14 Buddhist monks were invited to read Buddhist sutras for the benefit of a deceased person's soul on the seventh, the fourteenth, the twenty-first, the twenty-eighth, the thirty-fifth, the forty-second, the forty-ninth, and the one hundredth day after death. Another reading of sutras took place one full year after that person's death, and the cycle of ten Sevens concluded with a session at the end of the twenty-seventh month after that person's death.

15 "Yang Pass" here serves as a general reference to the border regions.

16 The Bodhisattva Guanyin is a common simile for perfect female beauty.

17 Long River (Changjiang) is the common designation of the Yangzi.

18 The steppes and deserts of Central Asia.

19 "A thousand pounds" here denotes the strength and energy needed to lift a weight of a thousand pounds.

20 The Giant Tortoise carries the earth on its back.

21 For emphasis or variety, the standard seven-syllable line of verse may be preceded by a group of three extra-metrical syllables. The short phrase appears in the translation as a separate line in smaller type.

22 In the sixth and fifth centuries B.C.E., the states of Wu (with its capital in Suzhou) and Yue (with its capital in Shaoxing/Guiji) were continuously at war. Eventually the king of Yue selected the most beautiful girl of his country, Xi Shi, and after training her in all the arts of seduction, offered her to the king of Wu. Soon seduced by her charms, the king of Wu neglected his duties, after which his country was utterly defeated by Yue.

23 The empress-dowager is the mother of the reigning emperor.

4 BORN FROM A GOURD

1 This text was donated to the library by Professor Patrick Hanan. By far the most readily available edition of this text is the one provided in Lu, *Meng Jiangnü wanli xunfu ji*, 219–40, based on a 1912 woodblock edition by the Yihuatang in Shanghai. As already pointed out by Ch'iu-kuei Wang, however, Lu Gong deleted considerable sections of the text, especially those dealing with the piety of Meng

Jiangnü's and Wan Xiliang's parents and their eventual deliverance by the bodhisattva Guanyin, greatly detracting from the religious coloring of this text.

2   The Star of the Great White (also Metal Star of the Great White) is the deity of
    the planet Venus. He appears on earth in a variety of unobtrusive guises and acts
    as a handyman for the Jade Emperor.

3   Ch'iu-kuei Wang, "From Pao-chüan to Ballad," 53.

4   Sprout Lad is perhaps best understood as a late-imperial manifestation of the
    God of Sprouts (Mangshen), also known as the God of Budding Sprouts
    (Goumangshen), the god of the first month of the year. In late-imperial illustra-
    tions of the Spring Buffalo, this god is often depicted as a young boy.

5   The Three Jewels of Buddhism are the Buddha, the Dharma (the body of his teach-
    ings), and the Sangha (the community of monks and nuns). A belief in the saving
    power of the Three Jewels ferries one across the sea of suffering to the realm of
    bliss. "Dharma King" refers to the Buddha.

6   The lowering of the screen in front of the emperor marks the formal end of the
    audience.

7   In this text, Meng Jiang is introduced as an incarnation of the Weaving Maid.

8   The Purple Tenuity Enclosure is the heavenly dwelling of the Jade Emperor, the
    highest authority in the cosmos.

9   Elongated earlobes are one of the signs of buddhahood and indicate good
    fortune.

10 The term "Five Mounts" here refers to the forehead, nose, chin, and two cheek-
    bones; their proper alignment predicts prosperity and high status.

11 The three parts are the upper, middle, and lower parts of the face.

12 A *kalpa* is an immeasurably long period of time, which ends in the destruction
    of the cosmos.

13 Menstrual blood and the blood shed by women in childbirth were widely
    regarded as a source of pollution.

14 I do not fully understand this line. Most likely the author wants to express the idea
    that the gourd by its very nature partakes of the elements of water and wood.

15 "Star of disaster" (*taisui*) is a common designation for a local bully. The village
    head might easily obtain a reputation for ruthless oppression, as he was respon-
    sible for the collecting of local taxes.

16 There was a drum in front of the office (yamen) of the district magistrate, and a
    person who suffered an injustice was free to sound the drum in order to appeal
    to the magistrate in his capacity as judge.

17 "Revert the light" and "reverse the glare" are the names of certain techniques of
    meditation.

18 In Chinese mythology, the moon (yin) is inhabited by a hare, and the sun (yang)
    by a crow.

19   Pears, which are dark on the outside but white on the inside, are called "joined" because they are considered a mixture of the elements of metal and wood; the jujube is called "fiery" because of its red color.

20   The dragon and tiger symbolize yang and yin; meditation aims for the union of both elements into the elixir of immortality, often envisioned as a spiritual embryo.

21   The Three Purities are the highest deities in the Daoist pantheon.

22   In Buddhist cosmology, Jambudvipa is the continent on which the historical Buddha Shakyamuni preached the Law and on which we mortals live.

23   The term "Golden Crow" refers to the sun.

24   The *Book of the Yellow Court* (Huangting jing) is not a Buddhist text but is one of the earliest Daoist works on the techniques of longevity.

25   Top-Graduate's Red and Golden Lion are two varieties of peony.

26   In a well-known Tang-dynasty classical tale, a young man on his way to the capital in order to take the examinations rests at an inn, experiences in a dream a complete career at court, with all its ups and downs, and realizes the vanity of all earthly glory. His little nap takes less time than needed to cook a dish of yellow-millet gruel.

27   King Yama is the main judge in the Underworld.

28   "Red dust" is a common term for this world of attachment and suffering.

29   "Mountain-Sea Pass" is a literal translation of Shanhaiguan.

30   In traditional China, years and days were counted using the sixty bisyllabic terms generated by the combination of the ten characters constituting the Heavenly Stems and the twelve characters constituting the Earthly Branches. This particular date makes no sense, as there is no *gengzi* year during the reign of the First Emperor (the nearest *gengzi* year is 201 B.C.E.).

31   In premodern China, the night was divided into five watches of equal length. In cities, the beginning of each watch might be sounded by beating the drum on the drum tower. The watches of the night might also be sounded by watchmen walking the streets. Songs on the theme of the five watches of the night form a tradition that can be traced back to at least the tenth century. In this case, each of the following five songs consists of four lines, a first line of five syllables, and three more lines of seven syllables each.

32   In this set of songs on the theme of the five watches of the night, each song consists of five lines; each first and fourth line consists of two half-lines of three characters each, while the three remaining lines consist of seven characters.

33   "Samsara" is the Buddhist term for the endless cycle of death and rebirth in the realm of suffering, where sentient beings are caught as long as they do not free themselves from attachment to this world of empty phenomena.

34 In Buddhism, the five *skandhas* are the five physical and mental components: form/matter, sensation, discerning, judgment, and cognition. The temporary combination of these components makes up a sentient being.

35 A *sarira* is a little pearl-shaped relic left when the body of a buddha is cremated. Here it would appear to refer to the eternal embryo that the practitioner forms inside the body through assiduous meditation.

36 The five elements are metal, wood, water, fire, and earth. Everything that exists is considered to be a combination of some of these elements (or states of energy).

37 In Confucian and Daoist cosmology, the Non-Ultimate (Wuji) is the highest principle of the universe, which generates all that exists.

38 The Tushita-heaven is the heaven in which the future buddha Maitreya awaits the moment of his birth on earth. Pious Buddhists pray for rebirth in the Tushita-heaven, so they may hear Maitreya's heavenly teaching and be reborn during his lifetime in order to achieve final enlightenment upon hearing his sermons on earth.

39 The *dhyana*-heavens are the lowest heavens, which are accessible through meditation (*dhyana*).

40 Maya is the mother of the Shakyamuni Buddha. She died seven days after his death and was transported to the Thayatrimsat-heaven.

41 *Pratyeka*-buddhas are persons who have achieved enlightenment by their own effort but do not teach.

5 BEING A FILIAL DAUGHTER-IN-LAW

1 Lu, *Meng Jiangnü wanli xunfu ji*, 59–64.

2 Zhanzhan Waishi, *Qing shi*, 222–23.

3 A tadpole script is an indecipherable script, so named after the wriggling shapes of tadpoles.

4 The Chinese mile, or *li*, measures about one-third of the English mile.

5 The Five Ranges are the mountain chains that separate the modern-day area of Guangdong and Guangxi from the Chinese provinces to the north. The term may also refer to the roads through the Five Ranges from the north into Guangdong. The Epang Palace was the imperial palace of the First Emperor near the capital Xianyang, on the southern bank of the Wei. The size and extravagance of Epang Palace were immortalized by the Tang poet Du Mu (803–852) in a famous and often anthologized rhapsody.

6 Wenjun is Zhuo Wenjun, the wife of the poet Sima Xiangru (179–118 B.C.E.).

7 The Graybeard of the Border (Saiweng) is depicted in *Master Huainan* (Huai-

nanzi), a philosophical work of the second century B.C.E., as an elderly man who knows that sudden misfortune may well spell fortune, but that good fortune may well be followed by disaster.

6 SWITCHING THE DRAGON-ROBES

1   Yet another precious scroll that derives its plot from the late-Ming *Precious Scroll as Spoken by the Buddha of the Chaste and Virtuous, Wise and Filial Meng Jiangnü at the Long Wall* goes by the simple title *Precious Scroll of the Long Wall* (Changcheng baojuan) and is preserved in a manuscript of around 1865. In this latter text, the story line is almost identical to that of the *Precious Scroll as Spoken by the Buddha of the Chaste and Virtuous, Wise and Filial Meng Jiangnü at the Long Wall*, but the elaborate sectarian teachings have been omitted, even though the character of the Eternal Mother still makes her appearance. Its most remarkable plot element may well be that Meng Jiangnü travels to the Long Wall in male disguise. In a formal respect, this precious scroll is remarkable because its verse sections are written primarily to the tune of "Shuahai'er," a melody that is more closely associated with Daoist traditions of storytelling.

2   Duan, *Hexi baojuan de diaocha yanjiu*, 180–81.

3   Ibid., 190–206.

4   The Tong Pass, situated between the mountains and the Yellow River, guards the border between the modern provinces of Shaanxi and Henan.

5   A *liang* is one Chinese ounce of silver.

6   The Gate of Ghosts is the entrance to the Underworld.

7   King Yama is the major judge in the Underworld.

8   In traditional China, the night was divided into five watches of equal length.

9   One *zhang* measures ten feet.

10 Carp that manage to jump across the Dragon Gate Rapids in the Yellow River were believed to turn into dragons.

11 The eighth day of the Fourth Month is widely celebrated as the birthday of the Buddha. The Mothers are the goddesses in charge of fertility and childbirth and are widely revered by women.

12 In many areas of northern China, people used to take "winter clothes" made out of paper to the graves of the ancestors and burn them there on the first day of winter.

13 Flowers are a common metaphor for women.

14 In some folktales, the immortal maiden who substitutes for Meng Jiangnü is pregnant when she returns, and her son Xiang Yu goes on to destroy the Qin dynasty. See Yang, *Meng Jiangnü yanjiu*, 256–58.

7 MOBILIZING THE GODS

1 *Zhongguo geyao jicheng: Henan juan*, 550–56.

2 A modern edition of this nineteenth-century ballad is included in Lu, *Meng Jiangnü wanli xunfu ji*, 55–58.

3 The term "four rites" refers to the rites of capping, marriage, burial, and ancestral sacrifice. It may also refer to the norms of behavior for a wife in serving her husband.

4 As a daughter, a woman should obey her father, as a wife her husband, and as a widow her son. The Four Virtues are wifely chastity, wifely speech, wifely appearance, and wifely work.

5 Looking Back Home Terrace is the place in the Underworld where the souls of the deceased are allowed one last glimpse of their homes and families. According to ancient Chinese beliefs, a person has, not a single soul, but three souls and seven spirits, which disperse upon death. One theory holds that one of the three souls resides in the ancestral tablet, one stays with the corpse in the grave, and one descends to the Underworld to be judged.

6 King Yama is the most powerful judge in the Underworld.

8 STEPPING INTO THE POND

1 *Meng Jiangnü ziliao xuanji*, 80–91. The same volume of this collection includes another ballad from the same region, with an identical title and very similar to the version translated here. The text of this other ballad is divided between the two protagonists, however, turning the ballad into the script for a play (92–105).

2 Ibid., 90.

3 *Zhongguo geyao jicheng: Hunan juan*, 778–88, contains a shorter version of this text, introduced as "(an) excerpt(s)." That version of the text was performed in 1977 by Gong Faxian and recorded by Jin Kejian. This version of the text most likely reflects an earlier draft of the version translated here, prepared by Jin based on his first fieldwork trip.

4 The ancient state of Chu covered most of the modern provinces of Hubei and Hunan.

5 During the reign of the mythic emperor Shun, China suffered from floods for nine years. Yu's father, Kun, tried to solve the problem by constructing higher and higher dikes, but without success. The problem of continuous flooding was solved only when Yu provided all the major rivers an outlet to the sea. Shun thereupon appointed Yu his successor, and Yu became the first emperor of the Xia dynasty.

6 The Old Gardener is Zhang the Old Gardener (Zhang Guolao), one of the Eight Immortals.

7   Sima Qian (145–87 B.C.E.), in his *Records of the Historian*, credits Huandou with opening up the jungle of the southern barbarians, including the area of modern Hunan.

8   Qu Yuan (fl. 300 B.C.E.) is credited with the authorship of "Encountering Sorrow" (Lisao), the opening poem in *Songs of the South* (Chuci), which contains the quoted phrase.

9   According to the tradition, the Double Fifth Festival was celebrated in memory of the poet Qu Yuan. The competing dragon-boats were said to reenact attempts to save Qu Yuan after he had thrown himself into the Miluo River.

10   Taigong (Jiang Ziya) had already turned eighty before he was employed as adviser to King Wen, and he was ninety when he assisted King Wu in the conquest of the Shang dynasty and the founding of the Zhou dynasty.

11   Seventh Sister is the Weaving Maid, who came down to earth to marry the filial son Dong Yong and assisted him in repaying the debt he had contracted in order to provide his parents with a proper funeral. She bore him a son and then returned to heaven. When the boy grew up and wanted to meet his mother, he went to a soothsayer, who told him to go to a certain pond, hide himself there, and wait for three heavenly maidens to come down from the sky and disrobe in order to bathe. The boy was instructed to grab the robe of a certain color, which he did, and the robe he grabbed turned out to belong to his mother, who then spoke to him.

12   The Bodhisattva Guanyin is widely venerated in China in female form and is often praised as the perfection of female beauty.

13   "Master of Life" is the official title of the god of the stove.

14   Xianyang, close to modern-day Xi'an, was the capital of the Qin dynasty.

15   The term "fire and water" summarizes all kinds of disaster that may befall a human being.

16   When two families have tentatively agreed to a marriage, the eight characters of the boy's and girl's dates of birth are submitted to a diviner to see whether the couple is compatible.

17   The character for "thought, thinking" (*si*) consists of the character for "field" (*tian*) above the character for "heart" (*xin*).

18   The word for "lotus root" (*ou*) has the same pronunciation as one of the words for "pair, a couple" (*ou*). The word for "thread" (*si*) and the word for "thought, longing" (*si*) also have the same pronunciation. Moreover, when lotus roots are broken, the fibers cling to one another.

19   In this line, the newlyweds most likely are being compared to the Weaving Maid and the Oxherd, two stars on opposite sides of the Heavenly River (Milky Way). The Weaving Maid and the Oxherd are united by an eternal love but are allowed to meet only once a year, on the seventh night of the Seventh Month, when magpies form a bridge between them.

1 This may be the reason why Zhao Liming did not include this text in her *A Collective Edition of Writings in China's Women's Scripts* (Zhongguo nüshu heji).

2 Zhao, *Zhongguo nüshu jicheng*, 655–66.

3 "Youzhou" refers to the northeastern section of the ancient Chinese world (modern-day Hebei and southern Liaodong). This was the area of the ancient state of Yan.

4 A *mu* is somewhat more than one-seventh of an acre.

5 "Eastern Capital" (Dongjing) is the common designation for Kaifeng as the capital of the Northern Song dynasty (960–1126) in ballad literature. Here it seems to be used in the general sense of a capital.

6 In some parts of the China, the sixth day of the Sixth Month was celebrated by praying to the god of crops for a bountiful harvest.

7 As noted by the modern editor of the text, there is a contradiction here with the earlier information that Fan Qilang hailed from Nanyang in Dengzhou.

8 Chang'an was the capital of both the Western Han dynasty (206 B.C.E.–8 C.E.) and the Tang dynasty (618–906). Here it is used as a general designation for the national capital.

9 Student Zhang and Cui Yingying are the main characters in the *Story of the Western Wing* (Xixiang ji), China's most popular romantic comedy. While staying temporarily at an out-of-the-way Buddhist monastery, Student Zhang and Yingying fall in love at first sight. Eventually they have a premarital affair, which Yingying's mother discovers. Student Zhang leaves for the capital to take part in the examinations and passes with flying colors. He then returns to claim Yingying as his bride. The earliest dramatic adaptation of this story is credited to Wang Shifu (fl. 1300).

10 A common metaphor likens a prostitute to a wildflower.

11 Zhao Wuniang and Cai Yong (Bojie) are the central characters in *The Story of the Lute* (Pipa ji), by Gao Ming (ca. 1307–ca. 1371). The young student Cai Yong is ordered by his father to travel to the capital to take part in the examinations and leaves his young wife Zhao Wuniang behind to look after his parents. Cai Yong passes the examinations with flying colors, but the prime minister then pressures him to marry his daughter and does not allow him to return home. Meanwhile, a patiently suffering Zhao Wuniang takes care of her suspicious parents-in-law. Only after the older couple dies during a famine does she manage to travel to the capital (she begs her way by singing the sad story of her life to the accompaniment of a lute), where she is reunited with her husband (and his second wife).

12 Middle Prime is also known as the Ghost Festival, as the ghosts of the deceased are welcomed back to their original homes; at the same time, hungry ghosts are treated to rich offerings.

13   Li Sanniang and Liu Zhiyuan are the central characters in *The White Hare* (Baitu ji), a very popular play dating from perhaps as early as the fourteenth century. Liu Zhiyuan is a poor farmhand whose future greatness is noticed by Li Sanniang and her father. But soon after the two marry, Li Sanniang's father dies, and her brothers make life so difficult for Liu Zhiyuan that he decides to join the army, leaving his pregnant wife behind. When a son is born, she has the baby taken to the father, who in the meantime has married the daughter of his commanding officer. When Li Sanniang refuses to remarry, her brothers force her to do the most demanding and demeaning work in the household. The couple is reunited twelve years later, when Liu Zhiyuan has risen to the rank of provincial governor, and a white hare leads their son to his mother, Li Sanniang.

10   FORBIDDEN DESIRES

1   An edition of this text is also included in *An Anthology of Materials on Meng Jiangnü* (Meng Jiangnü ziliao xuanji), 65–67, which identifies the genre of the text, however, as a *Wenzhou guci* (Wenzhou drum-ballad). The compilers note that this genre was widely popular on Dongtou wherever the Wenzhou dialect was spoken.

2   The text has "Fan Xiliang," but the context makes clear that the singers intended "Wan Xiliang."

3   The empress-dowager is the mother of the emperor, so this song imputes to the evil First Emperor of the Qin the desire to have sex with his mother.

4   Zhang San (Zhang Three) and Li Si (Li Four) are conventional names for any Tom, Dick, and Harry.

5   The Eastern Capital is Kaifeng as the capital of the Northern Song dynasty. In popular literature, the term "Eastern Capital" is often used as a general designation of the national capital irrespective of dynasty.

6   The devotions of the priests and monks are meant to secure the release of the deceased from the tortures of the Underworld so that his soul may be reborn in the Western Paradise.

7   "Seven Continents" is a reference to the fourth-century Eastern Jin regime, which had its capital at present-day Nanjing. The Eastern Jin was said to control seven of the twelve "continents" into which the mythical sage-emperor Shun had divided the world.

8   The term "Springs" refers to the Yellow Springs, the abode of the dead below the earth.

GLOSSARY

Aiqing xiaoshuo Meng Jiangnü 哀情小說孟姜女

Bai Juyi 白居易
Baitu ji 白兔記
Ban Zhao 班昭
baojuan 寶卷
baqi zidi 八旗子弟
bengcheng 崩城
bimuyu 比目魚
Bo Jinxing 柏金星

Cai Gengyao 蔡庚堯
Cai Yong (Bojie) 蔡邕伯喈
Changcheng 長城
Changcheng baojuan 長城寶卷
Chang'e 嫦娥
Changjiang 長江
Chitaoxian 敕桃仙
Chongbian Meng Jiangnü xunfu kudao wanli Changcheng zhenjie quanzhuan
重編孟姜女尋夫哭倒萬里長城貞節全傳

Chuci　楚辭
Chunqiu　春秋
Cui Yingying　崔鶯鶯

dagushu　大鼓書
Diaoyuji　琱玉集
Ding Lan　丁蘭
Dong Yong　董永
dongjing　東京
Du Mu　杜牧

Epang　阿房

Fan　范
fan Qi Liang　犯杞梁
Fan Qilang　范杞郎
Fengyue jinnang　風月錦囊
Fengyue zhuren　風月主人
Foshuo zhenlie xianxiao Meng Jiangnü Changcheng baojuan　佛說貞烈賢孝孟姜女長
　城寶卷
Fu Xi　伏羲
furen　夫人

Gan Bao　干寶
Ganyingpian　感應篇
Gao Ming　高明
ge　歌
gengzi　庚子
Geyao zhoukan　歌謠周刊
gezai ce　歌仔冊
Gong Faxian　龔法顯
Gong Sizhong　龔思忠
Gu Jiegang　顧頡剛
Guanxiu　貫休
Guanyin　觀音
Guo Ju　郭巨
Gushi bian　古史辨

Han Peng fu　韓朋賦
Han Ping　韓平

Lisao 離騷

Liu Fu (Bannong) 劉復半農

Liu Xiang 劉向

Liu Zhiyuan 劉智遠

Lü Buwei 呂不韋

Lu Xun 魯迅

Ma Hanmin 馬漢民

Mao Zedong 毛澤東

meng 孟

Meng 孟

Meng Guang (Meng Jiangnü's father) 孟光

Meng Guang (Liang Hong's wife) 孟光

Meng Jiang 孟姜

Meng Jiang xiannü baojuan 孟姜賢女寶卷

Meng Jiangnü 孟姜女

"Meng Jiangnü gushi de zhuanbian" 孟姜女故事的轉變

"Meng Jiangnü gushi yanjiu" 孟姜女故事研究

Meng Jiangnü ku Changcheng 孟姜女哭長城

Meng Jiangnü kudao wanli Changcheng 孟姜女哭倒萬里長城

Meng Jiangnü peifu xinge 孟姜女配夫新歌

"Meng Jiangnü shieryue huaming" 孟姜女十二月花名

Meng Jiangnü wanli xunfu 孟姜女萬里尋夫

Meng Qi 孟起

Meng Tian 蒙恬

Meng Xing 孟興

Meng Zi 孟姿

Meng Zong 孟宗

Mengjiangnü ku Changcheng baojuan 孟姜女哭長城寶卷

Miaoshan 妙善

Minnanyu suqu changben "Gezai ce" quanwen ziliao ku 閩南語俗曲唱本歌仔冊全文資料庫

mu 畝

Mulian 目連

nanci 南詞

nanxi 南戲

Neixun 內訓

nü 女

Nü jie 女戒

Nü Lunyu 女論語

nü shu 女書

Nü sishu 女四書

Nü Wa 女媧

Nü Xiaojing 女孝經

Nü'er jing 女兒經

ou (lotus root) 藕

ou (a pair) 偶

Pipa ji 琵琶記

Qi Liang 杞梁

Qi Zhi 杞殖

Qin Shi huangdi 秦始皇帝 *first emperor of the qin*

qing 情

Qing shi 情史

qingge 情歌

qingyu 青魚

Qishi'er chao renwu yanyi 七十二朝人物演義

Qiu Shou 丘壽

Qu Yuan 屈原

ruhua 入話

Saiweng 塞翁

sanggu 喪鼓

Sanzang 三藏

Shang Zhihe ji 尚志和記

Shan'ge 山歌

Shangshan zaoxing 商山早行

Shanhaiguan 山海關

Shengyu 聖諭

Shi ji 史記

Shuahai'er 耍孩兒

Shun 舜

si (thought, longing) 思

si (thread) 絲 *Silk*

si qing xing 思情性

Sima Qian 司馬遷

Sima Xiangru　司馬相如
Sizhou　泗州
Song Ruozhao　宋若昭
Soushenji　搜神記
Su Tong　蘇童
Su Wukong　孫悟空
sufu　俗賦

Taigong　太公
Taiping yulan　太平御覽
taisui　太歲
tanci　彈詞
tian　田
Tongxian ji　同賢記
Tongzhi　通志
toushui　投水
Tujia　土家

Wan　萬
Wan Xiliang　萬喜良
Wang Chuxue　王楚雪
Wang Shifu　王實甫
Wang Shunlong　王順隆
Wang Xiang　王祥
Wen Tingyun　溫庭筠
wenren　文人
Wenxuan　文選
Wenzhou guci　溫州鼓詞
Wu Cheng'en　吳成恩
wuji　無極

xi　喜
Xi Shi　西施
Xi yuan lu　洗冤錄
Xiang Yu　項羽
Xiang Zechang　向澤昌
xiangtu　鄉土
Xiaojing　孝經
Xiaoshi Meng Jiang Zhonglie zhenjie xianliang baojuan　銷釋孟姜忠烈貞節賢良寶卷

GLOSSARY

xin 心

Xinke Jiangnü ge 新刻姜女歌

Xixiang ji 西廂記

Xiyou ji 西遊記

Xu, Empress 許

Xu Mengjiang 許孟姜

xuanjiang 宣講

Xuanzang 玄藏

xunfu 尋父

Yao Yonggen 姚永根

ye 野

Yi Nianhua 義年華

Ying Zheng 贏政

yinyue jie fengqi 音樂界風氣

Yu 禹

"Yue zhi" 樂志

zhang 丈

Zhang, Student 張生

Zhang Chang 張敞

Zhang Guolao 張果老

Zhang Henshui 張恨水

Zhang San 張三

Zhang-Wang, Mrs. 張王

Zhao Gao 趙高

Zhao Wuniang 趙五娘

Zheng, Lady 鄭

Zheng Qiao 鄭樵

zhengqi 正氣

Zhong Jingwen 鍾敬文

Zhongguo geyao jicheng 中國歌謠集成

Zhongzi 仲姿

Zhou Shuoyi 周碩沂

Zhu Bajie 豬八戒

Zhu Honghua 朱洪華

Zhu Yingtai 祝英台

Zhuang, Duke 庄

Zhuo Wenjun 卓文君

zi 子
Zichu 子楚
zidishu 子弟書
Ziming 子明
Zuo zhuan 左轉

BIBLIOGRAPHY

Anonymous. *Meng Jiangnü wanli xunfu* 孟姜女萬里尋夫 [Meng Jiangnü travels a myriad of miles to find her husband]. Hong Kong: Kwong Chi Book Company, ca. 1960.

Appadurai, Arjun. "Topographies of the Self: Praise and Emotion in Hindu India." In *Language and the Politics of Emotion*, edited by Catherine Lutz and Lila Abu-Lughod. Cambridge: Cambridge University Press, 1990.

Berlin, Isaiah. *The Roots of Romanticism*. Princeton, N.J.: Princeton University Press, 1999.

Brokaw, Cynthia J. *Commerce in Culture: The Sibao Book Trade in the Qing and Republican Periods*. Cambridge, Mass.: Harvard University Asia Center, 2007.

Brown, Melissa. *Is Taiwan Chinese? The Impact of Culture, Power, and Migration on Changing Identities*. Berkeley: University of California Press, 2004.

Butler, Judith. *Antigone's Claim: Kinship between Life and Death*. New York: Columbia University Press, 2000.

Certeau, Michel de. *The Practice of Everyday Life*. Translated by Steven Rendall. Berkeley: University of California Press, 1984.

Chen Pingyuan 陈平原, ed. *Xiandai xueshushi shangde suwenxue* 现代学术史上的俗文学 [Popular literature in the history of modern scholarship]. Wuhan: Hubei Jiaoyu Chubanshe, 2004.

DeWoskin, Kenneth J., and J. I. Crump, Jr., trans. *In Search of the Supernatural: The Written Record.* Stanford, Calif.: Stanford University Press, 1996.

Duan Ping 段平. *Hexi baojuan de diaocha yanjiu* 河西宝卷的调查研究 [Fieldwork and research concerning the precious scrolls of western Gansu]. Lanzhou: Lanzhou Daxue Chubanshe, 1992.

Duara, Prasenjit. *Culture, Power, and the State: Rural North China, 1900–1942.* Stanford, Calif.: Stanford University Press, 1988.

Elvin, Mark. "Female Virtue and the State in China." *Past and Present* 104 (1984): 111–52.

Feld, Steven. "Wept Thoughts: The Voicing of Kaluli Memories." *Oral Tradition* 5 (1990): 241–66.

Geertz, Clifford. *Local Knowledge: Further Essays in Interpretive Anthropology.* New York: Basic Books, 1993.

Giddens, Anthony. *The Transformation of Intimacy: Sexuality, Love and Eroticism in Modern Societies.* Stanford, Calif.: Stanford University Press, 1992.

Gu Jiegang 顾颉刚. *Gu Jiegang minsuxue lunwenji* 顾颉刚民俗学论文集 [Articles by Gu Jiegang on folklore]. Edited by Qian Xiaobo 钱小柏. Shanghai: Shanghai Wenyi Chubanshe, 1998.

———. *Meng Jiangnü gushi yanjiu ji* 孟姜女故事研究集 [Studies on the story of Meng Jiangnü]. Shanghai: Shanghai Guji Chubanshe, 1984.

Gu Jiegang 顾颉刚, Zhong Jingwen 钟敬文, et al. *Meng Jiangnü gushi lunwenji* 孟姜女故事论文集 [Articles on the story of Meng Jiangnü]. Beijing: Minjian Wenyi Chubanshe, 1984.

Guan Dedong 关德栋 and Zhou Zhongming 周中明, comps. *Zidishu congchao* 子弟书丛钞 [A collective edition of youth books]. 2 volumes. Shanghai: Shanghai Guji Chubanshe, 1984.

Guo Shuzu 郭述祖. *Meng Jiangnü* 孟姜女 [Meng Jiangnü]. Beijing: Meishu Sheying Chubanshe, 1986.

Harbsmeier, Chistopher. "Weeping and Wailing in Ancient China." In *Minds and Mentalities in Traditional Chinese Literature,* edited by Halvor Eifring, 317–422. Beijing: Wenhua Yishu Chubanshe, 1999.

Huang Ruiqi 黄瑞旗. *Meng Jiangnü gushi yanjiu* 孟姜女故事研究 [A study of the story of Meng Jiangnü]. Beijing: Zhongguo Renmin Daxue Chubanshe, 2003.

Hung, Chang-tai. *Going to the People: Chinese Intellectuals and Folk Literature, 1918–1937.* Cambridge, Mass.: Harvard University Press, 1985.

Jay, Nancy. *Throughout Your Generations Forever: Sacrifice, Religion, and Paternity.* Chicago: University of Chicago Press, 1992.

Jiang Bin 姜彬, ed. *Jiangnan shi da minjian xushishi Wugeji* 江南十大民间叙事诗吴歌集 [The ten great popular epics of the Jiangnan area: A collection of Wu-dialect songs]. Shanghai: Shanghai Wenyi Chubanshe, 1989.

Johnson, Elizabeth L. "Grieving for the Dead, Grieving for the Living: Funeral Laments of Hakka Women." In *Death Ritual in Late Imperial and Modern China*, edited by James L. Watson and Evelyn S. Rawski, 135–63. Berkeley: University of California Press, 1988.

———. "Singing of Separation, Lamenting Loss: Hakka Women's Expression of Separation and Reunion." In *Living with Separation in China: Anthropological Accounts*, edited by Charles Stafford, 27–52. London: Routledge Curzon, 2003.

Klöter, Hennig. *Written Taiwanese*. Wiesbaden, Germany: Harrassowitz, 2005.

Lee, Haiyan. *Revolution of the Heart: A Genealogy of Love in China, 1900–1950*. Stanford, Calif.: Stanford University Press, 2006.

———. "Tears That Crumbled the Great Wall: The Archaeology of Feeling in the May Fourth Folklore Movement." *Journal of Asian Studies* 64, no. 1 (2005): 35–65.

Liu Jing'an 劉經菴. *Geyao yu funü* 歌謠與婦女 [Folksongs and women]. Shanghai: Shangwu Yinshuguan, 1927.

Lovell, Julia. *The Great Wall: China against the World 1000 BC-AD 2000*. New York: Grove Press, 2006.

Lu Gong 路工, ed. *Meng Jiangnü wanli xunfu ji* 孟姜女万里寻夫集 [Meng Jiangnü travels for a myriad of miles to find her husband]. Beijing: Zhonghua Shuju, 1958.

Luhmann, Niklas. *Love as Passion: The Codification of Intimacy*. Translated by Jeremy Gaines and Doris L. Jones. Cambridge, Mass.: Harvard University Press, 1986.

"Meng Jiang nü" shi yizhu zunru fanfa de da ducao 孟姜女是一株尊儒反法的大毒草 [*Meng Jiangnü* is one pro-Confucian, anti-legalist big poisonous weed]. Nanning: Guangxi Renmin Chubanshe, 1975.

Meng Jiangnü chuanshuo yanjiu zhuanji 孟姜女传说研究专辑 [Special issue of studies on the folktale of Meng Jiangnü]. *Minjian wenxue jikan*, no. 4 (1986).

Meng Jiangnü ziliao xuanji 孟姜女资料选集 [An anthology of materials on Meng Jiangnü]. Volume 1, *Geyao* 歌谣 [Songs and Ballads]. Compiled by the Shanghai branch of the Chinese Society for the Study of Folk Literature, internal publication, 1985.

Needham, Joseph, and Liao Hongying. "The Ballad of Meng Jiang nu Weeping at the Great Wall (A Broadsheet from the City God's Temple at Lanchow, Kansu)." *Sinologica* 1 (1948): 194–209.

Qishi'er chao renwu yanyi 七十二朝人物演义 [Vernacular tales on personalities of seventy-two reigns]. Edited by Li Zhizhong 李致忠 and Yuan Ruiping 袁瑞萍. Beijing: Shumu Wenxian Chubanshe, 1988.

Ren Jiahe 任嘉禾 et al., eds. *Kusangge* 哭丧歌 [Funeral lament songs]. Shanghai: Shanghai Wenyi Chubanshe, 1988.

Roberts, Claire, and Geremie R. Barmé, eds. *The Great Wall of China*. Sydney: Powerhouse Publishing, 2006.

Schneider, Laurence A. *Ku Chieh-kang and China's New History: Nationalism and the Quest for Alternative Traditions*. Berkeley: University of California Press, 1971.

Singer, Irving. *The Nature of Love*. Volume 2, *Courtly and Romantic*. Chicago: University of Chicago Press, 1984.

Stent, George Carter. *Entombed Alive, and other songs, ballads, etc. (from the Chinese)*. London: William H. Allen, 1878.

Sun Chongtao 孫崇濤 and Huang Shizhong 黃仕忠, eds. *Fengyue jinnang jianjiao* 風月錦囊箋校 [A brocade bag of breeze and moonlight, a critical edition]. Beijing: Zhonghua Shuju, 2000.

Tao Wei 陶玮, ed. *Mingjia tan Meng Jiangnü ku Changcheng* 名家谈孟姜女哭长城 [Famous scholars on Meng Jiangnü weeping at the Long Wall]. Beijing: Wenhua Yishu Chubanshe, 2006.

Taylor, Charles. *Sources of the Self: The Making of the Modern Identity*. Cambridge, Mass.: Harvard University Press, 1989.

Waldron, Arthur. *The Great Wall of China: From History to Myth*. Cambridge: Cambridge University Press, 1990.

Waley, Arthur. *Ballads and Stories from Tun-huang*. London: George Allen and Unwin, 1960.

Waltner, Ann. *Getting an Heir: Adoption and the Construction of Kinship in Late Imperial China*. Honolulu: University of Hawai'i Press, 1990.

Wang, Ch'iu-kuei. "The Formation of the Early Versions of the Meng Chiang-nü Story." *Tamkang Review* 9 (1978): 111–40.

———. "From Pao-chüan to Ballad, a Study in Literary Adaptation as Exemplified by Two Versions of the Meng Chiang-nü Story." *Asian Culture Quarterly* 9–1 (1981): 48–65.

———. "The *Hsiao-shih Meng Chiang Chung-lieh Chen-chieh Hsien-liang Pao-chüan*— An Analytical Study." *Asian Culture Quarterly* 7–4 (1979): 46–72.

———. "The Tunhuang Versions of the Meng Chiang-nü Story." *Asian Culture Quarterly* 5–4 (1977): 67–81.

Wang, C.K. "Reflections of the Meng Chiang-nü Story in Yüan *Tsa-chü*." *Studies in Language and Literature* 1 (March 1985): 48–63.

Wang Shunlong 王順隆. "Cong qi zhong quanben *Meng Jiang nü ge* de ciyu wenti kan gezaice de jinhua guocheng" 從七種全本孟姜女歌的詞語問題看歌仔冊的進化過程 [Looking at the process of development of ballad booklets from the problem of the language of seven complete editions of the *Song of Meng Jiangnü*]. *Taiwan wenxian* 48, no. 2 (June 1997): 165–77.

Wang Zhaoyuan 王照圓, ed. *Lienü zhuan buzhu* 列女傳補注 [Biographies of exemplary women, with commentary], Wanyou wenku. Shanghai: Commercial Press, 1937.

Wimsatt, Genevieve, and Geoffrey Chen (Chen Sun-han). *The Lady of the Long Wall:*

A Ku Shih or Drum Song, translated from the Chinese. New York: Columbia University Press, 1934.

Wu Ruishu 巫瑞书. *Meng Jiangnü chuanshuo yu Hu Xiang wenhua* 孟姜女传说与湖湘文化 [The folktale of Meng Jiangnü and Hunan culture]. Changsha: Hunan Daxue Chubanshe, 2001.

Xiang Chu 项楚. *Dunhuang bianwen xuanzhu* 敦煌变文选注 [An annotated anthology of transformation texts from Dunhuang]. Chengdu: Ba Shu Shushe, 1990.

Yang Zhenliang 楊振良. *Meng Jiangnü yanjiu* 孟姜女研究 [A study of Meng Jiangnü]. Taipei: Xuesheng Shuju, 1985.

Yao Yizhi 姚逸之 and Zhong Gongxun 鍾貢勛, comps. *Hunan changben tiyao* 湖南唱本提要 [Content summaries of Hunanese songbooks]. 1928 or 1929. Reprinted in Lou Zikuang 婁子匡 and Ruan Changrui 阮昌銳, eds. *Zhongshan daxue minsu congshu* 中山大學民俗叢書 [Folklore Series of Sun Yat-sen University]. Taipei: Fulu Tushu gongsi, 1969.

Zhang Daoyi 张道一, comp. *Lao xiqu nianhua* 老戏曲年画 [Traditional new year prints on theatrical subjects]. Shanghai: Shanghai Huabao Chubanshe, 1999.

Zhang Xishun 張希舜 et al., eds. *Baojuan chuji* 寶卷初集 [A first collection of precious scrolls]. 40 volumes. Taiyuan: Shanxi Renmin Chubanshe, 1994.

Zhanzhan Waishi 詹詹外史, ed. *Qing shi* 情史 [Anatomy of passion]. Shenyang: Chunfeng Wenyi Chubanshe, 1986.

Zhao Liming 趙麗明, ed. *Zhongguo nüshu heji* 中國女書合集 [A collective edition of writings in China's women's script]. 5 volumes. Beijing: Zhonghua Shuju, 2005.

———, ed. *Zhongguo nüshu jicheng* 中国女书集成 [A complete collection of writings in China's women's script]. Beijing: Qinghua Daxue Chubanshe, 1992.

Zheng Tuyou 郑土有. *Wuyu xushi shange yanchang chuantong yanjiu* 吴语叙事山歌演唱传统研究 [A study of the development and transmission of Wu-dialect narrative folksong]. Shanghai: Shanghai Cishu Chubanshe, 2005.

Zhongguo geyao jicheng: Henan juan 中国歌谣集成河南卷 [A complete collection of China's songs and ballads: Henan]. Beijing: Zhongguo ISBN Zhongxin, 1995.

Zhongguo geyao jicheng: Hunan juan 中国歌谣集成湖南卷 [A complete collection of China's songs and ballads: Hunan]. Beijing: Zhongguo ISBN Zhongxin, 1999.

Zhongguo geyao jicheng: Zhejiang juan 中国歌谣集成浙江卷 [A complete collection of China's songs and ballads: Zhejiang]. Beijing: Zhongguo ISBN Zhongxin, 1995.